The New
Millennium
Manual

D1310680

A BRIDGEPOINT BOOK

BridgePoint,
an imprint of
Baker Books,
is your connection
for the best in
serious reading
that integrates
the passion of
the heart with
the scholarship
of the mind.

The New Millennium Manual

A Once and Future Guide

Robert G. Clouse

Robert N. Hosack

Richard V. Pierard

A BridgePoint Book

Baker Books

A Division of Baker Book House Co
Grand Rapids, Michigan 49516

© 1999 by Robert G. Clouse, Robert N. Hosack, and Richard V. Pierard

Published by BridgePoint Books
an imprint of Baker Books
a division of Baker Book House Company
P.O. Box 6287, Grand Rapids, MI 49516-6287

Printed in the United States of America

Library of Congress Cataloging-in-Publication Data

Clouse, Robert G., 1931–
    The new millennium manual : a once and future guide / Robert G.
Clouse, Robert N. Hosack, Richard V. Pierard.
      p. cm.
    Includes bibliographical references and indexes.
    ISBN 0-8010-5848-1 (pbk.)
    1. Millennium. 2. Millennialism. 3. Two thousand, A.D. I. Hosack,
Robert N. II. Pierard, Richard V., 1934– . III. Title.
BT890.C57 1999
236'.9—dc21   98-48302

For current information about all releases from Baker Book House, visit our web site:
http://www.bakerbooks.com

To
Bonnidell Clouse
Charlene Pierard
Lisa, Alexandra, Emma, and Margaret Hosack
For now and forever

Contents

Acknowledgments

Of the making of books there is no end to all who could be thanked and acknowledged. After all, we work and create not in isolation but in community—a rich one of people, books, and ideas that planted the seeds of this project years ago. Thus our insights owe a debt of gratitude to the giants who have gone before us. Any failings or oversights are to be charged to us alone.

The mechanics of putting a book together are much more than putting words down on paper or fingers to the keyboard. Those behind the scenes who helped immensely were Wendy Miller of the Billy Graham Center Museum, who offered invaluable assistance in mining the resources of the collection, and Mary Ann Jeffreys of *Christian History* magazine, who provided helpful direction in tracking down hard-to-find photo resources.

In addition, two Baker Book House staff members were essential in making this book a reality. Thanks must go to Melinda Van Engen, an editor gracious and fair, who guided this book to a successful completion on a perilously short time schedule, and to Brian Brunsting, whose innovative interior design well matched the tenor of our text.

"In the end is my beginning," wrote Eliot. We share this sentiment in the temporal over the completion of this book, and we embrace this truth in eternity for it says in simple terms all we really need to know about the millennium and the return of our Lord.

Introduction

Millennial madness is upon us; the signs are all around. Newspapers and magazines, both religious and secular, regularly report on the coming year 2000 and all its implications. A spate of Bible prophecy books line the shelves, as well as the best-sellers' lists, of Christian bookstores. The Internet is teeming with millennial sites—Christian, New Age, and secular. The Y2K (year 2000) computer problem is covered by the electronic media with an apocalyptic fever pitch.

While there always has been an apocalyptic thread running through the history of the church, the turn to a new millennium—for the first time in a thousand years, after all!—is bringing an unprecedented interest in and speculation about the endtimes and the timing of the second coming of Christ.

In an arena in which Michael Drosnin's best-selling *The Bible Code* does battle with evangelical prophecy entrepreneur Hal Lindsey's *The Apocalypse Code,* do we really need another book? We think so, and

The New Millennium Manual is a testimony to our concern and passion.

Millennium watcher and historian Richard Landes has suggested that the history of the endtimes may be likened to the conflict between two birds in an eschatological breviary, the roosters and the owls:

> Roosters crow about the imminent dawn. Apocalyptic prophets, messianic pretenders, chronologists calculating an imminent doomsday—they all want to rouse the courtyard, stir the animals into action. . . . Owls are night animals; they dislike both noise and light; they want to hush the roosters, insisting that it is still night, that the dawn is far away, that the roosters are not only incorrect, but dangerous.[1]

Referencing Landes's analogy, we have written our book from the perspective of what we would like to call "evangelical owls." We believe the roosters have *some* good things to say; however, many can't hear them for all their crowing. And those who do heed their call seem to hear nothing else but their apocalyptic chorus. But it is the owls who write history. As evangelical owls we have sought to write a balanced, irenic work that treats the issues, people, and movements surrounding this coming millennium. We freely acknowledge that we are pandering to the ever increasing millennial speculations and date setting brought on by an artificial calendar change, but we do so as evangelical owls who give a hoot about the type of literature available for the church in these "last days." We embrace the rooster's call to action, but we argue, indeed, "no one knows about that day or hour" of Christ's return (Mark 13:32).

While in Christian parlance the millennium refers to the thousand-year golden age envisioned in Revelation 20:1–6 and its relationship to the return of Christ, the "millennial moment" extant in our broader culture is based on the historic calendar turn from 1999 to 2000 (we quibble with this dating of the new millennium in chapter 1) and all its myriad supposed implications. However, the dovetailing of interest in these two millenniums provides an excellent opportunity to reflect on their relationship in contemporary church and culture.

The New Millennium Manual does not present a wholesale history of endtime beliefs. Rather, our book combines church history, theology, and cultural analysis to introduce readers to the meaning (or lack thereof) of the coming millennial change. While informing readers of the highlights and lowlights of millennial meditation, we seek not to frighten anyone into the kingdom of God but to inspire commitment where it is lacking and to redirect and nurture it in those with misplaced millennial faiths.

To accomplish this goal we have chosen the theme of pilgrimage for this book. From Abraham's nomadic travels in the book of Genesis to Bunyan's Christian in *The Pilgrim's Progress,* the idea of pilgrims on a journey is a classic spiritual theme. In reality, all of us who enter into the third Christian millennium are fellow travelers. Whatever one's belief (or lack thereof) we are all pilgrims on the road to the new millennium. As we tour through church history past and apocalyptic speculation future, take time to enjoy the scenery. The many photographs, images, and cartoons have been carefully selected to enhance your pilgrimage.

In one of J. R. R. Tolkien's *Lord of the Rings* books, Frodo and his servant, Sam, travel deep behind enemy lines on a mission. Overwhelmed by dire conditions and certain they are doomed, Frodo confides to Sam, "I am glad that you are here with me. Here at the end of all things, Sam." However, "in the nick of time" tragedy turns to triumph for the pilgrims, "and the end of all things becomes a beginning."[2] As pilgrims entering a new millennium we can be confident that we enter "the end" together and that in God's kingdom this will be transformed into a new beginning. With this certain confidence, "let's boldly go where no one has gone before."

Travel on, pilgrim.

1

Apocalypse Wow
Approaching the New Millennium

The future ain't what it used to be.

Yogi Berra

In 1968 Stanley Kubrick released his now classic *2001: A Space Odyssey,* a film about space travel that evoked images of a time far in the future. Similarly, for years, A.D. 2000 has been a marker in the public consciousness for another, future generation. It is no longer difficult to imagine living in that future, for that future is now. We are on the threshold of a new millennium.

The arrival of the new millennium is being greeted with great anticipation. In the last years of the twentieth century, the outpouring of books, essays, sermons, dramas, films, and TV programs speculating on the topic has reached staggering proportions. No other issue in our time has quite seized the imagination of people in the same manner as this one. We look to the new millennium with hope but also with deep and profound apprehension. As one writer has keenly observed:

> For decades the phrase "by the end of the century" denoted something far distant. But it is distant no longer. Millennial predictions are proliferating with increasing speed as prognosticators try to get in under the wire. The Internet, that electronic jungle drum, vibrates to the beat of prophecy.[1]

In light of this fervor it's interesting to note the comment of an anonymous writer who declared in the *Atlantic Monthly* in 1891: "What the last decade is to a century, the last century is to a millennium."[2] This insight suggests that the final decade of a century tends to define one's percep-

15

tion of that century and provokes one to look forward to higher levels of achievement and greatness in the next one. The same idea would hold true with the last century of a millennium: It serves to define the millennium as a whole.

The second millennium of the Christian era is no exception to that rule. It is the twentieth century that has capped a thousand years of material progress, the spread of Christianity throughout the entire world, and the development of a global society. But at the same time, during this century humankind developed the tools of its own mass destruction in the form of nuclear weapons, the pillage of the environment, and unchecked population growth.

The transition to the new millennium takes on a special dimension because many Christians have linked this to speculation about the "endtimes" and the return of Jesus Christ. In the twentieth century an extraordinary amount of attention has been given to eschatological and apocalyptic speculation, and the quantity of literature and the intensity of preaching on these topics has increased dramatically during the final three decades. Christians of all stripes are deeply interested in the future and what it holds.

Prophetic Concerns

As the year 2000 approaches, the number of North Americans enthralled with biblical prophecies of the last days increases steadily. Those interested are not just members of groups traditionally known for these concerns, such as the Jehovah's Witnesses, Seventh-day Adven-

Fig. 1.1 Apocalypse Online. Armageddon Books, an online prophecy bookstore, offers testimony to the marketplace's interest in things millennial.

World's largest Bible prophecy bookstore featuring books, videos, & charts on armageddon, antichrist, 666, tribulation, rapture, revelation.

tists, and millennialist fundamentalists. They now include members of evangelical churches, mainline Protestant denominations, and growing numbers of Roman Catholics. This interest in apocalyptic themes regularly finds its way into American popular culture, as exemplified in studio films such as *The Omen, The Rapture, The Seventh Sign, Contact,* and *Armageddon;* best-selling books such as Michael Drosnin's *The Bible Code,* Stephen King's *The Stand,* and Clive Barker's *The Great and Secret Show;* and TV shows such as Fox's popular *Millennium.*

Recent Gallup Polls reveal that 62 percent of Americans have no doubts that Jesus will return again, and 52 percent "are absolutely convinced" that they will be called before God at the judgment day to answer for their sins.[3] A 1994 poll found that 16 percent think the world will end within the next one hundred years,[4] while in 1991 some 15 percent were convinced that the Gulf War was the fulfillment of the prophecy of the final great battle of Armageddon that would occur before the judgment day.[5]

Those who are endeavoring to forecast the endtimes basically follow one of two forms, or approaches, to prophecy. Biblically oriented individuals focus on the three apocalyptic books of the Bible—Ezekiel, Daniel, and Revelation—along with scattered apocalyptic passages in other books. The adjective *apocalyptic* and noun *apocalypticism,* as used throughout this book, refer to the prediction of imminent disaster and total destruction. In theological terms this means the climactic triumph at the end of the age of the forces of good over the forces of evil in fulfillment of the divine purpose. The bibli-

Fig. 1.2 The End Is Here. The fortress of Megiddo in the Jezreel Valley (thirty-five miles southeast of Haifa) is the site traditionally associated with Armageddon (Rev. 16:16), where the climactic battle between good and evil will ultimately take place.

cists apply the apocalyptic Scriptures to contemporary affairs by drawing analogies and interpreting metaphors. The other approach is that of direct revelation. The Marians, a rather diverse grouping within Roman Catholic circles, believe they are currently receiving revelation through visions of the Virgin Mary. Some New Age sects also concern themselves with future events. Baptized with a self-understanding of what is termed an "inner divinity," these New Agers claim direct revelation from disparate sources ranging from channeling to "crop circles" (the British phenomenon of mysterious formations found in farmers' fields). In their minds the control belief of inner divinity validates the authenticity of their revelatory claims.

Prophetic teachings have great power because they speak to a universal human desire to make sense out of history. We really want to believe that time leads to an ultimate end where good triumphs and evil is punished. Unfortunately, history is a study in chaos; no clearly identifiable pattern of movement automatically emerges from it. This was underscored by the rise of secular historical studies in the nineteenth century, which challenged the traditional Christian understanding of history as God-directed and moving toward a final fulfillment. Although devout believers were marginalized if not outright ostracized, they found hope through their faith. They believed that with the help of God's Spirit they could understand the prophetic portions of the Bible and discover that history indeed was going somewhere.

In the modern era of mass media that brings international events into the living rooms of millions, American Christians in particular struggle to find their own place and that of their country in history. No matter how complicated the world becomes, they trace time simply. Like the life of an ordinary human being, movements in history have a beginning, a middle, and an end. And like human life, the middle years are followed by a decline that results in death. Many Christians apply this historical scenario to their own nation. Yet, although they may live in the most corrupt of generations, they look forward to the blessed hope of redemption.

During the twentieth century many traumatic experiences tore at the fabric of world society and for many heralded decline. Among these experiences were two world wars; bloody revolutions in Russia and China; a major economic depression; the Holocaust; environmental and ecological disasters; a widespread dissatisfaction with democratic forms of government; the development and use of atomic, biological, and chemical weapons of mass destruction; unprecedented famine and hunger and the spread of old and new diseases; and repeated genocides. After witnessing the events of the twentieth century, many Christians place themselves squarely in the middle of the decline of history and emphasize that they are part of the last generation.

While for most people the events of the twentieth century represented a staggering challenge, as they had a more optimistic view of the future, these disastrous occurrences came as no surprise to those who believed in endtime prophecies. They had a way to bring meaning to current events. They understood why the restoration of the Jews to their homeland in Palestine was bitterly opposed by various forces. As foretold in Ezekiel 38, Russia and other haters of Jews were bent on destroying the Jewish state. Other troubles in the world could be blamed on the rise of the Antichrist, about which Daniel prophesied.

In the Book of Revelation Jesus' opening of the seven seals of the scroll that God had held in his right hand was a vision of the ghastly times that lay ahead—the four horsemen who bring tyranny, war, famine, and pestilence; the martyrs seeking revenge; earthquakes; hail, fire, and blood raining down from the skies; and the darkening of the sun and moon. With the opening of the seventh seal comes the trumpet judgments—hail and fire mixed with blood; a mountain falls into the sea, destroying life there; a poisoning of the earth's fresh water supply; the light of heavenly bodies extinguished; the torment of locusts with human faces and stinging tails; and the invasion of two hundred million horsemen from the East who kill a third of the earth's population. Although there is disagreement over how these visions are to be interpreted, they do instill in believers a confidence in the certainty

Fig. 1.3 Takes a Licking and Keeps on Ticking. The invention of the mechanical clock revolutionized the time business and influenced the development of standard calendars.

of God's judgment and an assurance of the end of the evils of the world.

The Problem of Calendars

Many Western Christian students of prophecy see all these events happening in conjunction with the turn to a new millennium. Unfortunately, such an approach confuses our calendar change to a new millennium with the historic Christian understanding of a future millennium (from the Latin *mille* for "thousand"), the thou-

19

sand-year reign of Christ on earth found in Revelation 20. We must emphasize that, although the practice of predicting dire futures is widespread in other cultures, the idea of tying such predictions to any definite date, let alone to a new century or millennium, is rather unusual. This is because throughout history every people group had some way of measuring time, a practice that was linked to a particular place and ethnic group. This was "local" time since "when" was linked to "where." Only with the invention of the mechanical clock could one separate time and space, since the clock could be used by anyone, regardless of where the person might live. The clock also enabled a more precise calendar than had been available before.

We have wrongly assumed that all people number the days, months, and years as we do. In reality, a large part of the world's population has always operated on calendars other than our Western one. However, modern international society requires the use of the same calendar (and standard time as well) for business, communications, and diplomatic relations. Thus, the "Christian" (more precisely, the Gregorian) calendar has been accepted as the standard, even by people who have little or nothing to do with Christianity.

The earliest calendars were based on observations of the moon, since its phases occur in a regular pattern. The month usually began when people could first see the "new moon," that is, a crescent moon. Be-

cause it was not possible to see the moon during cloudy weather, the beginning of the month was determined through calculation. Since a lunar month was only twenty-nine and one-half days, a lunar year would be almost eleven days shorter than a solar year. To keep in step with the sun it was necessary to add an additional (leap) month about every three years. Some calendars began the new year at the vernal equinox, others in the fall, and still others in January.

The Romans developed a calendar that was based on observations of the sun and the moon, but by the late Republic it deviated almost eighty days from the normal solar calendar. Thus, in 46 B.C. Julius Caesar, with the aid of a Greek astronomer, developed a new calendar that was based completely on the movements of the sun without reference to the moon. The so-called Julian Calendar was based on a year of 365 1/4 days, with an extra day added every four years as February 29. The new year began on January 1 instead of March 1 as was the situation before, a fact that can be seen in the names of the months from September to December (seventh to tenth month), and the years were grouped and counted by the reigns of the consuls. Some modifications were made in the length of the months, and two of them were subsequently named after Julius and the first emperor, Augustus.

The Christian church readily adopted the Julian calendar, but around A.D. 525 a Roman monk named Dionysius Exiguus

Pontius' Puddle

Fig. 1.4 When Does Your Millennium Begin? While the third millennium actually begins in 2001, popular culture's 2000 date has the devotion of the masses.

(Dennis the Short) first set forth the idea of a Christian era beginning with the nativity of Jesus. Instead of basing the numbering of years on the reigns of consuls or emperors, Dionysius Exiguus set the birth of Jesus as the year 1 (*anno Domini*—in the year of our Lord). The years before this were later labeled as B.C.—before Christ. More recently, however, scholars discovered that he had erred in his calculations. Jesus was actually born about four or five years "B.C." At least two hundred years passed before Christians began using the new dating system with any regularity. Historians credit the English monk and scholar Bede (c. 673–735) with institutionalizing the practice.

After a few centuries people began to notice a significant discrepancy between the actual solar time and the Christian calendar. The solar year is in fact slightly shorter than Julius Caesar had calculated, namely, 365 days, 5 hours, 48 minutes, and 46 seconds. Pope Gregory XIII sought the help of an astronomer to correct the calendar and in 1582 announced his famous calendar reform, which involved advancing ten days to catch up with solar time. On the night of October 4, 1582, people went to bed as usual, but they awoke the next morning to find that it was now October 15—eleven days later!

The calendar change was quickly accepted by Catholic countries, gradually over the next two centuries by Protestant ones, and only in the twentieth century by those in which Eastern Orthodoxy prevailed. By the twentieth century, the calendar used in Russia and other Orthodox lands was thirteen days behind that used in the West. The Gregorian calendar is now the standard civil calendar used throughout the world.

Because there was no year 0, the first Christian millennium started with the year 1: The world went from 1 B.C. right into A.D. 1. Although that means the third millennium technically begins in 2001, there are no signs that people will be deterred from celebrating its beginning in the year 2000. After all, MCMXCIX will become MM with the tick of a clock. The Millennium Society, a six-thousand-member group, began planning for its celebration in 1979. At the stroke of midnight twenty-four public celebrations are planned in each of the world's time zones at famed places such as the Taj Mahal, Times Square, the Eiffel Tower, and the Great Pyramid of Cheops.[6] The Artist Formerly Known as Prince's ode to the new millennium, "1999," will carry the spirit of the day as revelers "party like it's 1999."

It must be noted that throughout most of Christian history the concept of time was viewed differently than today. The date of an event was of far less importance than its theological significance. The writing of history and precision of dating took on importance during the Renaissance and Reformation, when papal tradition first came under attack. The papacy attempted to bolster its image by emphasizing an unbroken line of continuity in papal succession beginning with Peter. Nevertheless, historians still tended to put more emphasis on the ongoing work of divine providence than actual objective events. Only in the nineteenth century did people come to recognize the fundamental significance of historical perspective. When people became conscious of the reality and inevitability of change, they saw a need to trace its progress. The reconstruction of the past required the ready availability of historical data, thus resulting in the collection and publication of medieval documents and the search for new information about classical antiquity through archaeology.

However, most of the world's peoples continued to use calendars of their own for religious and ceremonial reasons. Many such calendars exist, but probably the most significant are the Hebrew, Islamic, and Chinese calendars. The Hebrew or Jewish calendar is a lunar-solar calendar that is based on the phases of the moon. In ancient times each month began when the moon's slim crescent was visible in the evening twilight, and the festival of the new moon was celebrated with solemnity. Nowadays the calculation of months and years is done with astronomical regularity. The civil year begins at the autumnal equinox (Rosh Hashanah) and the religious year at the vernal equinox. The civil year consists of twelve lunar months—Tishri, Cheshvan, Kislev, Tebet, Shebat, Adar, Nisan, Iyar, Sivan, Tammuz, Ab, and Elul—which are alternately twenty-nine and thirty days. To prevent this lunar calendar from deviating too far from the solar cycle, a thirteenth month, Veadar (second Adar), is added seven times during each nineteen-year cycle. The weeks, however, run in a continuous seven-day cycle, with the Sabbath, which begins at sundown on Friday, ending the week.

The numbering of years begins with the creation (*anno Mundi* or A.M.), which Jews believe occurred 3,760 years before the birth of Christ. This means that the year 2000 in the Western calendar will be A.M. 5760/5761 in the Hebrew one. The Jewish calendar is used today in Israel for all civil and religious purposes and by Jews everywhere for religious purposes. Some Jews utilize the Christian calendar but replace the terms B.C. and A.D. with B.C.E. (before the common era) and C.E. (of the common era).

The Islamic calendar is a purely lunar one. The year 1 began on the day and year (sunset, July 16, 622, as reckoned by the Gregorian calendar) when the Prophet Muhammad fled from Mecca to Medina. Known as the Hijra or Hegira, this is the defining event in Muslim history. Each year, which is labeled A.H. *(anno Hegirae),* has twelve lunar months, which alternate between thirty and twenty-nine days in length, thus making it 354 days in length. Because the Koran specifies that a year has only twelve months, there is no thirteenth month. This means that the months move backward through all the seasons and complete a full cycle every 32 1/2 years. The year 2000 in the Islamic calendar is A.H. 1420/1421.

A new month does not begin until the new moon has been sighted and the announcement made by some prominent figure in the Muslim community. The days run from sunset to sunset, and Friday, the day of worship ("day of gathering"), marks the beginning of the new week. Some of the more westernized Muslim countries

---

Time Is on Our Side, or Is It?

Our year 2000 on the Christian calendar is:

A.M. 5760/5761 in the Hebrew calendar

A.H. 1420/1421 in the Islamic calendar

4698 in the Chinese calendar (the Year of the Dragon)

2753 in the Old Roman calendar

1716 in the Coptic calendar

2544 in the Buddhist calendar

---

use the Christian calendar alongside the Islamic one.

Finally, the Chinese calendar is quite regular and is based on the motion of the sun, moon, and planets. Its use can be traced back to 2953 B.C., the mythical founding of the empire. The Chinese developed two systems of numbering, both of which covered a sixty-year cycle. One linked the twelve animals of the zodiac (rat, ox, tiger, hare, dragon, snake, horse, sheep, monkey, rooster, dog, and pig) with ten celestial signs of the Chinese constellations. The other used the five elements (wood, fire, earth, metal, and water). The date of the Chinese New Year varies within a thirty-day period from mid-January to mid-February. The New Year in 2000 will fall on February 4 and mark the beginning of the Year of the Dragon.

A variety of other calendars are in use in other countries, such as the Coptic calendar in Ethiopia, the Saka calendar in India, and various Buddhist calendars in Southeast Asia. Who knows what time it is? Our calendar tour makes one thing clear: The date 2000, which is so meaningful to us in the West, is an arbitrary milestone and of little importance to people in many other parts of the world.

End of the Century, End of the Millennium

While the word *millennium* carries with it significant religious and historical baggage, the term *century* is a modern notion in measuring time different from the season, reign, or era.[7] In fact, the last decade of the nineteenth century witnessed such a great outpouring of literary and artistic material in Europe that contemporaries gave the period a name—*fin de siècle* (French for "end of the century")—to acknowledge its influence in time. Intellectuals looked upon the last years of their century as an era of cultural decadence and despair, an age of anxiety. European bourgeois or middle-class society seemed to have lost its way. Unable to influence political developments in an age of mass society and faced with the mounting crises of imperialistic expansion in Europe and overseas, industrial growth and economic depression, and the worsening armaments race, intellectuals and artists retreated into

aesthetic or psychological pursuits. The most radical among them welcomed the imminent collapse of a "botched civilization," as poet Ezra Pound put it.

The prophets of the new age about to dawn were Nietzsche, Darwin, and Freud. It was a world of chaos. Neither God nor human reason counted. Impersonal forces determined human existence, both within the psyche and in society at large. Christianity was a "slave morality" that softened the resolve of humankind to deal with the demands of the age. Survival of the fittest was the law not only of the jungle but also of the realm of business and among the nations and races for mastery of the world. The easy optimism of the Victorian Era and the Gilded Age was fading. An age of accelerating growth and change lay ahead, but many feared it would be one of conflict—between labor and management, rich and poor, and the nations themselves.

Perhaps the ennui of the late nineteenth century was connected to the expectations that the age created. Never before had history come under such scrutiny. The modern era was not living up to the hopes of its prophets nor its participants. Such expectations were not a problem in previous centuries because people looked at time differently. In fact, the first instance we have of a new century being celebrated in the Christian calendar is the Jubilee of 1300, proclaimed by Pope Boniface VIII. The celebration was facilitated by the invention of the mechanical, weight-driven clock in the previous century that was

Fig. 1.5 The Great Conversion. Augustine, bishop of Hippo from A.D. 395 to 431, was once a premillennialist. His adoption of the amillennial view was significant, for his perspective was the dominant one in the church for centuries.

used in the monasteries to determine the times for worship and prayer during each day. As a result of the clock's influence, a "time consciousness" gradually developed that simply was not known before.[8] Subsequent popes declared Jubilees in each century year. Known as a "holy year," the faithful who made a pilgrimage to Rome during this time received a generous indulgence (reduction of the amount of time one would have to spend in purgatory before he or she went to heaven) for visiting various churches.

By the 1600s centuries were taking on an identity of their own. They had their own personalities, life courses (beginning, first half, middle, second half, end), and names, such as the Reformation Century or Century of Louis the Great (Louis XIV of France). Nevertheless, the century years were not yet occasions for major observances until the end of the eighteenth century. Then the French Revolution, the rise of Napoleon, and prophetic speculation made people much more conscious of the year 1800–1801, and considerable attention was paid to the passing of the old century and advent of the new—in both Christian and secular circles.

Thus, when the nineteenth century arrived, it had a distinctive identity, and even magazines and journals took its name, something that had not occurred in previous centuries. The most prestigious of the many periodicals that did so was *The Nineteenth Century,* founded in London in 1877. At midnight on December 31, 1900, it was renamed *The Nineteenth Century and After.*

As the twentieth century neared, people were quite aware of the approaching new era and keenly anticipated it. From this time forward, consciousness of the coming of the next century was an integral part of Western thinking about time and dates. Moreover, as the years passed, people increasingly discussed the prospects that the next millennium might hold for humanity and society. As will be shown below, this was also a time of intense and even anxious eschatological speculation as many eagerly looked for the return of Christ at the end of this millennial century.

A.D. 1000: Was Time of the Essence?

Some have argued that the century preceding the arrival of the second millennium of the Christian era also was marked by a time of anxiety. As the year 1000 approached, many in Europe were gripped by what one contemporary writer labeled as the "terrors." The primary source for this characterization of the times was the monk Radulphus (or Raoul) Graber, whose *Five Books of Histories* chronicled events during the period 900–1044. However, historians have vigorously debated just how true this characterization was. Asa Briggs and Daniel Snowden conclude that rumors of tenth-century apprehension did not circulate in Europe until the sixteenth century.[9]

While millennial speculation receded in the church after the time of St. Augustine, it did not die out. After all, Augustine, in his *City of God,* suggested that the thousand-year period since the birth of Jesus was the millennium mentioned in Revelation 20, and thus, 1000 or 1033 (the anniversary of the death of Christ) could be seen as a time for expecting the Antichrist and the last judgment.

In the tenth century this resulted in a groundswell of speculation that the world was drawing to a close. Various monastic writers predicted the imminent coming of the Antichrist and the end of the world, and this led to heightened tensions and fears as the year 1000 approached. Both in the years immediately preceding and following that fateful date, various signs such as a comet, meteors, and famines were seen as indications of the approaching apocalypse.

However, the documentary record is unclear as to how widespread the alleged "terrors of the year 1000" actually were. Papal statements between 970 and 1000 and the principal monastic documents (annals as well as biographies) make no mention of such a happening. One writer, Thietmar of Merseburg, referred to 1000 not as a year of horror but as the comforting anniversary of Christ's birth: "When the thousandth year since the salvific birth of the Immaculate Virgin had come, a radiant dawn rose over the world."[10] Another problem was the imprecision of dating. At least one important monastic writer at the time maintained the A.D. calculation currently in use was twenty-one years off. Most modern-day scholars agree that the "terrors" of 1000 have been overstated and that anxieties about the end of the world prevailed throughout the eleventh century. What should have been the decisive year turned out to be just one more year in a lengthy period of fear and anxiety.

Modern-day Apocalypticism

While the extent of apocalyptic speculation a thousand years ago is debatable, there is no question that it is widely prevalent today. To be sure, our world is vastly more complex and the varieties of Christian and secular apocalypticism have multiplied almost beyond comprehension. In fact, the interest in the future and the possibilities of global destruction have increased immeasurably as the end of the twentieth century has drawn near.

The signs of contemporary Christian apocalypticism are all around us. One need only spend a few hours listening to or watching preachers on Christian radio and TV or browsing the "prophecy" shelves in any religious bookstore to gain some idea of the vast extent of such thinking in conservative Christian circles. This includes both Roman Catholics as well as Protestant evangelicals and fundamentalists. Many of these manifestations will be examined in greater detail in chapter 4.

The Branch Davidians

Apocalypticism is also widespread among pseudo-Christian cults as well as certain secular movements. The Branch Davidians is one group that recently caught the public imagination. The founder was a Bulgarian immigrant named Victor Houteff (1886–1955), who at age thirty-two converted to Seventh-day Adventism because of the church's clean living habits and literal interpretation of the Bible. He eventually settled in Los Angeles, where he sold washing machines and began studying biblical prophecy intensively. He soon became disillusioned with the church's leaders, whom he identified with the lukewarm Laodicean church of Revelation 3:14–22. In 1929 he declared God had selected him as a messenger ("the kings of the east," Rev. 16:12 KJV) to reveal new spiritual truths from the Scriptures and direct the purification process that would enable Christ's return. He spelled this out in a work entitled *The Shepherd's Rod*. Houteff saw his divinely appointed mission as that of unlocking the endtime secrets contained in the seven seals in the Book of Revelation and gathering the 144,000 faithful who would be delivered from destruction at Christ's second coming and would enter into the theocratic kingdom of David in Palestine. The church leaders rejected his message and expelled him in 1934. He then formed a group called "Davidian Seventh-day Adventists," which referred to his teaching about the imminent restoration of the messianic kingdom.

A year later Houteff and his followers purchased some farmland on the Brazos River near Waco, Texas, and established a community called the Mt. Carmel Center. He believed this was only temporary and the group would soon move to Palestine, where they would proclaim the true gospel to the world and be taken up into heaven at Christ's return. When this did not happen, the Shepherd's Rod adherents cleared the land, erected several buildings, and set up a close-knit, self-sufficient community. They grew their own food, operated a school, limited outside sources of news, practiced vegetarianism, and engaged in evangelism among Seventh-day Adventists.

The group grew slowly and had about one hundred members by the end of the 1930s. In 1942 Houteff severed all remaining ties with the mainline Seventh-day Adventist Church, sought converts around the globe for his Davidian group, and developed a small, deeply committed international membership. He died in 1955, surprising his followers, who had expected him to reign over the kingdom that was about to be founded. His wife, Florence, took control of the organization, sold the original property, and bought a new and much larger tract of land farther away from Waco so they could maintain their distance from the ungodly. She announced that she had unlocked the biblical code in Revelation and discovered that Jesus would return on April 22, 1959, to establish his kingdom. Prior to this a war would occur in the Middle East, a purification of the Adventists would take place, and Victor Houteff would be resurrected. The membership soared to over a thousand, and hundreds of believers sold their homes and moved to Waco in an-ticipation of the endtime. When the magic date passed uneventfully, the group disintegrated, and only a small number remained at the Mt. Carmel Center.

Benjamin Roden then appeared as the new leader and urged the Davidians to "Get off the dead Rod and move into a living Branch" (a reference to Zech. 3:8; 6:12), thus anticipating the name by which the group would be popularly known. He wanted to lead the Davidians to the Holy Land and even spent some time in Israel. When he died in 1978, the leadership passed to his widow, Lois, who added a variation of her own to the group's doctrine: The Holy Spirit was the female component of the Trinity. She promoted her belief in a magazine named *SHEkinah,* a feminization of the Hebrew word for the manifested presence (or spirit) of God. Following her death in 1986, her weak and ineffective son, George, assumed control, but he was quickly shoved aside by the much more dynamic Vernon Howell, also known as David Koresh.

Born in 1959, Howell joined the sect in 1981 after having been removed from the rolls of the Seventh-day Adventist church in Tyler, Texas, for causing dissension. He carried on a sexual relationship with Lois Roden, forty-five years his senior, married a series of teenage girls by whom he had a number of children, and by 1990 had gained mastery over the community. He legally changed his name to David Koresh, the Hebrew form of Cyrus, the Persian king and messianic figure who allowed the Hebrew

Fig. 1.6 "For False Christs and False Prophets Will Appear . . ." David Koresh caught in an unguarded moment. His apocalyptic Scripture twisting later led to guarded days at the Davidian compound and ultimately the deaths of dozens of followers.

remnant to return to their land (Isa. 45:1). The name David suggested the renewal of the Israelite kingdom. He saw his own role as that of messiah rather than prophet and expected to be both messiah and king.

The Mt. Carmel community lived in the shadow of the endtime. While preparing for it, the members tried to be as self-sufficient as possible. They produced their food and clothing, operated an automobile repair business, and sold weapons at gun shows. Koresh became increasingly convinced that the apocalypse would occur in America rather than Israel, and the group stockpiled large amounts of food, weapons, ammunition, and fuel for the ultimate showdown.

During these years Koresh formulated an apocalyptic theology so intricate that no one could make a coherent statement about it. Koresh had a phenomenal knowledge of Scripture and a talent for making the most radical reinterpretations of it sound plausible to his highly suggestible followers. However, he did all this orally and wrote no books or essays expounding his belief system. The core of his beliefs was that prophecy was being fulfilled in our times, and the events described in the Bible would be reenacted by contemporary players. The central idea was the inevitability of the apocalyptic struggle between the forces of good and evil. He insisted that the prophecy of the seven seals (Revelation 6–8) was now being fulfilled. He focused particularly on the fifth seal, which portrays the souls of those who had been slain for the Word of God and who are told to wait a little longer until the deaths of their fellows who will be killed in the same way. His followers were put into this holding pattern and told that they faced a life-and-death choice between obeying the will of God or man. Soon he was defining this in terms of a violent conflict with the federal government.

The tragic, violent assault on the Waco compound that occurred conformed exactly to Koresh's endtime scenario. The Davidians were entitled to use any kind of force necessary to resist the enemy. The authorities who besieged the compound ignored the group's millenarian beliefs, but their demonstration of force increased the Davidians' resolve to resist and to respond with force themselves. The assembling of troops and tanks was proof to the faithful that the powers of the world were arrayed against them. It confirmed their prophetic beliefs about their importance in the cosmic struggle.

They were convinced this was a holy war, and they were not about to surrender to the federal agents who attempted to enter the headquarters building on February 28, 1993, to search the premises for illegal weapons. A shoot-out ensued, leaving four government agents and ten Davidians dead, and this was followed by a fifty-one-day siege. When on April 19 U.S. Attorney General Janet Reno ordered a full-scale assault on the compound, a raging fire swept the buildings, leaving eighty-six people dead, many of whom were women and children. For these followers of Koresh, this war with unbelievers truly signaled the end of the world.

The Christian Identity Movement

After the destruction of the compound, the Davidian movement declined, but another deviant group, Christian Identity, drew sustenance from the Waco tragedy. The roots of Identity lie in British-Israelism, a curious prophetic teaching that a remnant of the descendants of Jacob, the so-called Ten Lost Tribes—the northern kingdom of Israel that was carried into captivity by Assyria in 721 B.C.—found their way to the British Isles. Thus, the Anglo-Saxons are the true heirs of the covenants Yahweh made with ancient Israel. There is, so to speak, an "identity" of Britain with biblical Israel, and America, as a result of past British colonization, shares in this relationship.

The southern kingdom (Judah) shared a similar fate, being taken into exile by Babylonia a century later. After seventy years, however, a remnant was allowed to return and resume the temple worship. The area in which they lived was called Judea, and the people soon came to be known as Jews. They were eventually taken over by the Romans, and over time, many foreign racial elements entered into the population. As a result, few racially pure Israelites remained.

On the other hand, the Ten Lost Tribes maintained a separate existence, although after a time they forgot their Israelite heritage. They moved north, passing through the area north of the Black Sea, eventually taking on Caucasian features and finding their way to the Atlantic coast after a migration lasting perhaps centuries. They then went on to populate the British Isles.

Although over time they had lost their Jewish beliefs, the promises made to Israel were unconditional and thus still valid. The prophecies of Genesis 48:17–19 were fulfilled, as the English ruler was a direct descendant of the house of David (the daughters of the last king of Judah were taken to Ireland and the royal line continued through the Irish and Scottish monarchies). The blessings bestowed on the twin sons of Joseph, Ephraim and Manasseh, came to pass in the histories of Great Britain and the United States. God had prepared the British and American peoples to receive Christianity and to become a light to the nations. The true Israel in the world today is the Christian church. The Jews, on the other hand, are not genuine descendants of Israel because they diluted their bloodline by intermarriage, and after they refused to receive Jesus as the Messiah, God had rejected them. Jews could never be God's chosen people in a national sense; they can only come to God through faith in Jesus Christ, the Messiah whom they rejected.

Christian Identity takes this curious prophetic belief one step further and says that there are two groups in the world. One is the children of Yahweh, the true Israelites who are the "seed of the woman," and the other is the progeny of Satan, the "seed of the serpent." God first created a people and put the leading angel Lucifer in charge of them. These were the ancestors of the African and Asian peoples. But Lucifer rebelled and forfeited his right to be governor of the planet, so God created a second human pair, Adam and Eve, who were whites, or "Aryans." However, the evil Lucifer, also known as Satan, seduced Eve, and the result of their union was Cain. After the couple was expelled from the garden, God said he would put enmity between the seed of Satan and the seed of Adam. Cain went to live among the pre-Adamite peoples, who in turn endeavored to intermarry with the descendants of Adam through Seth and infect them with the satanic seed. The struggle between the mongrelized peoples who were descendants of Satan and the pure Aryans has continued throughout the course of history. Still, for the most part the white Anglo-Saxon, Celtic, Nordic, and Germanic peoples maintained their racial purity and thus are the true Israel. They have a racial destiny to fulfill in bringing in God's kingdom here on earth, but it has not yet happened.

Adherents of Christian Identity have a distinctly millenarian view of the future. They believe they are the elect people who will have to endure the great tribulation before they are able to establish God's kingdom. They have been called to fight against sin and the forces of the Antichrist. In fact, they are suffering now because of their sins—permitting the "strangers," Jews and others, to live among them, allowing interracial marriages, and tolerating the sodomites (homosexuals) to continue their evil practices. The Antichrist they are at war with is the U.S. government, which they have labeled the Zionist Occupation

Fig. 1.7 Patriotism as Racism. Here Aryan Nations founder Richard Butler poses with white supremacist followers at his Hayden Lake, Idaho, outpost.

Government. They believe they must arm themselves to do battle with this evil regime, which is out to destroy the pure Aryan race. They point to such events as the Ruby Ridge, Idaho, standoff between Identity member Randy Weaver and FBI agents in August 1992 and the Waco, Texas, siege of the Branch Davidian compound as proof that the fateful struggle between the forces of good and evil is now underway.

Christian Patriot and Militia Movements

Other more loosely knit apocalyptic groups are active today as well. Extremist ideas have fed into the Christian Patriot and militia movements. Many adherents of these groups reject the racial tenets of Christian Identity but still see

the federal government as the enemy. Some have adopted a passive survivalist stance and have holed up in the mountains of the Pacific Northwest to escape the world and ready themselves for the final assault by the forces of evil. Still others have organized citizens' militias to combat environmentalists, gun control laws, income taxes, and liberal social policies—things they identify with their consummate foe, the federal government. At the same time, they are arming for the ultimate showdown, the battle of Armageddon, against the government, the Antichrist. On all sides they perceive conspiracies that rob them of their freedom—Social Security numbers, microchips, UN troops in black helicopters, and so on. Thus, they remain ready and armed for the final struggle with evil, never knowing from where the attack will come.

Millennial Net Surfing

The Internet is teeming with millennial web sites; tens of thousands of hits can emerge with a search engine look for the word *millennium*. The sites range from the wacky to the reverent. Following is a select list of outposts in cyberspace worth visiting, if not for inspiration at least for information. Millennial pilgrims should proceed at their own risk; the views set forth are not necessarily those of the authors.

The Millennium Society:
http://www.millenniumsociety.org/
Primed to party at the tick of the clock, this is the place to learn about the group's planned international extravaganzas.

The Third Millennium
& Jubilee Year 2000:
http://www.nccbuscc.org/jubilee/
vatican/prayer.htm
The pope has declared the year 2000 a jubilee year for the Roman Catholic Church. Here the National Conference of Catholic Bishops reveals plans to celebrate the year.

Sixty Great Conspiracy Theories:
http://www.mille.org/sites.html
This site allows travels to the worlds of those who peddle latter-day paranoia and fear theories.

Calendarland:
http://www.juneau.com/home/
janice/calendarland/millennium/
Here is a guide to time with links to all things calendar related.

The Center for Millennial Studies:
http://www.mille.org
This sophisticated site provides information on the center's serious work of analyzing millennial and apocaylptic movements.

The Millennium Watch Institute:
http://www.channel1.com.mpr/
Browse this site for an overview of the myriad millennial cults that populate the planet.

Gary North, Y2K Concerns:
http://www.garynorth.com
Christian Reconstructionist economist Gary North offers disconcerting diatribes on the Year 2000 computer problem.

Armageddon Books:
http://www.armageddonbooks
.com
The on-line endtimes bookstore stocks a full line of apocalyptic literature and has links to popular Bible prophecy web sites.

Secular Apocalyptic Manifestations

The New Age Movement

Apocalypticism is not unique to religious groups; elements are found in a variety of secular movements as well. Among the most conspicuous of these is the diverse and complex phenomenon labeled *New Age*. The name comes from the millennial character of many of the traditions on which the movement draws.

In the early 1960s, astrologers predicted a move into the Aquarian age, a sort of millennium, and The Fifth Dimension thrust this concept into the popular culture as they sang about "the dawning of the Age of Aquarius," an idea promoted in the countercultural rock musical *Hair.* The growth of the counterculture has reinforced the idea that something new and revolutionary in society is underway. Human evolution has reached its culmination in the imminent transformation of the race. Eastern mysticism affirms the unity between humanity and deity, thus making humans divine and capable of fulfilling their own destiny. Occultism emphasizes that ultimate reality is hidden from ordinary perception, but it can be disclosed by persons who have access to the inner workings of the spiritual realm.

The New Age worldview emerged as an alternative to the Judeo-Christian tradition, and its impact can readily be seen throughout contemporary culture. There is no way of determining how many people are adherents to identifiable New Age groups, but the movement's influence is much greater than its numbers.

As Robert Burrows has aptly observed, the New Age movement is in many ways analogous to the evangelical Christian community. Like evangelicalism, the movement is not tied to any particular organization, has no overarching structure, is made up of people with diverse practices and beliefs, and has no official leadership, although it does have prominent spokespeople.[11]

It is linked to the philosophical traditions underlying it by a set of common assumptions about ultimate reality (or God), humanity, and the nature of human condition. One is monism, that is, all reality is single in character, whether it is identified as pure undifferentiated energy, consciousness, or life force. The polarities of life—light/dark, male/female, good/evil, aggressiveness/passivity—are dynamic interactions that in fact are different facets of the single reality from which all creation emanates. Humanity is an extension of God (or ultimate reality) and shares its nature and essential being. The human predicament is not alienation (sinful rebellion against God) but ignorance. Blindness to the essential unity of all that exists and to humanity's innate divinity is the root of all humanity's woes. The solution involves gaining experiential knowledge of the oneness of humanity and its essential deity. Through the use of psychospiritual techniques, one can rid the consciousness of the negative effects of reason and Christian beliefs. The full experience of the unity of reality and humanity's divinity is the path to godhood, self-realization, cosmic consciousness, enlightenment, and New Age transformation.

Perhaps the best expression of the millennial vision of the New Age movement is Fritjof Capra's *The Turning Point*.[12] He portrays history not as the story of humanity's fall into sin and restoration through God's saving acts, but rather as the story of humanity's fall into ignorance and gradual move upward into enlightenment. Humanity moves from a mind that divides to a mind undivided. The emergence of the latter is the culmination of history, the dawning of the New Age. He links the old order and the crises of our time to Newtonian physics, rationalism, and the Judeo-Christian tradition. Newtonian physics provided a mechanistic view of the physical world whose basic structure was comprised of separate and distinct atoms. Rationalism's exaltation of reason made it impossible to grasp the unity of all reality. The Judeo-Christian tradition severed God from creation, thereby depriving it of its sacred character and laying it open to unrestrained exploitation. Even worse, the tendency of Newtonian physics and reason to divide reality into unrelated bits is a masculine trait, and its most extreme expression of this can be seen in the patriarchal character of Judeo-Christian religion with its authoritative, male God.

The answer to this sorry situation, according to Capra, is to develop a model of culture that recognizes the unity of all reality and regards things in a holistic or unified way. Important components of this model include nuclear physics, which sees reality as vibrant, pulsating energy; intuitive ways of knowing, which directly com-

> Thank you all for visiting the
>
> ## World Peace Millennium Club
>
> I am sorry to inform you that, due to lack of support, WPMC has closed its doors.
>
> To those of you who support the world peace movement, we wish you all the best.
>
> If you wish to contact us, we can be reached at wpmc@tscnet.com

Fig. 1.8 Cosmic Disappointment. This inactive New Age web site shows the results of the failure of cosmic forces to align.

prehend the whole without the interference of reason; and a feminine spirituality based on the awareness of the oneness of all life and of the cyclic rhythms of birth and death. This approach to culture will restore creation and bring an end to humanity's alienation. With a nurturing goddess as the image of deity, a kind of millennial age of decentralized power and egalitarian social organization will unfold. This holistic vision of reality is the key to ushering in a social utopia.

New Agers also call for other actions to resolve the present human predicament. One is psychological in nature, that is, restructuring the mind. A person must clear his or her mind of its crippling clutter and move consciousness into a transformative mode. Drugs, music, chanting, sensory deprivation, self-mortification rituals, and directed meditation are various means to this end. When all the fragments that divide are removed from the mind, the individual is no longer in the way. Then intuition can operate freely, and one can apprehend ultimate reality.

A second line of action to prepare oneself for the future state of being is a careful "tuning" of the body to the forces of the cosmos. This may be done through yoga, exercise, massage, acupuncture, therapeutic touch, and movement therapies. These nostrums from the realm of holistic health operate on the New Age premise that reality is one and manifests itself as spiritual energy in the body, as it does in all creation.

A third action is the use of practical magic, namely, the use of objects whose patterns of energy and vibration supposedly resonate with the mind and body. They can have practical benefits, ranging from curing insomnia and cancer to aiding one's business deals or smoothing over troubled interpersonal relationships. Rock crystals, pyramids, colors, and flower essences are various mag-

ical devices that serve to connect people to higher realms of light and awareness.

A final action involves spiritism. The cosmos—the world in general—is seen as a multidimensional reality in which spirits of various kinds dwell. They are sources of power, instruction, and guidance for those who know how to contact them and enlist their services. This involves the assistance of mediums, spiritual teachers, and entities that are in the great beyond. The famous line from George Lucas's *Star Wars* film, "May the force be with you," popularized the concept of an energy force that resides in the cosmos, gives life to all, and can be tapped intuitively through one's feelings, and reflects the secular emphasis on the spiritual. The New Age vision of the future appeals to people in many ways and on a multitude of levels.[13]

The Third Wave

Another secular millenarian view is the Third Wave, popularized by futurologist Alvin Toffler in his long, rambling book of the same name, published in 1980.[14] He argues that if we take the "long view" of the prospects of human civilization, there is no reason to be pessimistic. The First Wave of civilization was the agricultural phase, in which life was based on land and its use, and the Second Wave was the industrial phase, with life based on technology and the social organization oriented toward production. The Third Wave of change will bring about a totally new way of existence, one founded on diversified, renewable energy sources, new production methods, an end to the nuclear family, and radically changed schools and corporations. The new civilization will topple bureaucracies, reduce the role of the nation-state, give rise to semiautonomous economies in a postimperialist world, and lead to governments that are simpler, more effective, and more democratic than any known today.

This utopian society of the future will be a "practopia," a society that is both practical and preferable to the one we have. It will not be free of social problems, but at the same time it will not be static or frozen in some kind of unreal perfection or modeled on some imagined ideal of the past. The new civilization will not be antidemocratic or militarist, nor will it reduce its citizens to faceless uniformity, destroy its neighbors, and degrade the environment. It is one that will make allowance for individual differences and embrace racial, regional, religious, and subcultural variety. While innovative, it will yet provide relative stability. Instead of channeling its energies into marketization, this new civilization will direct great passion into art. New ethical or moral standards will be invented to deal with complex social issues. It will be in better balance with the biosphere. In this secular, decentralized world all that was bad or undesirable in the agricultural and industrial societies will be replaced with desirable and humane qualities. Obviously this best-selling book is one of the most extraordinary faith statements about the future ever made.

Catastrophe Theories

In sharp contrast to Toffler's enthusiastic portrayal of what lies ahead are the various catastrophe theories. These theories are not so much linked to particular official movements as to schools of thought. In each case they expound pessimistic prophecies of the future that qualify them as apocalyptic. The most extreme theory is the fear that the earth will collide with an asteroid or supermeteor. This is the stuff of science fiction, but many people take seriously the prospect of such a disaster. Astronomers have identified thousands of rocks circling around in space, one of which is 785 miles in diameter. About forty of these rocks intersect with the earth's orbit as they travel through space, and in 1989 one passed within five hundred thousand miles of our planet. Such an object could do great damage if it were to strike the earth. For instance, an asteroid one kilometer in diameter would explode with an energy force approaching one million megatons of TNT. (In contrast, the largest nuclear weapon ever tested only reached fifty-seven megatons.) The impact would throw so much dust into the air that sunlight would be greatly reduced, causing a rapid drop in temperatures and catastrophic losses of food crops. A meteor significantly larger than this could destroy human life completely because of the breakdown in the food chain that would result. Although this scenario seems highly unlikely, many scientists now feel that a major impact about

Startling photos from Iraq reveal that SADDAM HUSSEIN is rebuilding the lost city of Babylon. The Bible says Babylon will be rebuilt in the last days. *Could ours be the last generation?*

THE RISE OF BABYLON

SIGN OF THE END TIMES

CHARLES H. DYER ᵂᴵᵀᴴ ANGELA ELWELL HUNT

Fig. 1.9 Saddam as the Sign. During the Persian Gulf War of 1991, Iraqi leader Saddam Hussein was thought by many to be the Antichrist. This 1991 title, picturing Saddam on the cover, was only one of several books that fueled such speculation.

that will guarantee them the means of livelihood. In most of these areas, however, population growth regularly exceeds economic growth, thus rendering it impossible for people to rise out of poverty.

This impoverishment of a large portion of humanity is reflected in the increasing disparity in wealth between the developed and developing world. The gap between the rich and the poor nations is widening, not narrowing, and within the developed countries a similar situation is occurring between the most and least affluent segments of the populace. The ability to slow the birth rate and obtain a population balance is undermined by poverty. It is a formidable barrier to raising the standard of health care, something that is absolutely necessary if family planning is to become a realizable goal.

Linked with the population explosion and wealth disparity is the threat of the exhaustion of natural resources. The consumption of resources is currently taking place at an unsustainable rate. Simply put, we are depleting that which should be available for future generations. This catastrophe could lead to bitter wars, as the haves and have nots struggle to preserve or increase their shares of the earth's mineral and biological resources.

Also, serious changes are taking place in the earth's climate due to the burning of fossil fuels (coal, oil, and gas), as well as

sixty-five million years ago caused the extinction of 50 percent of all species on the earth, including the dinosaurs.

Another catastrophe threatening life on earth is the population explosion. Early in the twentieth century there were about two billion people in the world. By the end of the century the number will have risen to six billion, and within another fifty years it could reach ten billion. Most of the growth will be in the developing countries, which in 2020 will contain about 85 percent of the world's people. These people will make demands for food, energy, and employment plant materials. The delicate balance between the different forms of life and the physical and chemical environment that surrounds them on the planet is in jeopardy, and it seems the threat of global warming can no longer be ignored. A significant increase in the atmospheric carbon dioxide levels due to the burning of fossil fuels is causing surface temperatures on the earth to rise, a situation known as the greenhouse effect. An overall increase in temperatures of just a few degrees would affect rainfall patterns in many parts of the world, turning agriculturally productive areas into deserts. At the same time, the melting of the polar ice caps would raise the ocean levels and water would cover land currently inhabited by millions of people. The competition for the remaining space would become even more intense than it already is.

All of the above factors—unchecked population growth, high levels of poverty, competition for scarce resources, and climatic changes due to increased consumption levels—can lead to conflicts among the world's peoples. However, these conflicts have the potential to become struggles of apocalyptic proportions because of the kinds of weaponry now available. The idea of war in the modern world is that victory is all important, and no amount of violence is too great to obtain it. This was clearly the pattern in both the First and Second World Wars. There was no longer a meaningful distinction between offensive and defensive weapons, and civilian populations were just as subject to the horrors of war as armies and navies.

Even worse, new types of weapons have become available that are far more deadly than anything used in the past. In the last days of World War II, the first nuclear bombs were used on the Japanese cities of Hiroshima and Nagasaki. In the subsequent years, nations have built even larger weapons, and humankind now possesses the power to destroy life on the planet. The balance of terror during the Cold War forestalled the two superpowers, the United States and the Soviet Union, from using their weapons. Both sides realized that a nuclear exchange would deplete the ozone layer and spew deadly radiation into the atmosphere. This would cause a nuclear winter, whereby the smoke and ashes produced from the explosions would block the sun's rays, cool the surface temperatures dramatically, and cause crop failures and environmental damage in far distant areas. However, other nations and even terrorist groups have access to nuclear technology, and in spite of the nuclear nonproliferation treaties, some of these individuals may decide to use it for purposes of national aggrandizement, acquiring resources, or advancing a religious ideology. Throughout the 1990s, Iraqi leader Saddam Hussein has posed the most prominent threat, flirting with the abuse of nuclear technology to the horror of the watching world.

In addition to nuclear armaments, several nations have developed chemical and biological weapons that use chemical substances and biological organisms to kill plants, animals, and humans. Chemical warfare began in World War I and resulted in heavy casualties. Researchers during World War II developed even more lethal chemical weapons such as nerve gases that are so toxic that one drop on a person's skin will result in death in less than four minutes. The warring powers were reluctant to use such gases because of the fear of massive retaliation, but since then, countries such as Iraq have done so. Scientists during World War II also experimented with biological toxins such as anthrax, tularemia, and fungus agents and substances that cause animal diseases and destroy crops. To this point, only the Japanese have used such agents, albeit in a limited fashion, in China.

The "ABC" weapons (atomic, biological, and chemical) have raised the stakes in warfare to levels beyond all imagination. The apocalyptic struggle envisioned in the Book of Revelation is now very much within the realm of possibility. Given the competition for scarce resources and the ever expanding population, a cataclysmic conflict launched by people who have little to lose is no longer simply the stuff of science fiction. The new millennium could see the total elimination of human life on earth, or at least its reduction to a primitive existence. The catastrophists view the new millennium with deep pessimism, not optimism. Aldous Huxley's "brave new world" of technological advance and creature comforts is for them an illusion. As

Fig. 1.10 Mark Your Calendars. New Year's Eve, December 31, 1999, is likely to be Dick Clark's biggest celebration in years.

Christians would put it, sinful humanity now holds the key to its own destruction.

Conclusion

With this opening chapter we have sought to set the stage for the coming millennium. Whether you are an avid student of the Bible or a measured millennial cynic, we trust you have already learned a few new things through this overview. After all, we are all pilgrims on this journey into a new millennium. What will it bring? We can't predict for certain. But the Big Calendar Turn is an unprecedented event in our lifetimes. The title of James Finn Garner's recent, whimsical look at the coming millennium perhaps best sums up our ultimate expectations: *Apocalypse Wow!*[15] Something big is going to happen. But can we be certain of what or when? The Bible has a great deal to say about the endtimes, and there is no shortage of disagreement over how to interpret its message. Join us on our pilgrimage as we turn to chapter 2 and a tour of what various Christians have to say about the return of Jesus Christ and the beginning of a millennial age.

40

2

The Eschatological Smorgasbord
The Major Varieties of Millennialism

> The only place in the Bible that speaks of an actual millennium is the passage in Revelation 20:1–6. Any millennial doctrine must be based upon the most natural exegesis of this passage.
>
> George Eldon Ladd

"The world is coming to an end," shouted the street corner preacher, confronting a surprised Blondie and Dagwood. They had heard the same message many times before, so they let the minister know of their skepticism regarding his reliability. Downcast, he admitted he was on a losing streak, packed up his soap box, and optimistically opined, "Maybe I'll get lucky tomorrow."[1]

While the preacher's approach was a bit misguided, he was right about one thing: The world is coming to an end—some-time, according to the Bible. Concern with the future naturally raises a number of questions. What happens at death? Do people enter into another state of existence, or does life terminate completely at death? And if the human soul continues to exist after death, what does it encounter beyond the grave? Is the whole of creation moving toward some point of divine fulfillment, an "end" designed for it by God? Will the generations that have come and gone through the ages participate in this grand climax?

Theologians employ the term *eschatology* for matters having to do with the future or the study of last things. Such an interest in future events is not unique to Christianity; most major world religions wrestle with questions about the final destiny of the individual person and the di-

Fig. 2.1 Eschatological Evangelism. The Mayes tracts, placed in unusual places—here a two liter pop bottle—remind those who discover them of the imminent return of Christ and the need to repent.

rection in which humanity is moving. Key to understanding the Christian interpretation of the end involves understanding the various eschatologies.

What Is Eschatology?

Christians believe that in the future the work of God will be summed up or arrive at a state of completion. The endtimes are seen as the point at which God is finally and perfectly glorified in all of his creative activities. The destructive influence of sin is at last overcome, and the saving work of Jesus Christ is crowned with victory. Those who have been God's covenant people through faith in the atoning death of his Son experience their long-awaited redemption and glorification. God's saving plan is fulfilled, and his people enter into personal and permanent communion with him. Christians see this not as an ideal but as a reality that will come to pass at, what theologians call, "the consummation of all things."

In Greek, the word for "the last" is *eschatos,* and from this we derive the term *eschatology.* The concept of eschatology is rooted in Scripture passages that speak of "the last days" (Isa. 2:2; Micah 4:1; Acts 2:17; 2 Tim. 3:1; 2 Peter 3:3), "last times" (1 Peter 1:20; Jude 18), and "the last hour" (1 John 2:18). Although people in Old Testament times thought only in terms of "this age" and "the coming age," New Testament writers distinguished between a first and second coming of the Messiah. For them, the last days was the period immediately preceding the return of Christ and the end of this present world.

To be sure, Christians live with the consciousness that the kingdom of Christ has come, they now possess eternal life, and the Holy Spirit is the earnest of their heavenly inheritance. It is apparent, as the New Testament suggests, that the *eschaton* (the "last thing") has already begun. Further, though these aspects of Christianity cannot be empirically demonstrated through modern social science, Christians do have experience of them through revelation and by faith. A person cannot see or enter the kingdom except through experiencing the new birth through Christ. His or her participation in death to the old existence and resurrection to the new eschatological life is a present reality even if only in a spiritual sense.

Jesus fulfilled the Old Testament messianic prophecies and through his resurrection triumphed over sin and death, and the time of the new covenant has begun. Nevertheless, Satan's power is not yet eliminated and the fallen world order is a historical reality that challenges the Christian's existence. The kingdom has not become a visible, universal institution, death is still a fact of life for all human beings regardless of their spiritual condition, and the church (the Christian community) has not attained to the fullness of Christ's perfection. This reflects the tension be-

The Bible and Predictions: Some Statistics

- Amount of predictive matter in the Bible: 8,352 verses, out of its total of 31,124
- Proportion that is predictive: 27%
  Old Testament: 28 ½%
  New Testament: 21 ½%
- Books with the most predictive matter:

  Old Testament
  Ezekiel: 821 verses
  Jeremiah: 812 verses
  Isaiah: 754 verses
  New Testament
  Matthew: 278 verses
  Revelation: 256 verses
  Luke: 250 verses

- Books most highly predictive according to the proportion of verses involving forecasts of the future:

  Old Testament
  Zephaniah: 89% predictive
  Obadiah: 81% predictive
  Nahum: 74% predictive
  New Testament
  Revelation: 63% predictive
  Hebrews: 45% predictive
  2 Peter: 41% predictive

- Books with the most predictions in symbolical form: Revelation, 24; Daniel, 20

Source: J. Barton Payne, *Encyclopedia of Biblical Prophecy* (Grand Rapids: Baker, 1980), 681–82.

tween what is commonly called the "already" and the "not yet" in New Testament eschatology. But in the end God's victory through Christ will be exhibited before the entire world. Eschatology, therefore, encompasses matters linked to the second coming of Christ, including the climactic event that will mark the close of human history and open the door to the eternal joy that believers will experience in God's perfect kingdom.

The Role of History

Christians do not see history as an unending cycle but rather a definite process that moves toward a divinely determined end. The end God has in mind is not an evolutionary transition but a crisis event. At this specific point in time, Jesus will return to earth in power and glory, the dead shall rise, the last judgment will occur, and the members of his church, that "called-out assembly" from every tongue and nation, will live and reign with him in the new heaven and new earth that shall never end. God will separate the disobedient and unbelieving from his children, and those separated out will be excluded from his presence forever. The creation will be liberated from the power and effects of sin, and evil will be banished to the outer reaches of the universe. Then at last, when God has reconciled all things to himself in Christ, the kingdom of this world shall become the kingdom of our Lord and of his Christ, and over it he will reign for ever and ever (1 Cor. 15:24, 28; Eph. 1:10; Rev. 11:15).

There is agreement among biblical scholars about the general outlines of the eschaton. However, differences arise when they seek to spell out a more detailed map of the future. What is the nature of Christ's return? What will take place on what in the New Testament is called "the day of Christ" (Phil. 1:6, 10), "the day of the Lord Jesus" (2 Cor. 1:14; cf. 1 Cor. 1:8), and the "day of the Lord" (Acts 2:20; 1 Thess. 5:2; 2 Peter 3:10–12)? What will happen at the resurrection, who will participate in it, and precisely when will it occur? How will the divine wrath be poured out on evildoers? Will Israel, God's covenant people of the Old Testament, return to the land of their ancestors, and, if so, under what conditions? Who is the Antichrist, and what will he do? Will the church be taken up to be with Christ before God's wrath is poured out on earth, or will he allow believers to be subjected to all the furies of hell before he finally rescues them? These and many other questions have been the grist for the mills of eschatological speculation, as revealed in the plethora of sermons, books, tapes, and films on the topic and through the chatter on radio programs, TV talk shows, and the Internet.

Fig. 2.2 The Binding of Satan and Vision of the Future. Albrecht Dürer's classic 1498 woodcut represents an angel's hurling of the devil into the abyss as described in Revelation 20:1–6 and another angel showing John the New Jerusalem.

The Messianic Kingdom

An important element in eschatological thinking is the messianic kingdom, commonly referred to as the "millennial" kingdom because of the six references in Revelation 20:1–10 to the thousand-year reign of Christ. As the end of the second millennium of the Christian era has drawn near, theorizing on this matter has increased at an exponential rate. Before examining in closer detail the various positions that theologians have taken regarding the thousand-year kingdom, let us briefly survey Revelation 20, the Scripture passage that sets forth the concept.

Revelation 19 has just given a dramatic description of the victorious return of Jesus Christ. The narrative then turns to the ensuing events. It relates that an angel came down from heaven who held the key to the bottomless pit (the abyss) and a large chain. The angel seized the dragon or serpent that is called the devil or Satan, bound him and threw him into the pit, and shut and sealed it so that he could not deceive the nations. Those who had given their lives because of their witness to Jesus and for the Word of God and who had not worshiped the Beast (Antichrist) or received its mark were resurrected and reigned with Christ for a thousand years on thrones that had been set up for that purpose. They who shared in this first resurrection were called blessed and holy. They would never again be subject to death (the second death). Instead they would be priests of God and of Christ and

reign with him for a thousand years. When the thousand years came to an end, Satan escaped and tried to deceive the nations again, but he and his minions were destroyed and thrown into the lake of fire and brimstone where they would suffer eternal torment.

Premillennialism

Throughout the history of the church, the events described in Revelation 20 have been interpreted in different ways. One group, the premillennialists, holds that Jesus will personally and physically return to earth and immediately establish the millennial kingdom. Most premillennialists interpret the thousand years literally, but some see it symbolically as an extended period of time. The reign will be inaugurated in a cataclysmic way, and Jesus will personally exercise control over all the earth and its inhabitants.

The second coming will be preceded by a series of dramatic signs—wars, famines, and earthquakes, the preaching of the gospel to all nations, a great spiritual apostasy culminating in the appearance of the Antichrist, and an intense persecution of the church. Just when all seems to be lost, Christ will gloriously descend from the sky, smite his foes and place Satan under lock and key, and take charge of the world that is rightfully his. This will usher in a period of peace and righteousness under his firm but benevolent direction. These events will take place suddenly, by God's direct action, rather than gradually over a long period of time through the conversion of individuals. Those who have died in Christ in ages past will be resurrected, and they will join with the living believers at their Lord's side to rule the world.

This future age will be one of great happiness and joy, and even the Jews will figure prominently in it. They will at last acknowledge their Messiah and once again occupy a prominent place in God's plan for the world. The territory of their kingdom, with the Son of David as its omnipotent monarch, will far exceed that of Solomon (Ps. 72:8–14). In fact, many of the details about life in the kingdom are found in the Old Testament. People will have long lives (Isa. 65:20). Wild animals will be tame (Isa. 11:6–9). The curse will be removed from nature, and even the desert will produce abundant crops (Isa. 35). The weather will be ideal, and light will be continuous (Zech. 14:6–7). The world will be free from war and violent conflict, and all will dwell together in peace (Isa. 2:4; Micah 4:3–4). In other words, through his power and authority, Christ will restrain evil and ensure happiness.

Despite these idyllic conditions, a final rebellion against Christ and his saints will occur at the close of the thousand years. Satan, now unbound, will launch one last, desperate attempt to regain his former power. However, God will utterly vanquish the Evil One, call forth the unbelieving dead from their graves (the second resurrection), bring everyone before the final judgment, and consign those who had rejected him to everlasting punishment. His children will then enter into the New Jerusalem and enjoy the eternal state of happiness and bliss.

Premillennialists read the Scriptures quite literally and generally interpret the Book of Revelation in a futurist sense; that is, they see the events described in it as occurring in the endtimes and as the consummation of the history of redemption. Other Bible scholars, however, take the preterist, historicist, or idealist approach. Those who hold the preterist approach believe Revelation 20 portrays events that happened at the time it was written and insist the book was intended to encourage Christians who were undergoing persecution in that period—and by implication, throughout all ages. According to the historicist explanation, the events described in Revelation 20 should be interpreted in a prophetic sense. They actually happen in the future but over a long course of church history. The idealist interpretation entirely dehistoricizes the events and sees them as purely symbolic representations of truths that are timeless in character.

Central to the premillennial position are the two resurrections. The first resurrection is that of the saints, who are to rule with Christ (Dan. 12:2; Matt. 19:28; Luke 14:14; John 5:28–29; 1 Cor. 6:2–3; 15:23–26; Phil. 3:11). Up to this point in time, Christ has been reigning at his Father's right hand in

Fig. 2.3 Saints in the Hands of a Biblical Postmillennialist. Jonathan Edwards, perhaps the foremost eighteenth-century American theologian, was an influential advocate of postmillennialism.

heaven. Now he is on earth, exercising his authority in triumphal majesty. Everyone on the planet sees the power and glory of his sovereignty. Thus, the millennium is linked to the resurrection; it is the age of his manifested rule. It is an absolute kingdom; every knee shall bow to him (Phil. 2:10–11). However, his reign will be one of justice and righteousness—not arbitrary whim—and peace among people and harmony within the creation will prevail. The saints themselves will share in what their Lord does. Only after the millennium has ended will those who have died without Christ be resurrected and that only for judgment. Christ's own children will go on to live with him in the eternal city whose builder and maker is God (Heb. 11:10).

Postmillennialism

At the opposite end of the millennial spectrum are those who believe that the kingdom of God is now being extended in the world through the preaching of the gospel and the saving work of the Holy Spirit in the hearts of individuals. The postmillennialists hold that the world will eventually be Christianized, thereby bringing in a golden age of spiritual prosperity. Then Christ will return. Thus, the millennium expected by the postmillennialists deviates from that of the premillennialists both with regard to the time and manner in which it will be set up and in the nature of the kingdom and way in which Christ exercises his control.

Postmillennialists anticipate a golden age that will not differ significantly from our own time as far as the basic facts of existence are concerned. The present age has been and will continue to gradually merge into the millennial age as an increasing proportion of the world's inhabitants turn to the Christian faith. Marriage and family life will continue, and new members will be added to the human race through the natural process of birth. Sin will not be eliminated altogether, but it will be reduced to a minimum as the moral and spiritual environment of the earth becomes increasingly Christian. Social, economic, and educational problems will remain, but their unpleasant features will be reduced and desirable features heightened. Christian principles of belief and conduct will become the accepted standard.

The nature of life during the millennium will be better than that in today's world, therefore, in the sense that existence within a Christianized community is preferable to that in a pagan or irreligious community. Although the present age is anything but the best of all possible worlds, Christians are engaged in proclaiming the truth, and the gospel is becoming increasingly more influential in the lives of people. Even now Christians function as the outward and visible manifestation of the kingdom of God, and over the course of time they will produce a transformed political and social order whose values are those of Christ.

Gradually Christians will bring in the millennium of Christ's rule in the hearts of men and women. It will be a period of genuine peace in which conflicts among nations and frictions among social classes and races will cease. There will be no labor disputes, and all races will live together in harmony. Even religious competition and denominational rivalries will become a thing of the past. It will be the fulfillment of the vision of harmony pictured in Isaiah 11:6, in which the wolf will live with the lamb, the leopard will lie down with the goat, the calf and the lion will feed together, and a little child shall lead them. He who said "peace I leave with you; my peace I give you" (John 14:27) will carry out that promise.

Not only will Christ's reign over the earth be the result of forces now active in the world, but it will also last an indefinitely long period of time, perhaps much longer than a literal one thousand years, the number used in Revelation 20. The millennium's length will be difficult to determine because it has no clear beginning point. The kingdom will arrive by degrees not instantaneously. Eventually the era of peace and harmony will conclude with the personal and visible return of Christ, just as the Bible has foretold. This will be followed by the resurrection of both the righteous and unrighteous. All will be judged and consigned to one of two permanent states—eternal punishment or eternal happiness.

Most postmillennialists agree that even though the millennium will be a golden age, a time of apostasy and resurgence of evil will occur just before Christ's return. This limited manifestation of evil will serve to show once again what a terrible matter sin is and how much it is worthy of punishment. Still, those who call themselves postmillennialists place a strong emphasis on the universal character of Christ's redeeming acts. There is hope for the salvation of an incredibly large number of humankind. It was the world, or the human race, that fell through Adam's sin, and this is the object of Christ's redemption. That does not mean that every individual will be saved but that humankind, as a race, will be redeemed. The Scriptures portray Jehovah not as a tribal deity but as "the great King over all the earth" and "the Lord of all the earth" (Pss. 47:2; 97:5). The salvation he has in mind cannot be limited to a small select group or a favored few. The good news of the gospel was not merely "local" news for a few villages in Palestine but a worldwide message. The abundant testimony of Scripture is that the kingdom of God is to *fill* the earth, "from sea to sea and from the River to the ends of the earth" (Zech. 9:10).

> After this I looked and there before me was a great multitude that no one could count, from every nation, tribe, people and language, standing before the throne and in front of the Lamb. They were wearing white robes and were holding palm branches in their hands. And they cried out in a loud voice: "Salvation belongs to our God, who sits on the throne, and to the Lamb."
>
> Revelation 7:9–10

God has chosen to redeem untold numbers of human beings. While postmillennialists acknowledge that they have not been told what proportion of the populace will be included in his purposes of mercy, given the future days of prosperity that are promised to the church, they infer that the great majority will be found among that number.

Christians have an important role to play in God's plan of redeeming humankind. The Great Commission, which Christ gave to his disciples just before he departed the earth, made clear the task of the Christian: "All authority in heaven and on earth has been given to me. Therefore go and make disciples of all nations, baptizing them in the name of the Father and of the Son and of the Holy Spirit, and teaching them to obey everything I have commanded you" (Matt. 28:18–20). Christ's followers are to take the gospel to all nations and to all persons so that their hearts and lives may be transformed by the gospel. His authority lies behind this evangelization. Jesus will not have any more authority in the future than he now has, for he has all there is. We do not have to look for a future age when he will bring in the reign he has prophesied. Christ the King is as capable of doing things now as he will be in the future.

The redemption of the world is a long, slow process that has been taking place throughout the centuries. From a human point of view, it has often appeared as though the forces of evil were about to gain the upper hand, but as one age has succeeded another, postmillennialists believe progress has occurred. Consider, for instance, the horrendous moral and spiritual conditions that existed on earth at the time of the first coming of Christ. The world groped helplessly in pagan darkness. Slavery, polygamy, exploitation of women and children, ignorance, grinding poverty, and primitive health care were the lot of nearly all those except members of the ruling class.

Now the world at large is on a far higher plane of existence. Slavery and polygamy have disappeared except in areas that are under the sway of false religions. The status of women and children have been elevated in an extraordinary fashion. Social and economic conditions have improved everywhere in the world. The spirit of in-

Fig. 2.4 The Sound of Postmillennialism. Ernest Shurtleff's militant hymn of victorious social progress reflects the influence of postmillennial themes.

the new covenant blessings. Godliness and sober living bring their own reward. "Seek first his kingdom and his righteousness, and all these things will be given to you as well" (Matt. 6:33). "Godliness has value for all things, holding promise for both the present life and the life to come" (1 Tim. 4:8). "The desert and parched land will be glad; the wilderness will rejoice and blossom" (Isa. 35:1). By properly managing the earth, the task that had been assigned to the first humans, the restoration of plant and animal life will become possible. Once the sin condition in humankind is remedied, a marvelous transformation will take place in nature. In fact, the resources that have been squandered on war will be increasingly dedicated to healing the environment.

ternational cooperation has reduced the number and intensity of wars.

According to postmillennialists, the great material prosperity that the Bible says will characterize the millennial era will be to a large extent the natural result of the high moral and spiritual life of that time. Numerous prophecies affirm that temporal blessings follow in the wake of

Postmillennialists also cite the veritable revolutions in transportation, communications, and the realm of labor-saving devices occurring during the twentieth century as proof for their claims. New energy sources continue to be discovered and exploited, and the whole field of electronics has transformed how people live. As one new discovery follows another, postmillennialists see ever more clearly the tremendous possibilities for good, potentials that through all the preceding centuries remained unrealized. No matter how marvelous this material prosperity may be, it must be seen as the by-product of the moral and spiritual prosperity that already has come to characterize the partially Christianized nations.

Until the time of the Reformation, the Bible had been a book for priests only. It was written in Latin, and the Roman Catholic Church would not allow it to be translated into the languages of the common people. But this all changed when the Protestant Reformers came on the scene. The Bible was quickly translated into all the vernacular languages of Europe. And wherever the light of the Reformation went, the Bible became the book of the common people. The decrees of popes and church councils gave way to the Word of Life. Ever since then, the spread of the Scriptures has continued unabated. Bible societies now circulate more Bibles each year than were produced in the fifteen centuries prior to the Reformation. Today the Bible is available in whole or in part in the tongues of all but a handful of the world's people. None of the so-called best-sellers even approach the sales figures that the Bible attains each year. The worldwide spread of knowledge and literacy has made the message of Scripture, the saving gospel of Jesus Christ, accessible to all peoples.

Moreover, the new electronic media enables the gospel to be preached throughout the world. Because of this, Billy Graham has reached more people with the gospel than any other evangelist in history. Thanks to the worldwide missionary outreach that has carried the Bible and gospel to every corner of the earth, the number of Christians has grown more in the last one hundred years than in the preceding nineteen hundred. Christianity has almost as many nominal adherents as the combined total of any other two world religions.[2]

Although some postmillennialists tend to jump to conclusions about how soon the kingdom will be ushered in, most concede that they really do not know whether the time will be long or short. But above all, they do not despair of the power of the gospel to win the world. They believe it cannot be defeated, and eventually the goal will be reached.

Amillennialism

A third widely held position concerning the future kingdom's timing is amillennialism. Adherents to this branch of eschatology believe there will be no literal thousand-year reign of Christ on earth. The second coming of Christ will be a dramatic, visible occurrence that will be followed immediately by a general resurrection of all the dead, both believers and unbelievers. Meanwhile, the Lord Jesus will instantaneously transform and glorify the living believers. Then the last judgment of all men and women will take place, and they will be consigned to their eternal rewards. Unbelievers and all who have rejected Christ will experience the second death and spend eternity in the outer darkness, permanently separated from the holy God. The names of those who during their lives received Christ as their Savior and Lord have been recorded in the Book of Life, and they will enter into everlasting happiness in the New Jerusalem, the holy city that dominates the landscape of the new earth.

Amillennialists regard the first coming of Christ as more important than the second coming. When the Son of God came to earth, he lived a sinless life, died on the cross as the atonement for our sins, and rose triumphantly from the grave. In the process, he overcame sin, the devil, and death itself. Because of the victory of Christ, the ultimate issues of history have already been decided. It is now only a matter of time until his work is consummated.

Amillennialists believe the kingdom of God is both present and future. Christians embrace the present by following Jesus and the future by expecting his return. The bridge between present and future is faith in Christ. What we do today anticipates what will occur in the future.

Christ taught that the kingdom was already present during his earthly ministry:

Fig. 2.5 An Amillennial Backlist Favorite. William Hendrickson's *More Than Conquerors,* a classic defense of amillennialism, was the first book published by Baker Book House. This 1939 book went through eleven hardcover printings before being released in a paper edition in 1998.

"But if I drive out demons by the Spirit of God, then the kingdom of God has come upon you" (Matt. 12:28). When asked by the Pharisees when the kingdom would arrive, Jesus responded: "The kingdom of God does not come with your careful observation, nor will people say, 'Here it is,' or 'There it is,' because the kingdom of God is within you" (Luke 17:20–21). However, he also stated that in some sense the kingdom of God was still future. "Many will come from the east and the west, and will take their places at the feast with Abraham, Isaac and Jacob in the kingdom of heaven" (Matt. 8:11). Paul also described the kingdom as both present and future: "For he [God] has rescued us from the dominion of darkness and brought us into the kingdom of the Son he loves" (Col. 1:13) and "The Lord will rescue me from every evil attack and will bring me safely to his heavenly kingdom" (2 Tim. 4:18).

Since the kingdom of God has a sense of both present and future, we live in a tension between the "already" and the "not yet." We are now in the kingdom and share its blessings, but still we await its total and complete victory. Since the precise time of Christ's return is not known, Christians live with a continuing sense of urgency, realizing as they do that the end of history may be near. At the same time, however, they continue to plan and work for the future on this present earth because it could very well last a long time.

According to amillennialists, as far as the one thousand years of Revelation 20 are concerned, we are now in the millennium. Christians today enjoy the benefits of this period because Satan has been bound. It does not mean that the Evil One is not active in the world, but rather that during this period he cannot deceive the nations, namely, he cannot prevent the spread of the gospel. The binding of Satan makes possible missions and evangelism. This greatly encourages and motivates the

church for service. At the same time, the souls of believers who have died currently live and reign with Christ in heaven while they await the resurrection of the body. Their state is one of blessedness and happiness, but their joy will not be complete until they are restored to their bodies. This, too, is a comfort to those whose loved ones have died believing in the Lord.

Adherents to this position hold that certain signs will precede the final return of Christ. These include the preaching of the gospel to all nations, the fulfillment of the promises to Israel through the church, the great apostasy, the time of tribulation, and the coming of the Antichrist. However, one must not see these as referring exclusively to the endtime. In some sense they have been with us from the very beginning of the Christian era and are present now. This reinforces Christ's command to be ready and to watch for his return. Never should we in our thoughts push it into the far-distant future. Nevertheless, these signs of the times will experience a climactic fulfillment just before Christ returns. This fulfillment will not be something totally new but rather an intensification of those signs that have been present all along.

Amillennialists agree with postmillennialists that both the second coming and the general resurrection will be single events. There will be no separation between believers and unbelievers within the timing sequence of either one. After the resurrection, believers who are still alive shall be transformed and glorified. As Paul states in 1 Corinthians 15:51–52: "We will not all sleep, but we will all be changed—in a flash, in the twinkling of an eye, at the last trumpet. For the trumpet will sound, the dead will be raised imperishable, and we will be changed." Both groups of believers, those who have died and those who are still alive, will then meet their Lord, rejoicing in their new resurrection bodies.

On the other hand, amillennialists agree with premillennialists that a worldwide growth of righteousness extending to every realm of society is not likely to occur and that the faith of many Christians will grow cold. Most of them doubt that a worldwide evangelization resulting in the conversion of nearly everyone is likely to take place. Both groups also acknowledge that Christ could come at any time. However, amillennialists believe that the Old Testament prophecies have been fulfilled in the church or will be so in the new earth described in the Book of Revelation. Thus, they are not preoccupied with biblical prophecy and the signs of the times and have little to say about the deterioration of world conditions and the present culture. What social criticism one hears from amillennialist preachers is far more likely to be based on considerations of human sin than prophetic passages in the Scriptures.

Amillennialists see the Book of Revelation as a continuing recapitulation of events taking place in the life of the church not in some far-removed future time. Also, they believe it is a highly symbolic book whose images should be taken figuratively not literally. They do not see Satan bound with a literal iron chain or the bowls, seals, and trumpets as literal objects. Thus, the number one thousand is also a figurative concept. It is seen as the symbolic number of perfection. Amillennialists and postmillennialists alike set forth the argument that the numbers three and seven are both sacred, and added together they total ten, the number of holy perfection. The num-

"It has to do with eschatology!"

Fig. 2.6 The Great Millennium Match. A lighthearted look at the debates and infighting that has marked end-times thinking throughout church history.

ber ten cubed (that is, to the third power) is one thousand, and this can be understood as the number of absolute completeness. It represents the totality of Christ's triumph over Satan and the forces of evil, and it is the completeness of the glory of the redeemed in the new heaven and earth.

Dispensational Premillennialism

The dominant force in prophetic teaching today is actually a variation of premillennialism known as dispensational premillennialism. Whereas the other strains of millennial thought all have deep roots in the history of the church, the dispensational variety is of recent origin. During the later nineteenth century, a renaissance of premillennial thinking took place in Britain and North America, fostered by a number of Bible and prophecy conferences. These interdenominational meetings focused primarily on the second coming of Christ, but at first they were only vaguely premillennial in their emphasis. By 1910, however, a radical change had occurred in the Bible and prophecy movement. The founders had passed from the scene, and a new generation had taken up the reins of leadership. The young leaders accepted the teaching of John Nelson Darby, an influential British leader of the separatist Plymouth Brethren, and became thoroughgoing dispensationalists. Darby's

unique influence will be more closely examined in chapter 3.

It must be emphasized that all dispensationalists are premillennialists, but many premillennialists do not subscribe to the dispensationalist view of the future. To be sure, there is a small group of "progressive dispensationalists" who have recently proposed a number of modifications to the classical form of the doctrine of dispensationalism. But this group remains in the minority, and its influence has not filtered down to the televangelists, preachers, and writers who promote dispensationalism at the grassroots level. Above all, dispensationalism is an entire system of theology, of which eschatology is only one element, and it is firmly based on a distinctive approach to interpreting the Bible.

Biblical Interpretation

Dispensationalists talk about "rightly dividing the word of truth" (2 Tim. 2:15 KJV), not only into compartments of time but also into sections that apply to Israel, the church, and the Gentiles. They insist that not all portions of Scripture apply equally to the believer. Further, they stress literalism as the basic principle for interpreting the words of Scripture. The literal, normal, or plain interpretation of whatever text may be under consideration is the most desirable approach.

Dispensationalists affirm that the writers of the various Old Testament books stressed they were speaking the word of the Lord to his people, and the New Testament authors declared their message was intended for the saints of the church. The Word of God was transmitted to the people so that they would gain various moral and spiritual benefits. They were instructed in the will of God and shown the way of salvation. They received guidance, encouragement, and comfort and were warned of the perils that lay before them. They were given hope in the midst of the darkness and dread of this world.

If the message was to reach the minds of the people and accomplish what God had intended, it had to be given in a simple, straightforward, and clear way. God providentially determined that the message was written in the common language of the people to whom it was originally addressed. The Old Testament was written in Hebrew, which was familiar to the Jewish people, and the New Testament was written in Greek, the vernacular of a major segment of the population of the Roman Empire. The divine message was accessible to the rank and file of God's people. No special class of prophets, teachers, theologians, or ecclesiastics stood between the people and the divine Word.

That is precisely why the literal method of interpretation brings the meaning of the Bible down to the level of the ordinary person. The historical and doctrinal sections are to be taken literally, and the same is true for the moral and spiritual information and prophetic material. To be sure, there is figurative language in the Bible, but dispensationalists maintain it is sim-

CYRUS I. SCOFIELD

Fig. 2.7 A Dispensational Portrait. A disseminator of dispensationalism through his highly influential *The Scofield Reference Bible,* C. I. Scofield and his prophetic position continue to influence many readers today.

ply an application of the literal method to interpret such passages in a figurative way. However, when it comes to the millennial kingdom, all passages referring to it are to be interpreted literally.

Dispensations

In biblical history, God revealed his will to humanity in various ways, and each of

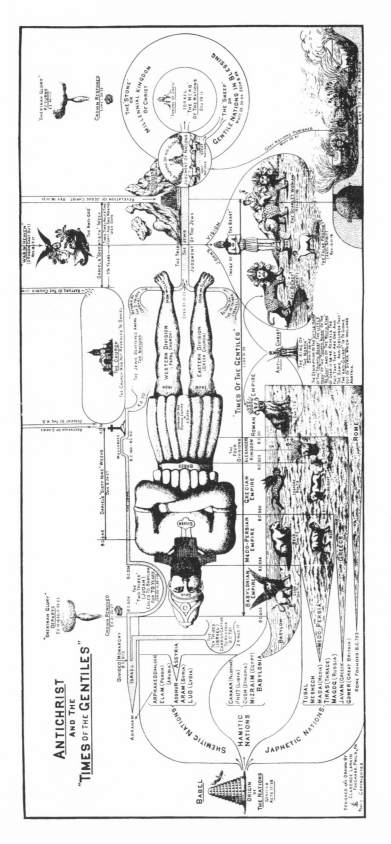

Fig. 2.8 Charting the Dispensations. This chart is representative of American Baptist Clarence Larkin's (1850–1924) popular efforts to visualize "dispensational truth."

these ways is called a *dispensation*. The term is found in the King James Version (1 Cor. 9:17; Eph. 1:10; 3:2; Col. 1:25), and it refers to the administration of God's earthly household (*oikonomia*). Modern Bible versions translate the word *oikonomia* as "stewardship," "commission," or "administration."

Dispensationalists divide history into different eras of God's dealings with humankind and thereby distinguish the different economies (dispensations) he uses in directing his total program for the world's history. C. I. Scofield, whose *The Scofield Reference Bible*—a King James Version with his annotated notes—was the most influential exponent of the viewpoint, defined a dispensation as "a period of time during which man is tested in respect of obedience to some *specific* revelation of the will of God."[3]

Although the number of dispensations vary from writer to writer, Scofield's listing of seven dispensations is probably the most widely accepted—innocency (Garden of Eden), conscience (Adam to Noah), human government (Noah to Abraham), promise (Abraham to Moses), law (Moses to Christ), grace or the church age (from Christ's first to second coming), and the kingdom age or millennium. In each of these periods salvation is by faith. That is, new light was shed upon the relationship between God and man, but no new way of entering into that relationship was ever instituted. Also, the moral law of God applies to all dispensations, although its precise content and emphasis may differ from one epoch to another.

Israel

The most distinctive feature of this system of biblical interpretation is its insistence that the terms *Israel* and *church* be kept separate. Israel stands for an earthly, theocratic kingdom, while the church represents a spiritual and heaven-oriented people. Throughout the ages God has simultaneously pursued two distinct purposes, one that is oriented to the earth and its people and the other that deals with heaven and those in spiritual union with him there.

Israel was the earthly people whom God had selected to be his own, and this was sealed in covenants with Abraham, Isaac, Jacob, Moses, and David. The promises God made were never invalidated, even though he expelled the people of Israel from the Promised Land because of their sins. The unfulfilled prophecies in the Old Testament that are addressed to Israel will come to pass during a future time after the people have returned to the land of Palestine.

When Jesus came as the Messiah, he offered the kingdom to the people of Israel. Had the people received him, he would have inaugurated his kingdom right then. But their refusal to accept Jesus as king led to their expulsion from the land by the Roman authorities and postponement of that kingdom. Since God's covenant with Abraham was unconditional, the promises remain eternally valid. They will eventually

DISPENSATIONS IN THE DISPENSATIONAL TRADITION

J.N. Darby (1808–82)	J.H. Brookes² (1830–97)	E.W. Bullinger⁴ (1837–1913)	C.I. Scofield⁵ (1843–1921)	I.M. Haldeman (1845–1933)	Wm. Graham Scroggie (1877–1958)
Paradisaical State¹	Innocence	Innocence	Innocency	Edenic	Adamic
Conscience¹	Conscience	Patriarchal	Conscience	Antediluvianm	Antediluvian
Noah	Patriarchs		Human Government	Patriarchal	Noachian
Abraham			Promise		Patriarchal
Israel 1. Law 2. Priest 3. Kings	Law	Law	Mosaic		Sinaitic 1. Mosaic 2. Gideonic 3. Davidic
Gentiles					
Spirit/ Christian Church	The Lord	Grace	Grace	Messianic	Christian
Grace	Grace	Judicial⁴		Holy Ghost	
Millennium	Millennial Age	Millennial	Kingdom	Restitution	Millennial
		Glory		Eternal State	Final

1. Darby taught that these situations were not "dispensations." See Larry Crutchfield, *The Origins of Dispensationalism* (Lanham, Md.: Univ. Press of America, 1992), 67–75.
2. From James Hall Brookes, *I Am Coming*, 7th ed. (Glasgow: Pickering and Inglis, n.d.). The outline given by Arnold Ehlert, "A Bibliography of Dispensationalism," *Bibliotheca Sacra* (1945), 327, and reproduced in C. Ryrie, *Dispensationalism Today* (Chicago: Moody, 1965), 84, is the same in structure but different in nomenclature. Brookes attributed that outline to W.C. Bayne of McGill University. Brookes agreed with the structure but changed the nomenclature. The final outline is much closer to that eventually adopted by Scofield.
3. The dispensational schemes from Bullinger to Scroggie can be found in Ehlert, "A Bibliography of Dispensationalism."
4. The Day of the Lord.
5. This outline has been adopted and followed by many including Arno C. Gaebelein, H.A. Ironside, and Lewis Sperry Chafer.

Fig. 2.9 Dividing the Dispensations. This chart compares the schemes of noted dispensational teachers. Even dispensationalists have not agreed on the number of divisions in biblical history.

be fulfilled even though Israel is now suffering punishment for its disobedience.

What followed Israel's rejection of the Messiah was a "parenthesis" known as the church age. After his chosen people rejected his kingdom, Christ turned in another direction to accomplish his purpose. He announced that he would build the church, a new society of believers (Matt. 16:13–20), even though this required his death and resurrection (Matt. 16:21; 17:22–23; 20:17–22, 28; 21:33–42). But he assured his followers that he would return in glory to establish his kingdom. With the transfiguration he gave them a preview of the kingdom's nature and promised them a share in it (Matt. 19:27–28; Luke 22:28–30). In other words, the Gentiles were welcomed into God's spiritual kingdom through faith in the shed blood of Jesus and grafted on to the unfruitful stump of Israel (Rom. 11:11–24). In this way, those who trusted Christ would also enter into a relationship with God as his children.

In the New Testament and during the church age, Israel and the church are two separate entities. The promises made to Israel cannot be transferred to the church. The church is a "mystery that has been kept hidden for ages and generations, but is now disclosed to the saints" (Col. 1:26) and something that was not foreseen in the Old Testament. The church is built upon the resurrection of Christ and was inaugurated at Pentecost by the Holy Spirit (Acts 2). Its functioning hinges on the gifts that Christ gives to its members and his intercession for them at the right hand of the Father. The church is something distinct to this age and was hidden to Old Testament believers. It is a parenthesis that lies between the sixty-ninth and seventieth week of Daniel 9:25. No prophecy referring specifically to Israel has been fulfilled since Christ was on earth; the prophetic clock has not ticked since Pentecost. During the sixty-nine prophetic weeks, God dealt with Israel. Then the clock stopped and the church age began. When the church is removed from the earth, however, the clock will start again and the seventieth week will occur.

Where then are the people of Israel? They are currently dispersed among the peoples of the world, suffering divine punishment for their unbelief and rejection of their Messiah and King. They are being relentlessly persecuted for having turned away from God, as Moses had prophesied: "The LORD will scatter you among all nations, from one end of the earth to the other." Among these nations "you will find no repose, no resting place for the sole of your foot" (Deut. 28:64–65). The people will live in constant despair and anxiety.

However, Romans 11:2 underscores the point that God did not forever reject or cast away his people whom he foreknew. Further in the chapter it states, "Israel has experienced a hardening in part until the full number of the Gentiles has come in. And so all Israel will be saved." Then "the deliverer will come from Zion; he will turn godlessness away from Jacob" (vv. 25–26).

That means we can look forward to a national reconciliation of Israel to its promised Messiah.

Dispensationalists assert that all the Old Testament prophecies relating to the first coming of Christ have been fulfilled to the minutest detail. So, then, why should the same not be true for the unfulfilled prophecies regarding the Jewish people and their nation, for example, Ezekiel 11:17–20?

> This is what the Sovereign LORD says: I will gather you from the nations and bring you back from the countries where you have been scattered, and I will give you back the land of Israel again. They will return to it and remove all its vile images and detestable idols. I will give them an undivided heart and put a new spirit in them; I will remove from them their heart of stone and give them a heart of flesh. Then they will follow my decrees and be careful to keep my laws. They will be my people, and I will be their God.

Although Israel has been forced from its God-given home, it still exists as a conscious entity dispersed among the nations of the world. Jews have always survived in a Gentile-ruled environment, no matter how harsh anti-Semitic persecution might be. Those peoples who sought the destruction of the Jews have themselves suffered God's judgment. Spain, once the wealthiest power of Europe, is now a backwater because its rulers killed or expelled its Jewish population during the fifteenth and sixteenth centuries. Germany was reduced to a land of smoking ruins in World War II because its leaders perpetrated the Holocaust. As Elwood McQuaid stated, "If anyone is to destroy Israel, he must control the universe and dethrone God himself."[4] In fact, "the credibility of the Bible is placed squarely on the pedestal of Jewish preservation."[5]

Israel's Return

The Bible emphasizes that Israel will be restored to the land whose boundaries were delineated in the promise to Abraham in Genesis 15:18: "from the river of Egypt to the great river, the Euphrates." We are today witnessing the fulfillment of the prediction that Jesus made in Matthew 24:32–33 about the budding of the fig tree, or as contemporary translations put it, the tree is putting out its branches and leaves. That tree is the divine symbol of Israel. According to dispensationalists, it is no exaggeration to say that the creation of a Jewish state in Palestine is the greatest miracle since the resurrection of Jesus Christ.

At the beginning of the twentieth century, large numbers of Jews began leaving their European abodes because of the brutal pogroms in Russia and pervasive anti-Semitism elsewhere. Although a large number of them sought freedom in America, many fled to their ancestral home in Palestine, an area that was under foreign rule—first by Ottoman Turkey, then by Great Britain under the League of Nations and later a United Nations (U.N.) man-

Fig. 2.10 Representing the Rapture. Distributed by the Bible Believers' Evangelistic Association, here is one artist's vision of what an urban rapture-in-progress scene might look like.

date. They established homes and farms and turned the desolate countryside into a model of prosperity. God frustrated the diabolical scheme of the Nazis to kill all the Jews of Europe, but this horrible event made Jews even more conscious that they needed a territorial base if they were to survive as a people in the modern world.

After World War II, Jews streamed into the land from all over the world. Violence between the Jewish and Arab inhabitants escalated to the point that Britain decided to give up its U.N. mandate over Palestine. As soon as the British left, the Jewish leaders proclaimed their independence. And so on May 15, 1948, the new state of Israel was born. After a year of fighting between the Israelis and the neighboring Arab countries, the two parties agreed to a partition of Palestine. Although the Palestinian Arabs regarded the Jews as interlopers, Holy Scripture specified that the land belonged to the Jewish people (Gen. 17:20–21). In fact, God granted the descendants of Ishmael (the Arabs) vast tracts of land in the Middle East, but that small sliver of territory

1 False Christs	5+1	18 World Church	5	35 The Antichrist	1
2 Occult	2	19 Globalism	4	36 Volcanoes	5+1
3 Satanism	2	20 Tribulation Temple	5	37 Earthquakes	4
4 Unemployment	2	21 Anti-Semitism	3	38 Hurricane/Torn	5
5 Inflation	1	22 Israel Unrest	3	39 Persia (Iran)	5+1
6 Interest Rates	1	23 Russia (Gog)	5	40 Famine	5
7 Economy	5	24 Less Civil Rights	3	41 Drought	4+1
8 Oil Supply/Price	1	25 The False Prophet	1	42 Plagues	4
9 Debt	5	26 Nuclear Nations	5	43 Climate	5
10 Financial Unrest	4-1	27 Global turmoil	5	44 Food Supply	3
11 Leadership	4+1	28 Arms Build Up	5	45 Floods	5
12 Drug abuse	2	29 Liberalism	2		
13 Apostasy	5	30 The Peace Process	5+2	Rapture Index	169
14 Supernatural	2	31 Kings of the East	5	Net Change	+6
15 Moral Standards	5	32 Mark of the Beast	5		
16 Anti-Christian	4	33 Beast Government	5	Updated: 26 Oct 98	
17 Crime Rate	2	34 Date Settings	5		

Record High 170	Record Low 57	1996 High 152	1997 High 168	1998 High 170
Jan 12 98	Dec 12 93	1996 Low 111	1997 Low 137	1998 Low 152

The Purpose For This Index

The Rapture Index has two functions: one is to factor together a number of related end time components into a cohesive indicator, and the other is to standardize those components in order to eliminate the wide variance that exists with prophecy reporting. The Rapture Index by no means is meant to predict the rapture, however, the index is meant to measure the type of activity that could act as a precursor to the rapture.

Rapture Index of 85 and Below:	Slow prophetic activity
Rapture Index of 85 to 110:	Moderate prophetic activity
Rapture Index of 110 to 145:	Heavy prophetic activity
Rapture Index above 145:	Alert zone

Fig. 2.11 Are You Rapture Ready? The Rapture Index is taken from the Rapture Ready web site at http://www.novia.net/~todd/, which promises: "Here's a site that offers a way to get other people rapture ready." By assigning ratings to contemporary events, the index seeks to track and measure prophetic activity that could lead to the rapture. The index is updated regularly in light of changing world events.

known as Palestine was reserved for his chosen people.

The ancient city of Jerusalem remained divided between the two competing nations. During the Six-Day War in 1967, however, the Jews reclaimed this and other portions of their heritage, resulting in continued Arab hostility toward the Jewish state. After failing to destroy the Jewish state in the 1973 Yom Kippur War, the Arabs had to face the reality that Israel was there to stay.

It is clear to every student of prophecy that God's hand was protecting his chosen people, even though they had returned to their homeland in unbelief. Especially significant for Israel's survival has been the support of biblically oriented evangelical

Christians in Western countries, especially the United States, who believe they understand God's purposes in the Middle East. They essentially forced their own national leaders to support the existence of the Jewish state.

The Rapture of the Church

Since dispensationalists make a definite distinction between God's program for Israel and his program for the church, they believe the church will be removed from the earth so that Israel's destiny may be fulfilled. This event, commonly called the rapture (the translation of the Greek word *parousia* in 1 Thess. 4:17), marks the end of "the times of the Gentiles," which Jesus mentioned in Luke 21:24. During the rapture, believers will be caught up (or taken up) from the earth to meet Christ in the air. The unbelieving world will not see this take place, but they will witness its effects—the sudden and mysterious disappearance of many people.

This is the blessed hope of the believer and is something that can happen at any time. No preconditions exist that require the Lord to delay coming for his church. He will come suddenly, like a thief in the night. Those believers who are alive at the time will be translated, that is, they will take on the condition that will be theirs throughout all eternity. At the same moment, those saints who have already died in Christ will be resurrected and will join the living believers as they proceed up-

Fig. 2.12 Drivers (and Passengers) Beware! This bumper sticker warns of the rapture's impact on unbelieving commuters.

ward to meet their Lord in the air. Then all Christians will appear before the "judgment seat of Christ" (2 Cor. 5:10) and will be rewarded for the good works they had accomplished on earth. All unbelievers will remain behind and will go through the tribulation period, the time when the wrath of God will be poured out on the earth (1 Thess. 1:10).

A minority of dispensationalists hold to variant positions concerning the rapture. Some believe that only those who are faithful and watching will be called up (Heb. 9:28). Those careless Christians who are indifferent to his return will go through the tribulation. Another view is that the rapture occurs midway through the tribulation period. The resurrection trumpet that is sounded in Revelation 11:15 is the same as the "last trumpet" of 1 Corinthians 15:52. The trumpet will sound after three and a half years, that is, in the middle of the great tribulation. A third position is that the church will go through the tribulation (Matt. 24:22) and receive supernatural protection

Antichrists We Have Known*

Nero
Domitian
Frederick II Hohenstaufen
Saladin
Charles I
George III
Napoleon
The Roman Papacy
Benito Mussolini
Adolf Hitler
A Common Market Computer
Anwar Sadat
Henry Kissinger
Mikhail Gorbachev
Ronald Reagan
Sun Myung Moon
Saddam Hussein

*A short list

from Christ. The saints will go to meet their Lord just before the second coming.

The Great Tribulation

Once the church has been raptured, the Holy Spirit will remove his restraining hand (2 Thess. 2:6–7) and all hell will literally break loose on earth. Now the prophetic clock starts ticking again; the seventieth week begins (Dan. 9:26). The preeminent world power will be a revived Roman Empire consisting of a ten-nation confederacy led by a ruthless king who even before the rapture will have been crushing his associates in an

effort to establish absolute rule (Dan. 7:7–8, 23–24). In all probability the United States (that is, the "isles") will be aligned with the new Rome (Ezek. 39:6). The ruler of the empire, who is called the "Beast" in Revelation 13, is also portrayed as the "man of lawlessness" in 2 Thessalonians 2:3–4 and the Antichrist in 1 John 2:18. He is the very personification of Satan himself. The emergence of the Antichrist will begin the seven-year period of tyranny and incomprehensible horror known as the tribulation or the great tribulation.

The Antichrist's activity will center around a relationship that he will establish with the newly restored nation of Israel. The Antichrist and Israel will work out a diplomatic agreement that permits the Jews to reconstruct the temple and restore their sacrificial system, and he will move his capital to Jerusalem. However, three and a half years after signing the treaty, the Antichrist will doublecross his Jewish allies (Dan. 9:27). He will defile the temple by entering it, even though he is a Gentile, and will order the immediate suspension of the sacrifices. He will declare that he himself is God and demand the worship of all people on earth. He will be the "abomination that causes desolation" described in Daniel 11:31 and Matthew 24:15.

To carry out his blasphemous demands, the Antichrist will turn to an associate called the False Prophet and delegate authority to him to compel all people to worship the Beast. He will do this through naked force, utilization of miracle-working powers (including a counterfeit resurrection), and economic pressure. The latter is the infamous "mark of the Beast," the mysterious symbolic 666, which dispensationalists equate with a world government that will regulate, in a computerized age, all aspects of one's economic and business life. For three and a half years those who refuse to give their allegiance to the Antichrist will be subjected to a reign of terror.

During the tribulation, many people will turn to Christ after hearing the gospel message through the preaching of the "two witnesses" (Rev. 11:3–12), and they will be relentlessly persecuted. As believers they will oppose the Beast's rule, and as a result, they will not be able to buy or sell goods or hold jobs. They will be hunted down and executed. Only those who have hidden away food and other necessities of life in secret caches will be able to escape the clutches of the Beast's enforcers.

Now begins what Jeremiah 30:7 calls "a time of trouble for Jacob." As Isaiah 28:15 predicted:

> You boast, "We have entered into a
> covenant with death,
> with the grave [hell] we have made
> an agreement.
> When an overwhelming scourge
> sweeps by,
> it cannot touch us,
> for we have made a lie our refuge
> and falsehood our hiding place."

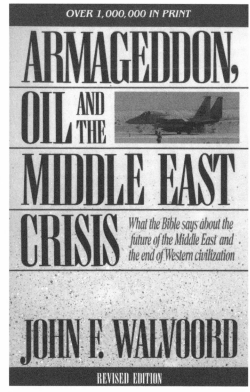

Fig. 2.13 Armageddon: Prophets or Profits? John F. Walvoord's *Armageddon, Oil and the Middle East Crisis* was conveniently published in 1990 during the Persian Gulf War. Essentially a presentation of classic dispensationalism, because of its title and timing it sold over a million copies in its short but financially rewarding life.

Israel has tied its fate to the deified world dictator, but his reign starts to unravel. The second of the dreaded four horsemen of the Apocalypse, the red horse, rides forth, an action symbolizing the unleashing of war on the earth (Rev. 6:4).

In spite of the Antichrist's enormous political power, a few places will remain outside his authority. Thus, an all-out war

When Does Christ Return?

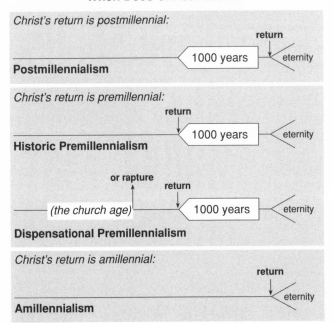

Fig. 2.14 The Millennial Maze. The four major millennial views are distilled here in shorthand form.

will break out when a northern confederacy under Russia's leadership, the "King of the North" of Daniel 11 and Ezekiel 38–39, moves south on Israel in a lightning offensive, hoping to fulfill the dream of both the Tsarist and communist rulers of securing control of the Middle East and its vast wealth and resources. According to *The Scofield Reference Bible*[6] and many other commentators, the Gog and Magog mentioned in Ezekiel 38–39 are the prince and land of Russia.

Convinced that the Antichrist will not mount an effective defense of the corrupted Jewish state, the Russian leader will join forces with the "King of the South," an Arab-African confederacy (Dan. 11:40),

and assault the Antichrist's seat of government in Jerusalem. However, the godless master of Jerusalem will launch a successful counterattack, which in turn will provoke certain "kings of the East." As a result, two hundred million Chinese soldiers will cross the Euphrates River and march toward Palestine (Rev. 9:13–16; 16:12).

With the armies of the leading world powers converging on Palestine, a showdown will be imminent. What began as a conflict between the Antichrist and the northern confederacy will escalate into an all-out war, the goal of which will be to destroy every Israelite. Anti-Semitic frenzy will grip the armies as they turn upon the Jews, many of whom will have vainly fled to desert refuges in hope of escaping the impending disaster in their land. The armies will besiege Jerusalem first (Zech. 14:2) and then assemble in the valley of Megiddo, a place called in Hebrew, *Armageddon,* or the Mount of Slaughter. It is the last day of Daniel's seventieth week.

Jesus Comes Again

At the very moment when it seems God's chosen people will be destroyed in a second holocaust, Jesus, the son of David, will suddenly appear in the sky to execute vengeance upon the Antichrist and his armies and allies. Mounted on a white horse, he will be called "Faithful and True," and with justice he will judge and make war. His eyes will be like blazing fire, and on his head he will wear many crowns. He will be dressed in a robe dipped in blood, and his name will be the Word of God. On his robe and thigh will be written: "KING OF KINGS AND LORD OF LORDS." The armies of heaven, his saints, will follow behind him riding on white horses and dressed in fine linen, clean and white. A sharp sword will come out of the mouth of the Lord, and in one fell swoop he will strike down the nations and thereafter rule over them with an iron scepter (Rev. 19:11–16). He will deliver the Jewish remnant that the Gentile world powers, led by the Beast and False Prophet, had besieged. The Beast and False Prophet will be summarily cast into the lake of fire.

Thus, the battle of Armageddon will end in the greatest slaughter in the history of humankind (Rev. 19:17–21). So many people will be killed that the pool of blood in the valley will reach to the horses' bridles. Seven months of sustained labor will be required to bury the dead. The birds and wild animals will have an enormous feast: "You will eat the flesh of mighty men and drink the blood of the princes of the earth as if they were rams and lambs, goats and bulls" (Ezek. 39:18).

The Kingdom

Jesus then shall stand on the Mount of Olives and take possession of his kingdom (Zech. 14:4). The survivors of Israel will be regathered and judged, as will the Gentile nations (Ezek. 20:37–38; Matt. 25:31–46). Then the thousand-year reign of Christ will begin, while Satan is bound and placed in "the Abyss" (Rev. 20:3). The Abrahamic and Davidic covenants will be fulfilled, and the people of Israel will receive their Messiah.

Many Old Testament prophecies describe the millennial kingdom as a glorious time of political justice, social harmony, material prosperity, and spiritual renewal (Ps. 72; Isa. 2:1–4; 11; 65:17–25; Jer. 29:10–14; 33:10–16; Ezek. 11:14–21; 34:20–31; Hosea 14:4–7; Joel 3:18–21; Amos 9:11–15; Zeph. 3:9–20; Zech. 14:9–21). Both dispensationalist and historic premillennialists agree that the kingdom will be a golden age and that Israel will turn to God and be restored to the land. Christ's rule will be firm but benevolent.

At the end of the millennium Satan will escape from captivity and lead a brief rebellion. His forces will besiege the saints, but God will send down fire from heaven to devour them. Satan will then be dispatched to the lake of fire, where he will remain forever. This is followed by the resurrection of all the unrighteous dead. They will stand before the great white throne, where they will be judged according to their works before they are sentenced to eternal damnation. Then the new heaven, new earth, and New Jerusalem will appear, becoming the eternal dwelling place of all those from every age who have been saved by their faith. This group of believers will include the Old Testament saints, members of the church from every part of the world, Jews who were faithful to God during the tribulation and acknowledged Jesus as their Lord and Savior when he appeared, and even those born during the millennium whose hearts were genuinely obedient to Christ.

Conclusion

Adherents to all of the foregoing millennial views are in full agreement about how the endtimes story concludes. As 2 Peter 3:10–13 assures us, the old heaven and earth shall pass away and the new one will be the home of righteousness. Never again will there be rebellion against God. Justice, security, peace, harmony, and joy will be the lot of humankind throughout all eternity. Of this beatific vision we can all be certain; it's just the details about which there is disagreement.

Now that we have surveyed the Bible's teaching on the end of the world, we must point our journey in still another direction. We are not the first pilgrims to contemplate millennial issues. Throughout church history, groups, both orthodox and cultic alike, have been fascinated by endtime scenarios. Chapter 3 will take a panoramic look at the characters and groups espousing millennialism in Christian history and speculate on the movement's resurgence as we enter the twenty-first century.

3

It's the End of the World as We Know It

Millenarianism in the History of the Church

This is the way the world ends
Not with a bang but with a whimper.

T. S. Eliot

A recent Associated Press (AP) poll of Christian adults discovered that nearly one out of every four—estimated at over twenty-six million people—expect Jesus to return in their lifetime. For many evangelical Christians a focus on the second coming is what the new millennium is all about as 40 percent believe Jesus will return in the twenty-first century, if not before.[1] Clearly the end is on the minds of many.

A database search of Armageddon Books, an online book distributor devoted to endtimes literature, shows the end is not only on the minds of the masses but also on the minds of many writers: *The End of the Age, The End: Why Jesus Could Return by* A.D. *2000, The End Times Blood Bath, The End Times Are Here Now, End-Time Visions,* and *End Time Events* are recently published titles on apocalyptic themes. And this partial list only chronicles endtimes books with the word *end* in the title. A closer analysis reveals over 350 books currently available on apocalyptic topics, the vast majority of which have been penned in the last ten years.

The appetite for new books containing ever more fantastic predictions of the future seems almost insatiable, and publishers gladly respond to the demand of this market. Although those who have little contact with evangelicals condescendingly regard millennial speculation as a quaint novelty of our times, it actually has had a long tradition in Christian history.

Throughout church history each of the three main endtimes interpretations has had its share of adherents, although generally one view tended to predominate at a given time. As one observer noted, "Time and again there seems to be a connection between eschatology and the church's perception of itself in its historical situation" to the extent that "eschatologies have been a reflection of the current mood or *Zeitgeist*."[2] For example, during the first three or four centuries of the Christian era the premillennial position occupied center stage in the thinking of most theologians. Beginning with Augustine in the fifth century, amillennialism came to the fore and thereafter served as the primary position of Roman Catholics and later many Lutheran and Calvinist (Reformed) thinkers as well. The seventeenth century witnessed both a revival of premillennialism and the emergence of a full-blown postmillennialism. The latter predominated in Anglo-American Protestantism until the end of the nineteenth century. Then in many quarters it was supplanted by dispensational premillennialism. Today this interpretation has a substantial following among evangelicals, particularly those in Great Britain, North America, and other parts of the world influenced by missionaries from these lands.

Moreover, a variety of millennial views have emerged in contemporary Roman Catholicism, Protestant sectarianism, and non-Western independent churches. These will be discussed in the next two chapters.

Voices in Early Christianity

Following the apocalyptic context in which the gospel was first proclaimed, the early Christians continued in the belief that they were living in the last days. As mentioned above, while various biblical books describe the circumstances surrounding the endtime, the twentieth chapter of the Book of Revelation (also commonly known as the Apocalypse) specifically mentions a thousand-year reign of Christ, which commentators referred to as the millennium. From early on in the church's history, thinkers speculated on the meaning of the millennium.

Papias

The first post–New Testament writer to express millennial views was Papias (c. 60–130), a bishop in Asia Minor who had had personal contact with the disciples of Jesus, especially John. He stated "the Lord used to teach concerning those [end] times" that during the period of a thousand years after the resurrection of the dead, the kingdom of Christ would be set up in material form on this very earth. Drawing upon various Old Testament texts and Revelation 20, he said miracles and natural blessings would characterize the golden age of the personal rule of Christ. Not only would the earth yield abundant crops, but animals and humans would live in a peaceful relationship.

The *Epistle of Barnabas*

The *Epistle of Barnabas,* a theological tract written in the early second century, maintained that the six days of creation are actually a period of six thousand years because a thousand years are like one day in the eyes of God (2 Peter 3:8). In six days, that is, in six thousand years, everything will be completed, after which the present evil time will be destroyed. The Son of God will come again, judge the ungodly, and change the sun, moon, and stars. On the seventh day he will truly rest, and the sabbath of the millennial kingdom will dawn.

Irenaeus

Irenaeus (c. 130–c. 200), bishop of Lyons in southern Gaul (modern-day France), was the first significant theologian of the early church fathers. Although he was born and educated in the East (one of his teachers was Polycarp, who had sat at the feet of the apostle John), he became one of the most important Western fathers. His principal work is a book entitled *Against Heresies,* which was directed at Gnosticism, the prime competitor to Christianity in the second century. Because his theology pointed toward what would become the main line of Christian thought, subsequent writers appealed to him as an authority. In a long passage in book 5, chapter 32 of *Against Heresies,* Irenaeus made the strongest case for premillennialism of any of the church fathers.

Barnabas's Year-Day Tradition

What some argue for as an early expression of dispensationalism is found in the *Epistle of Barnabas.* It is the beginning of the so-called "year-day" tradition, which holds that the six days of creation and seventh day of rest symbolically correspond to thousand-year periods of human history. Thus, the world would endure for six thousand years in anticipation of a thousand-year golden age. Following is Barnabas's history outline:

- Days 1–5 (5,000 years) = the past human history
- Day 6 (1,000 years) = the present (understanding Christ's return to be imminent, Barnabas viewed the church as being at the close of day 6)
- Day 7 (1,000 years) = the millennium
- Day 8 (endless time) = the eternal state

Source: Larry V. Crutchfield, "Millennial Year-Day Tradition," in *The Dictionary of Premillennial Theology,* ed. Mal Couch (Grand Rapids: Kregel, 1996), 265–66.

Irenaeus begins with Revelation 20 and fills in the details about the millennium from the Old Testament. He portrays the reign of Christ as a paradise on earth. The righteous have risen again, received their rewards for what they had given up for Christ and done for the poor, and now rule the earth, which has been restored to its condition prior to the fall of Adam. The millennium is the time of redemption of the children of God that Paul referred to in Romans 8:19. The capital city of the kingdom is Jerusalem, and the Lord Jesus manages the affairs of the earth from there. After Christ's thousand-year reign, the final judgment will take place.

Justin Martyr

Justin Martyr (c. 100–c. 165), the greatest of the second-century apologists (writers who defended Christianity against its critics), was a liberally educated philosopher who taught in Ephesus and later in Rome. Although he held no formal position in the church, he engaged in debates with prominent enemies of Christianity. During his life, public profession of the Christian faith was a crime under Roman law, and he eventually sealed his testimony with his blood, thus earning the name "Martyr" (witness). Among those with whom he debated was Trypho, a Jewish intellectual.

In the course of the disputation, Trypho asked him if he believed in a second coming of Christ. Justin responded with a ringing yes and went on to explain that Christians believe there will be a millennial reign on earth: "I and others are right-minded Christians in all points and we are assured that there will be a resurrection of the dead and a thousand years in Jerusalem, which will then be built, adorned, and enlarged."[3]

Tertullian

Tertullian (c. 160–c. 220), a distinguished lawyer and teacher in North Africa, was one of the most prolific writers of the early church. According to him, the process of attaining righteousness takes place through successive stages of growth. It began in the rudimentary stage of a natural fear of God and moved through the law and prophets to the fervor of youth, the period of the gospel, and then to the mature stage of the Holy Spirit, the Paraclete. The Spirit succeeds Christ on earth and proclaims him to all people. Another historical period, the stage of the visible reign of Christ on earth, will follow. This kingdom will be established after the resurrection and exist for a thousand years. It will be the divinely built city of Jerusalem that descends from heaven. In fact, Tertullian said, the soldiers of the army of the Roman emperor Septimius Severus, who were serving in Palestine, actually saw the New Jerusalem hovering in the morning sky for forty days.

Tertullian described what will happen during and after the millennium. Christians will be raised at various times during the thousand years, sooner or later according to what they have done during their lives on earth. The New Jerusalem will receive the resurrected saints and provide them with the blessings they had to forego on earth because of their witness for God. The kingdom on earth assures that the just are rewarded at the very scene of their sufferings for Christ. At the end of

Fig. 3.1 An Early Premillennialist. Tertullian, influenced by the Montanists, was an early church father who advocated a premillennial eschatology.

the millennium the world will be destroyed by fire and the wicked brought before the final judgment. All believers will instantly become like angels, that is, given an incorruptible nature, and enter into heaven where they will spend all eternity.

Hippolytus

Hippolytus (c. 170–c. 236), the most important theologian of the third-century Roman church as well as a bishop, was a prolific writer and the first person who utilized mathematical calculations with regard to the second coming. He placed the return of Christ and the resurrection within the framework of a universal week of seven thousand years and argued that

Christ would return in the year 500. He assumed that God made all things in six days and rested on the seventh (Gen. 1–2) and that these days symbolized a thousand years each (Ps. 90:4). Thus, six thousand years after the creation would come the time for the sabbath rest of a thousand years.

Hippolytus believed that Christ was born 5,500 years after the creation. He drew this idea from the dimensions of the ark of the covenant, which Moses had constructed in the wilderness. According to Exodus 25:10, the ark was to be two and a half cubits in length, a cubit and a half in width, and a cubit and a half in height. When these are added together, the sum is five and one-half cubits. Hippolytus multiplied this by one thousand, which gave the figure 5,500. Utilizing this calculation, he suggested the period from his own time to the second coming of Christ would be about 250 years.

Methodius of Olympus and Victorinus

Methodius of Olympus (c. 260–c. 311), a bishop in the Near East who apparently suffered martyrdom during the persecutions sponsored by the Emperor Diocletian, had his own unique view of millennialism. Like Hippolytus, he believed that the seventh day of creation pointed to the universal millennial sabbath. However, in the Old Testament he saw another type of millennium in the wandering of the Israelites in the wilderness before they en-

75

tered the Promised Land. When they reached the border of Canaan, they halted and observed the Feast of Tabernacles. In a similiar manner, Christians are also wandering pilgrims on their way to the celestial city, and they will celebrate their "feast of tabernacles" after the first resurrection when they are spending a thousand years with Christ on earth. He went on to say that the thousand years will be the "day of judgment" for professing Christians, while for true believers, those who have really stood for Christ in this life, it will be the "first day of the feast," the beginning of the eternal state of blessedness.

A contemporary of Methodius, Victorinus (d. c. 304), bishop of Pettau in the central Danube region, suggested that the reign of Christ on earth will begin with the resurrection of the just in the seventh millennium of the world's existence. He used the week of creation and the symbolic emphasis placed on the number seven as the basis for his theory.

Commodianus

Commodianus, a Christian Latin poet of the mid-third century, was the early church father who set forth the most detailed millennialist system. He identified numerous signs that would precede the Anti-

christ and showed that the Man of Sin was predicted in Isaiah. He spelled out in detail the Antichrist's reign and military campaigns and that he would say, "I am the Christ to whom you always pray." Commodianus noted that the Antichrist's False Prophet and talking image will convince many to believe in him. However, the almighty Christ will come down from heaven to his elect people, defeat the forces of the Antichrist, and throw him and the False Prophet into hell, where they will be tormented with their followers.

He followed Hippolytus's millennial sabbath theory and argued that those who have been devoted to Christ, the martyrs, will experience the first resurrection. They will rise again and become incorruptible. At that moment, the city prepared for the people of God will descend, one that is twelve thousand cubits long, broad, and high, and it will reach up to heaven. All the good things of earth will be at the martyrs' disposal. They shall receive the blessings that had been denied to them because of their sacrificial deaths, such as marriage and offspring. Universal peace will prevail, the earth's climate will be ideal, and the land will bear fruit in abundance. Certain classes of sinners, especially those who were higher on the racial and social scale, shall provide the saints with servants during the thousand-year reign. These sinners will be given a chance to repent, but Commodianus was not specific on this matter. After the millennium will come the final judgment. The earth and sky will be burned up, sinners will be sent away to the second death, and the righteous will receive their eternal reward.

Lactantius

Lactantius (c. 250–c. 325) was from Africa and experienced conversion as an adult. He was so well trained in rhetoric that he earned the name "Christian Cicero." He lived during the last of the great Roman persecutions and the legalization of Christianity under Constantine. Then he became the tutor of the emperor's son, Crispus. His most famous work, the *Divine Institutes,* is the first attempt at a systematic Christian theology. In this book he describes the millennium, but he adds to the customary biblical material of the Hebrew prophets and the Book of Revelation details from the Sibylline Oracles (religious utterances made by prophetesses in pagan Rome). His statement about the millennium is one of the most lucid of the early fathers:

> But He, when He shall have destroyed unrighteousness, and executed His great judgment, and shall have recalled to life the righteous, who have lived from the beginning, will be engaged among men a thousand years, and will rule them with most just command.[4]

Just as God rested on the seventh day after he finished his work, so at the end of six thousand years of human history he will abolish all wickedness from the earth and Christ will reign a thousand years. He will raise all the righteous from the dead, and they will reign with him. People will not die in this age but bear children and raise up a large and godly population. Satan will be bound and the heathen will become the slaves of the righteous. The very earth itself will be transformed. There will be no darkness, but there will be an abundance of rain and agricultural fruitfulness. Honey will drip from rocks, and wine and milk will flow like rivers. The dominion of evil will be broken and peace will rule in the animal kingdom. Beasts and birds will no longer feed on other creatures, and lions and calves will live together. At the end of the millennium the prince of the devils will be loosed. He will assemble the nations and make war on the holy city of the righteous, but God will send earthquakes and scorching showers of brimstone and fire to destroy the satanic hosts. Then the second resurrection for the unrighteous will occur, and they will be judged and dispatched to everlasting punishment. Heaven and earth will be renewed, and humans will be transformed into the likeness of angels, white as snow.

Alternative Visions

While the above champions of millennialism were undoubtedly orthodox, others held more questionable views. By far the most significant of the theological deviants were the Montanists. Their beliefs arose from the teaching of Montanus, an obscure ascetic who appeared in Phrygia in Asia Minor around the year 170. He and his followers claimed to receive direct revelations from God and called for an extremely puritanical lifestyle. A fanatical preacher, he fell into trances during which he saw himself to be the special instrument of the Holy Spirit. He was joined by two women, Priscilla and Maximilla, who were converted to his beliefs and left their husbands. They went around prophesying in the Spirit and speaking in unknown tongues (glossolalia).

The Montanists insisted they were simply continuing the gifts of the early church, especially that of prophecy. They cited scriptural examples of prophets such as John (Revelation), Agabus (Acts 21:10), and the four daughters of Philip (Acts 21:8–9) as evidence that their ecstatic utterances were divinely inspired. More importantly, they taught that the millennial reign of Christ was about to begin. However, this would occur not at Jerusalem but in Pepuza, a small village in Asia Minor.

This message, propagated with enthusiasm and accompanied by frenzied prophesying, spread to Rome and North Africa and caused turmoil in the church. The church councils and bishops who had to deal with the New Prophecy (as Montanism was often called) generally denounced the movement as the work of demons and ex-communicated its followers. The Montanists' tendency to see themselves as spiritually superior to other Christians alienated them from the main body of the church.

Their fanaticism was linked to the belief in the imminent coming of Christ. They rejected the pleasures of life, condemned works of art, and expected women to wear plain clothing and virgins to be veiled. They believed that fasts and other disciplinary exercises were the best way to prepare for Christ's return. Martyrdom was encouraged and any effort to escape persecution was seen as a denial of Christ. Central to all this rigorous behavior was the teaching that Jesus would reward every sacrifice when he erected his earthly kingdom. The Montanists lived with the expectation that the present age was about to end and the millennium to begin. Thus, they were contemptuous of all efforts to bring about change or improvement in the social order. When Christ did not return as the Montanists had prophesied, support for the movement rapidly waned and within two or three centuries it died out completely.

While there were some exceptions, the evidence overwhelmingly shows that the early church fathers were mainly premillennialists. They stressed the literal interpretation of the Old Testament and insisted that the prophecies not be spiritualized, as they would find fulfillment in the millennium. They generally believed there would be a personal Antichrist whom Christ would defeat, the physical resurrection of the righteous would occur at his second coming, and his millennial reign would be inaugurated. At the end of his reign, the second resurrection would take place followed by the final judgment and the beginning of the eternal state of bliss. The fathers derived most of the details about the millennial kingdom from the Old Testament prophetic books, Jewish apocalyptic works, and pagan sources such as the Sibylline Oracles. Thus, the eminent Reformed scholar D. H. Kromminga correctly insists that the ideas of modern premillennialism were in all their essentials present in the early church.[5]

The Shift to Amillennialism

The great appeal of premillennialism was that it met the spiritual needs of Christians who lived under the constant threat of persecution and war. Its promise of an earthly millennial kingdom and emphasis on the connection between the Antichrist and the Roman Empire were clear and memorable images that were easily understandable. Chiliasm (belief in millennialism) was popular religion at its best, and it nourished the spirits of Christians during times of danger and strengthened their wills to persist in the faith.

However, other forces were at work in the third century that were undermining faith in millennialism. For one thing, Mon-

tanism, with its claim that the New Jerusalem would come down from heaven in Pepuza and its attempts to set a specific date for the second coming, turned some people away from chiliasm. Moreover, the teachings of the theologian Origen (c. 185–c. 254) cast doubt on accepted millennial beliefs. He advocated the spiritualizing of the teachings of Scripture, had a low opinion of the material world, claimed it was possible for all to come to Christ, and viewed history as a series of cycles rather than a linear process. To be sure, his views were not universally held in the church, but they did lead many to question the idea of a future kingdom of material prosperity and happiness for the elect company of believers.

But the really crucial development was the accession of Constantine (c. 275–337) to the imperial throne. Although the degree of his Christian commitment is a matter of considerable historical debate, his edict in 313 allowing toleration of the church and his other actions favoring Christians placed them in a new relationship to the Roman state. For example, he gave the Lateran Palace to the bishop of Rome, legalized the giving of monetary gifts to churches, began the construction of church buildings, and supported clergy, single women, and widows from public funds. Thus, fewer Christians were inclined to regard Rome as a force of evil and the emperor as the Antichrist. Moreover, millennialists had predicted that Christ would return and

Fig. 3.2 The Emperor's New Clothes. The emperor Constantine's toleration of and openness to the church directly influenced eschatological currents.

formed an unlikely combination. One was Tyconius (d. c. 390), a lay member of the breakaway Donatist church, and the other was Augustine, bishop of Hippo (354–430), the leading adversary of the Donatists and one of the truly landmark figures in the history of Christianity. Both in his own theory of biblical interpretation and in his eschatology, Augustine was greatly indebted to Tyconius and utilized his opponent's ideas and methods.

Tyconius

Tyconius is remembered for two works. In the *Book of Rules,* the first manual of scriptural hermeneutics written in the Western (Latin) church, he argued that the biblical prophecies are fulfilled "spiritually" in the church. Then, in a commentary on the Book of Revelation, the Donatist thinker rejected the literal interpretation of the thousand-year reign of Christ. He maintained that the millennium described in Revelation 20 is actually the present age in which, with divine help, the saints can overcome sin. The first resurrection is the transformation from the death of sin to the new life of righteousness. The blessed (Rev. 20:6) are those who are born again through baptism.

end the persecution of the church, but this did not harmonize with the events that had transpired.

The millennial hope had thrived while people were under the pressure of persecution, but now in the newly "Christianized" Roman world, official hostility was past and there was a lessened need for such endtime teaching. The time was ripe for a new eschatology to replace chiliasm. Its pioneers lived in North Africa, and they

According to Tyconius, the millennial rule of the church is symbolic; it will last until the end of the age when the second resurrection, a literal event, will take place. The twelve thrones on which the saints will sit and judge the twelve tribes of Israel (Matt. 19:28; Rev. 20:4) are within the church and represent the apostolic power that the church exercises. Christ has authority over this body, one in which all are called to repentance and mutual love. The souls of the righteous (Rev. 20:4) are those who die with Christ now. The figure 1,000 represents the perfect rule of the church age, which will last until Christ's second coming.

Augustine

Augustine admitted that at one time he had been a millennialist, but the "immoderate, carnal" extremism of some of its advocates had turned him against it.[6] In the book that most scholars regard as his greatest work, *The City of God,* Augustine adopted the symbolical-mystical interpretive system of Tyconius. He declared that the thousand years designated the period "from the first coming of Christ to the end of the world, when He shall come the second time."[7] The binding of Satan (Rev. 20:2) began when the church carried the gospel message beyond Judea into the other nations of the world. This fulfilled the statement of Jesus: "In fact, no one can enter a strong man's house and carry off his possessions unless he first ties up the strong man" (Mark 3:27). The strong man is Satan, and this tying up of the Evil One is repeated whenever people are won to the Christian faith.

Augustine refused to speculate about when the final events might occur ("It is not for you to know the times or dates the Father has set by his own authority," Acts 1:7), and although the Roman Empire was

in danger of collapsing, he did not speak of the nearness of the second coming. Rome was not the source of the Antichrist—there would be no revived Nero—but the power that restrained his coming. Augustine believed the New Jerusalem was already present. Whenever grace enters the hearts of people, they become citizens of the heavenly city. At the last judgment the New Jerusalem will appear with greater clarity, and the bodies of its inhabitants will become incorruptible and immortal. After the final judgment God will wipe away the tears from their eyes, and there will be no more death, grief, or sorrow.[8]

Augustine spiritualized the millennium—hence he denied that there would be a literal reign of Christ on earth at some point in the future. Instead, during the present age the "city of God" exists alongside the "city of man," that is, the world. There are two distinct societies of people: one will reign eternally with God and the other will suffer eternal punishment. The earthly city is that of Cain and the heavenly one that of Abel. Now the city of God is the church, and its citizens are repentant and forgiven sinners. The citizens of the earthly city are destined to never-ending punishment with the devil. This godless city is the "beast coming out of the sea" (Rev. 13:1). When Christ came the first time, he placed Satan in chains. However, in spite of the devil's limited power, he is still able to seduce people. When he is set free at the end of the age, he will regain his full powers and launch a final persecution. The wicked na-

Fig. 3.3 The New Jerusalem. Gustave Doré's vision of the holy city shows the place where believers will reside for eternity.

Popular Millennialism

Joachim of Fiore

The Augustinian view on millennialism was amazingly influential and held the majority position in the church for the next twelve centuries. There were, however, some dissenting voices, the most significant of which was Joachim of Fiore (c. 1135–1202), a Cistercian monk in southern Italy who was renowned for his piety and deep knowledge of the Scriptures, as well as for his ties with leading figures in both church and state. In less than four years in the 1180s he produced three important works: *Book of the Harmony of the New and Old Testaments, Exposition of the Apocalypse,* and *Psaltery with Ten Strings.*

tions, symbolized by Gog and Magog, will attack the city of God, but they will be defeated. The dead will be raised, all will be judged, and the unrighteous will be consigned to everlasting torment. The faithful will be given new bodies, both physical and spiritual, and they will enjoy endless happiness with God.

The central idea of Joachim's position is his "trinitarian" conception of history. He divided history into three clearly overlapping epochs or ages (status) that were comparable to the three persons of the Trinity. The first, that of the Father, was the age of law and the Old Testament, and it stretched from Adam to the coming of Christ. The second, that of Christ, was the age of the gospel, the church, and the New Testament. Its beginnings lay in the time of Elijah, a type for Christ, and would last until the second coming. Since the Western church taught that the Holy Spirit proceeded from both the Father and the Son, Joachim argued that the third age, that of the Spirit, could be traced back to the time of Elijah and Benedict of Nursia, the founder of Western monasticism (c. 500), but reaches far into the future. This age will be one of freedom. It will be characterized by a spiritual church, a spiritual understanding of both the Old and New Testaments—the documents of the first two ages—and the joyful contemplation of heavenly things. It will be a reign of peace that lasts until the great persecution under Gog and Magog, the final judgment, and the end of the created world as we know it today.

His most original and controversial idea was that of the approaching third age of the Spirit. He agreed with Augustine that Satan was only partially bound at the death of Christ. He will only be bound completely and thrown into the lake of fire when all the Beast's seven heads have been destroyed. Then the millennium in its fullness will begin. The life of the church will be transformed from one of activity to that of contemplation. Two new spiritual (that is, religious) orders will appear on the scene to lead the church through the time of tribulation caused by the Antichrist into the peace of the third age. A hermit order will pray unceasingly for the church during this time of trouble, while a preaching order will labor in the world on its behalf.

He treated the Book of Revelation as a detailed account of history. The seal visions described events in the first age from the time of Jacob until the Roman conquest of Palestine and, at the same time, happenings in the time of Christ. The Beast with the seven heads referred to persecutions endured by Christians in the Roman era, struggles against heresy, conflicts with Arabs and Turks, and two more recent figures, Emperor Henry IV, who challenged papal authority, and Saladin, who recaptured Jerusalem from the Crusaders. By identifying Revelation with the church's policies in the West and East, he made it an instrument for the defense of the papacy. The two witnesses (Rev. 11:3–12) represented the two religious orders of spiritual people. The approaching period of the Holy Spirit would probably begin in the year 1260, a number that he derived from Revelation 11:3 and 12:6.

Joachim himself died peacefully in 1202, his ideas causing little stir. However, the prophetic character of his interpretation made it attractive to reformers who came after him. They transformed his spiritual age into one that was physically located in time. The prophecy of the two witnesses was fulfilled in the Dominican and Franciscan orders, founded shortly after his death. There had been many antichrists, but the greatest was yet to come. He will be like a usurping pope (an antipope) who exercises dominion over all the earth, but he will be opposed by a saintly pope, the

Fig. 3.4 A Monk's Work Is Never Done. An early woodcut shows a monk hard at work. Monks such as Joachim of Fiore offered alternative views to the presiding Augustinian position.

angel that comes "from the east" (Rev. 7:2) and prophet of the new age.

Joachim's doctrine of the third age suited the prevailing mood of dissatisfaction in his day—the threat of Islam, controversies between popes and emperors, and discontent with the church's leaders by various factions. He set a precedent for later thinkers to interpret the events of the Book of Revelation in light of happenings in their own times—a tradition that has continued unabated to our own day. Various writers utilized his idea of the angelic pope and the last world emperor for their own purposes. Finally, his optimistic view of the future age has ap-

pealed to visionaries from his day to the twentieth century.

Francis of Assisi

The emergence of Francis of Assisi (1181–1226) enabled Joachim's ideas to experience a degree of influence that no one could have foreseen. Francis seemed to be the leader in the new age of the Spirit. Although he, too, passed from the scene and the year 1260 came and went without any noteworthy happening, a group of his disciples known as the Spiritual Franciscans tried to follow literally his ideals of poverty. Because they saw themselves as the vanguard of the new order in the church and St. Francis as their messianic head, they quickly fell into disfavor and suffered persecution. Accordingly, they turned to the prophecies of Joachim for spiritual sustenance in their struggle with the papacy during the late thirteenth and early fourteenth centuries.

Since the Spiritual Franciscans believed they lived in the third age in which knowledge of God could be obtained directly through contemplation, they rejected preaching, the sacraments, and the clerical hierarchy, including the pope. They utilized the Book of Revelation to exalt Francis and contrast his life with the lives of the popes. One person even claimed Francis was the angel of the sixth seal (Rev. 7:2). Another Spiritual pointed to Joachim's prophecy of a future false pope and identified the beast from the sea with worldly Christians. He included among them prominent princes and clergymen. A third writer compared the coming of Francis with the advent of Christ twelve centuries earlier and claimed the mystical number 666 meant *benediktos*, the Greek name of Pope Benedict XII (1334–42). Offshoots of the Spiritual Franciscans, the Beguines and Beghards, identified the Roman church with the whore of Babylon and said there were two antichrists—Pope John XXII (1316–34) and a second who would appear by 1335. The Spiritual Franciscans were a countercultural "people's religion" that existed alongside the main church during the Middle Ages, and they were only one of many such groups.

The Hussites and the Taborites

At times, popular millennialism took on a violent character. The best example of this was the Hussite struggle in Bohemia (modern-day Czech Republic). Here the church was enormously wealthy and most of the higher clergy were foreigners (Germans) and quite corrupt. The leading Bohemian reformer, University of Prague philosophy professor Jan Hus (1373–1415), declared that the pope "is the messenger of Antichrist and an adversary of Peter."[9] After the church council at Constance in 1415 ordered Hus's execution for his allegedly heretical views, a mass revolt of townspeople and peasants broke out in Bohemia.

The most radical of the rebels, the Taborites, called for a thoroughgoing social and economic revolution, and they steeped their insurrection in millennial language. They fortified several hilltop towns, one of which they named Tabor after the Palestinian mountain of the same name, which according to church tradition was the site of the transfiguration and the place where Jesus appeared to his disciples after the resurrection.

In late 1419 a preacher said that in the following February God would destroy by fire every town except the Taborite strongholds, and a large number of people at once fled to the hills. The Taborites said that as soon as the world was free of sinners, Christ would appear on Mount Tabor and take over as ruler of Bohemia. The third of Joachim's ages would begin, there would be no need for the church, and everyone would be healthy, free, and equal. However, when Christ did not come in 1420, the various Bohemian factions formed armies and a bloody civil war ensued. The more moderate Hussites won out and their reformed faith held sway in Bohemia until the Thirty Years' War in the seventeenth century when the region was reconquered by the Catholic forces of Habsburg Austria.

The Protestant Reformation

Martin Luther

Although the Reformation turned much of the church on its head, its proponents continued to hold the Augustinian view of the millennium. Never-

Fig. 3.5 Antichrist Superstar. During the time of the Reformation the pope was often villified as the Antichrist, thus beginning a long-standing Protestent tradition of anti-papal sentiment.

he so deeply disliked the papacy, he interpreted the book as a prophetic history of the church and tried to correlate the various symbols in it with events in church history. For him the golden age of the church was in the patristic era, and it ended with the triumph of the papacy. Thus, he would not go along with the millennial view of the late-medieval followers of Joachim and anticipate a future era of peace and righteousness on the earth. At the same time, he did look for the second coming of Christ, the eschaton that would bring all things on earth to a final end. He often emphasized that the event could not be calculated, but on occasions he would engage in such speculation. He developed a chronological table of world history in which he theorized that the world would come to an end in 2040, near the end of its sixth millennium. Also, in one supper table conversation with his theology students in 1538, he suggested that the end would occur in about twenty years. However, he did not place theological significance on these statements.

Although Luther himself was not a strict millennialist, his more literal approach to the Bible and the attention that he called to its prophetic portions led some Lutheran scholars to adopt a millennialist interpretation.

theless, they suggested changes in eschatological interpretation that led to a renewal of premillennialism in the seventeenth century. As mentioned above, the medieval dissidents did not attack the papacy as an institution but only the moral failures of individual popes, and those influenced by Joachim of Fiore looked for the rise of an "angelic" pope who would bring about renewal. However, Martin Luther saw the very institution of the papacy as the Antichrist, and other Protestant writers followed his lead. Since the Antichrist was identified as an ecclesiastical institution, one could attack and destroy this foe.

Second, Luther took a more literal approach to the Book of Revelation. Because

Columbus and the *Book of Prophecies*

Those who write about Christopher Columbus (1451–1506) usually depict him as a rational geographer who overcame ignorance and religious superstition to convince Isabella and Ferdinand to finance his voyage to America. This image is quite far from the truth, for in reality he was encouraged to his mission by a mystical assurance drawn from a study of Holy Scripture and its commentators.

Columbus was an avid Bible student aided by medieval Bible scholars such as Nicholas of Lyra and Pierre d'Ailly. His journals and private letters show a great devotion to Christ and knowledge of the Bible. This is especially the case in the *Libro de las Profecias,* or *Book of Prophecies,* a careful compilation of Bible passages on such subjects as the earth, distant lands, oceans, population movements, prophecies of the spread of the gospel throughout the world, and the end of the age and beginning of the earthly kingdom of Jesus Christ. Columbus believed that the prophecies about the end of the world could not be fulfilled until all nations and peoples had been evangelized. In fact, he felt his own name, Christophorus (Christ-Bearer), was a special sign that God had predestined him to reach the "distant isles" with the message of Christ. Late in his life he wrote, "God made me the messenger of the new heaven and the new earth of which he spoke in the Apocalypse of St. John after having spoken of it through

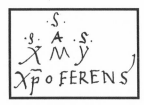

Fig. 3.6 Sign on the Dotted Line. Columbus signed his name along with Greek and Latin abbreviations that represented his mission as the bearer of Christ.

the mouth of Isaiah; and he showed me the spot where to find it."

The *Book of Prophecies* helped Columbus convince the Spanish sovereigns to fund his voyage, which was in fact part of a far grander plan, "the Enterprise of the Indies." In his mind it was the first step in a crusade in which Isabella, Ferdinand, and Columbus would restore the Holy Land to the Christian faith. With the fall of Granada in 1492 and the explorer's subsequent discovery of the sea route to the Indies, the Spanish monarchs would have access to the riches of the Indies to fund this grand scheme. Throughout his last years of failure, Columbus still believed himself guided by God's providence and biblical prophecy in all his undertakings. In times of distress, such as during his fourth voyage (1502–4), the tired old mariner heard voices and saw visions. The message he received from God was, as always, a positive one.

Source: Pauline Moffitt Watts, "Prophecy and Discovery: On the Spiritual Origins of Christopher Columbus's 'Enterprise of the Indies,'" *American Historical Review* 90 (February 1985): 102.

John Calvin

John Calvin, like Luther, was not impressed with millenarian views. The violence caused by radical sectarians in the 1520s and 1530s had soured both Reformers on prophetic speculation. Calvin himself dismissed such teaching as a childish fantasy without scriptural support. He condemned millenarians as being ignorant of divine things and as malignant perverts who attempted to overthrow the grace of God. His concern was for the appearance of the Lord to bring about a general resurrection and the last judgment, and he felt that millennialism was a poor substitute for this hope. Calvin was also against using biblical numerology in speculations about the end of the age. Commenting about Daniel 12, a favorite for such predictions, the Genevan reformer stated: "In numerical calculations I am no conjurer, and those who expound this passage with too much subtlety, only trifle in their own speculations, and detract from the authority of prophecy."[10] With this attitude, it is no surprise that he never wrote a commentary on the Book of Revelation.

The Transition to Premillennialism

Johann Heinrich Alsted

An important German Calvinist scholar, Johann Heinrich Alsted (1588–1638), dissented significantly from his master on the question of chiliasm. Originally a professor of theology at the Reformed Academy of Herborn in the Rhineland, in 1624 he accepted an appointment at a new school in Transylvania in Eastern Europe to escape the violence of the Thirty Years' War.

In 1627 he published a book defending premillennialism, which soon was translated into English under the title *The Beloved City,* and it deeply influenced the thinking of the post-Reformation generations. In it he laid down guidelines for studying biblical prophecy and insisted that the Thirty Years' War devastating his homeland was indeed the end of the age.

The book is a careful exposition of Revelation 20. Alsted followed the customary path of laying out the events of the chapter—the imprisonment of Satan in the abyss that allows the church outward peace for a thousand years, the resurrection of the righteous dead, and the conversion of multitudes to Christ. At the end of this period Satan will be released, Gog and Magog will make war against the church and will be defeated, the final judgment will take place, and evil will be banished forever. He also completed a word study of the chapter to support millennialism, and a logical analysis of the text, and he introduced a large number of the standard prophetic passages in the Old Testament to explain the nature of the millennial reign. Then, in a complicated numerical section, he calculated the beginning date of the millennium as 1694. Alsted is, therefore, a major transitional figure in Protestantism. His work marked the recovery of the premillennialism of the early church fathers, and henceforth Protestants would be deeply divided on the issue of the coming kingdom of God.

Joseph Mede

Joseph Mede (1586–1638), called by some the greatest biblical scholar that the Anglican church has ever produced, popularized Alsted's premillennial views in the English-speaking world. In his book *The Key of the Revelation* he set forth the idea of the "synchronism" of prophecies, meaning that many of the prophetic teachings of the Apocalypse apply to the same time period and describe individuals and events during that time span.

He said that the book has three divisions and each of these begins with a voice sounding forth as a trumpet from heaven to the apostle John. The three divisions are the messages to the seven churches, the vision of the seals, and the opened book. He does not explain the first section, but the second division deals with the Roman Empire and the third reveals the future of the Christian church. The first six seals picture the fate of pagan Rome, culminating in the conversion of Constantine. The seven trumpets arising from the seventh seal were fulfilled by the Germanic invasions, the division of Rome into ten successor states, the extinction of the Western empire, the war between eastern Rome and the Ostrogoths, the rise of Islam, the Turkish invasions, and the coming of Christ. When the sixth trumpet sounds, six vials or bowls of judgment are poured upon the anti-Christian world. The first was the late medieval reformers who denounced the pope as Antichrist and Rome as Babylon. The next was Luther's action in destroying the authority of the Roman church over large areas of Europe. The third, the rivers of blood, referred to Catholics killed by European Protestant rulers. The other four remained to be emptied on papal Rome. They would destroy the Austrian ruling family (the protectors of the pope), level the city of Rome, send the Jews to attack the papacy, and prepare the nations for the battle of Armageddon.

The seventh trumpet begins the battle of Armageddon, at which time the papacy and all the other enemies of the church are destroyed and the earth is prepared for the thousand-year reign of Christ and his saints. Then comes the first resurrection, the thousand years granted to the bride of Christ to live in peace and prosperity on the earth, the final resurrection of the damned and their judgment, and the taking of the saints into heaven to live with Christ forever.

Mede's work was extremely popular, both in his own lifetime and in the following years. During the seventeenth-century Puritan revolution his ideas helped fan the fire of prophetic enthusiasm. Although the actions of some radical groups during the revolution (such as the Fifth Monarchy Men and the Diggers) tended to discredit premillennialism, many influential people continued to adhere to it, such as Isaac Newton in England and Cotton Mather in Massachusetts.

The Emergence of Postmillennialism

Daniel Whitby

Although premillennialism found a secure place among the seventeenth-century Puritans, postmillennialism had arisen at the same time and proved to be a formidable rival. The major exponent of this position was Daniel Whitby (1638–1725), rector of St. Edmund's Church, Salisbury, who published the two-volume *Paraphrase and Commentary on the New Testament* in 1703. He held that the earth's population would be converted to Christ, the Jews restored to the Holy Land, the pope and Turks vanquished, and then the world would enjoy a thousand-year golden age of universal peace, happiness, and righteousness. At the close of this period Christ would personally come to earth and the last judgment would take place. Whitby's more optimistic outlook continued to be influential as his work was reprinted into the mid-nineteenth century.

Jonathan Edwards

During the eighteenth century Whitby's eschatology proved to be quite popular, and several noteworthy commentaries on Revelation advanced the same view. One of the most brilliant American philosophers and theologians of all times, Jonathan Edwards (1703–58), best known to students of American literature as the author of the sermon "Sinners in the Hands of an Angry God," also adopted postmillennialism.

For three decades he kept a journal on the Book of Revelation in which he analyzed its contents, took notes from commentators, and recorded the signs of the times that he believed were leading to the millennium. He also set forth his millennial ideas in *Some Thoughts Concerning the*

Present Revival of Religion in New England (1742) and the sermons of 1739 posthumously published in 1774 as *A History of the Work of Redemption*. These writings, which grew out of the revivals of the Great Awakening of the 1740s, painted a postmillennial vision on the landscape of the New World.

In these books Edwards stated that the church would achieve a golden age on earth through the process of preaching the gospel in the power of the Holy Spirit. The destruction of the Antichrist, whom he identified with the pope, would usher in this period. It was papal oppression that had forced people into superstition and ignorance and had taken the Bible out of the hands of laypeople. Fortunately, the Protestant Reformation (which he identified with the fifth bowl judgment in Revelation) had resulted in the reestablishment of sound doctrine, the propagation of the gospel to the heathen, and the pietist movement. Learning had been revived, the power of the papacy reduced, and persecution diminished.

He calculated from Revelation 16:1 that the papacy would continue in power for 1,260 years and then expire either in 1866 or 2016, depending on which date one selected as the point at which the institution came into existence. At that time a great outpouring of the Holy Spirit would destroy the Antichrist. A revival resulting from the preaching of the gospel would overthrow Satan's visible kingdom, the apostate church, and a great age of human happiness would follow. He saw himself as living in momentous times, as the Great Awakening was taking place around him. He argued that the Scripture prophecies of the "latter-day outpouring of the Spirit" applied to America. It would be the scene of the prelude to the great manifestation of the power of God.

During the millennial period he argued that heresy, infidelity, and superstition would be eliminated, Islam destroyed, the Jews converted, and the heathen of Africa, America, and India won to Christ. The holiness and commitment to Christ of this age would be accompanied by a vast increase in knowledge and learning. International peace and understanding would prevail, and along with it would come the greatest prosperity the world had ever known. It would also be a time when Christianity and the church would be the most respected institutions in society.

At the close of the millennial age much of the world would fall away from Christ and his church. Gog and Magog would be able to recruit vast numbers for their armies because people had abused the prosperity of the era to serve lust and corruption. But then Christ would come, crush the rebellion, and carry out the last judgment. The church would be caught up in the clouds to meet its Lord in the air, the world would be set on fire, and it would become a great furnace in which the enemies of Christ would be tormented forever.

A Resurgence of Premillennialism

Although Jonathan Edwards was the most outspoken postmillennialist of his time, there were still individuals who faithfully preached premillennialism. Among these were the father of German pietism, Philipp Jakob Spener (1635–1705), the distinguished New Testament scholar Johann Albrecht Bengel (1687–1752), and some of the Methodists. Even John Wesley (1703–91) in his early ministry preached premillennialism, only to abandon it in his later years.

The number of premillennialists increased markedly in the early nineteenth century as the French Revolution fostered a renewal of interest in prophecy and speculation about the end of the world. This was particularly so because Roman Catholic power in France had been destroyed. During the revolution church properties were seized, including the papal territory at Avignon, many priests were sent to the guillotine, a "religion of reason" was founded, and the pope was exiled from Rome. Because they believed the millennium would not come until the papacy had been destroyed, many Bible scholars concluded that the end of the age was near. They believed they were witnessing the "deadly wound" inflicted on the papacy as foretold in Revelation 13, and their calculations of biblical numbers seemed to point to the eighteenth and early nineteenth centuries as the decisive period for the establishment of the millennium.

Henry Drummond

Great Britain was the center of the new prophetic movement, and a vast amount of literature on millennial themes was written there in the first half of the nineteenth century. Most of the writers belonged to the Church of England and the Presbyterian Church of Scotland. Not only were they convinced that Christ would return to set up the millennium, but they were also concerned about the conversion of the Jews and their return to the Holy Land.

Beginning in 1826 Henry Drummond (1786–1860), a banker and occasional Tory member of Parliament who had an ongoing interest in prophecy, sponsored prophetic conferences at his Albury Park estate. Drummond summarized the conclusions reached at the meetings:

1. This "dispensation" or age will not end "insensibly," but cataclysmically in judgment and destruction of the church in the same manner in which the Jewish dispensation ended.
2. The Jews will be restored to Palestine during the time of judgment.
3. The judgment to come will fall principally upon Christendom.
4. When the judgment is past, the millennium will begin.
5. The second advent of Christ will occur before the millennium.
6. The 1,260 years of Daniel 7 and Revelation 13 ought to be measured from the reign of Justinian to the French Revolution. The bowls of

wrath (Revelation 16) are now being poured out and the second advent is imminent.[11]

Eleazar Lord and David Lord

Two brothers from the United States, the banker Eleazar Lord (1788–1871) and writer David Lord (1792–1880), popularized British premillennialism in their homeland through various books and *The Theological and Literary Review,* a quarterly that appeared between 1848 and 1861. David systematized premillennial teachings more than any previous writer, and he developed an ingenious scheme for the literal interpretation of prophetic Scriptures.

He distinguished between "language prophecies," which conformed to the accepted rules of language and grammar, and "symbolic prophecies," which were revealed in dreams or visions. According to his method it was possible to distinguish the literal from the figurative expressions in the prophets and make their meanings clear and demonstrable. In his opinion, this effectively countered postmillennial interpretations that were based on spiritualized predictions. His explanation of the Book of Revelation showed the futility of optimistic views of the present. Every period of revival has been followed by backsliding, and the purpose of the trials of our present age is to prepare the way for the world to be redeemed. Christ will return, inaugurate the millennium, reign in person, and bring salvation to all nations.

Lord's system attracted followers not only among his fellow New England Calvinists, both Presbyterians and Congregationalists, but also other groups. In fact, premillenarians were soon to be found in all the major denominations. They included Joseph Seiss (Lutheran), R. C. Shimeall (Episcopalian), John G. Wilson (Methodist), James Inglis (Baptist), and John Demarest (Dutch Reformed). The premillennialists encountered hostility within their denominations, however, and as a result, created their own alternative structures, such as the Premillennial Advent Society of New York City, and held separate millenarian Bible conferences, the best-known being the Niagara Bible Conference. Although the dominant view among the denominational leadership was postmillennialism, the premillenarians had a well articulated theology and a solid core of supporters.

The Turn to Dispensational Premillennialism

Postmillennialism prevailed in the middle and later nineteenth century among such orthodox theologians as A. A. Hodge and B. B. Warfield of Princeton Theological Seminary, W. G. T. Shedd of Union Seminary, and A. H. Strong of Rochester Theological Seminary. The conservative variety stressed that God's power over his enemies will become more fully manifest as the time of Christ's return draws near,

Fig. 3.8 A Millennium Bible. Long before the contemporary era of specialty or niche Bibles, William Biederwolf's (1867–1939) *The Millennium Bible* appeared. First published in 1924, it was a commentary of prophetic passages that advanced the premillennial dispensational viewpoint. After coming back into print in 1964, it was later released as *The Second Coming Bible, The Amazing Prophecy Second Coming Bible,* and *The Second Coming Bible Commentary.*

and it served as a motivating force in the great foreign missionary outreach. But a liberal postmillennialism was also gaining ground as the new century approached. The primary source of this optimistic approach was not the Scriptures but the merging of the eighteenth-century view of human goodness with the nineteenth-century myth of progress.

John Nelson Darby

Against this backdrop, the rising pace of eschatalogical expectations led to the development of dispensationalism, and with it came a division in the ranks of the premillennialists. This new school of belief in the second coming was both a system of biblical hermeneutics and a philosophy, crystalized in the 1830s in Great Britain by John Nelson Darby (1800–82) and the group he led, the "Plymouth" Brethren. As mentioned earlier, dispensationalists rejected the traditional view that the church had superseded Israel in God's plan for the ages. Instead, they recognized the Jewish people as both the historical Israel and the object of the Old Testament prophecies concerning the restoration of the Davidic kingdom in the endtimes. Moreover, the true church of Christ was in no way the same as the official church establishment, or the "professing church," as dispensationalists liked to label it. The church was that body of believers who found Christ through faith, and they alone would pass through the final judgment and enter into eternal life.

The Darbyite Brethren never became a mass movement in Great Britain, but their anti-institutional ideas fell on fertile ground among laissez-faire evangelicals in nineteenth-century America.[12] Its impact was typified in the experience of A. T. Pierson, the foremost promoter of foreign missions in the late nineteenth century. A conservative Presbyterian postmillennialist who was committed to evangelical doctrine and the winning of souls, he met in 1879 with the prominent Brethren personage, George Müller of Bristol, England, who was known for his orphanages. Pierson told his visitor from abroad that Jesus would return to earth after the "thousand year period of prosperity brought in by human effort and benevolent Christian civilization." Müller, however, silenced the American's arguments with one statement: "My beloved brother . . . not one of them is based upon the word of God." From that time on, Pierson was a staunch premillennialist.

The historic premillennialists, such as A. J. Gordon, a prominent Baptist pastor and Bible teacher in Boston who founded a college to train missionaries, soon lost out to the new wave of dispensationalism. These premillennialist teachers had held to the idea of progressive fulfillment of prophecy in church history, saw the signs of hope in the imminent return of Christ, and rejected the idea that the church was a small faithful remnant who would survive the "great apostasy" in the last days. But Darby's books on eschatological themes became quite popular in the English-speaking world, and his lineage could be traced through such influential prophecy preachers and writers as G. Campbell Morgan, W. H. Griffith Thomas, Harry A. Ironside, Arno C. Gaebelein, William L. Pettingill, William E. Biederwolf, Reuben A. Torrey, and James M. Gray. Moreover, the two leading evangelists of modern times, Dwight L. Moody and Billy Graham, adhered to this teaching. The most significant figures in the popularization of dispensationalist eschatology in late-nineteenth- to early-twentieth-century America, however, were William E. Blackstone (1841–1935) and C. I. Scofield (1843–1921).

Fig. 3.9 A British Import. John Nelson Darby, a leader in the British Plymouth Brethren movement, was without question the leading nineteenth-century proponent of dispensationalism and the individual responsible for bringing its message to America.

JOHN NELSON DARBY
1800-1882

William E. Blackstone

William E. Blackstone was born into the home of a humble tinsmith in Adams, New York. His family were devout Methodists, and after his conversion at age eleven, he became a lifelong member of the Methodist Church. He did not attend college or receive any formal ministerial training, but he was a lay Bible teacher, preacher, and superintendent of a Sunday school. After service in the Civil War, Blackstone relocated to Illinois and from 1870 lived in Chicago, where he became quite successful through building ventures and property investments. During the 1870s he moved in a social circle that included several prominent dispensationalists, among them D. L. Moody, and he lectured widely on Christ's imminent return.

In 1878 he felt called by God to end his business career and devote himself full time to evangelistic witness. In the sub-

PLAN OF THE AIONS.

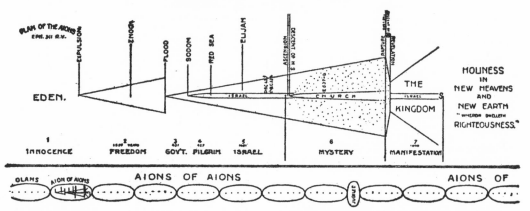

Fig. 3.10 Blackstone's Chart. Another dispensational chart is shown here, this one from the best-selling *Jesus Is Coming* by William E. Blackstone (or W.E.B. as he was listed on the cover and title page).

sequent years he published several books and tracts promoting premillennialism, the best known of which was *Jesus Is Coming*. Originally published in 1898, the book was translated into forty languages and eventually sold a million and a half copies. Although Blackstone lacked academic credentials, he was a polished author with a thorough knowledge of the Scriptures, and he corresponded with public figures throughout the world.

The book affirmed the dispensational premillennial view of the second coming and refuted the other positions. It also spelled out the signs of the times, which pointed to Christ's speedy coming: the growth of knowledge, the worldwide travel network, expansion of mass communications, perilous times (natural disasters, evil political ideologies, the militarization of Europe, lawlessness), spiritualism (linked with Christian Science and Buddhism), apostasy of the churches (due to the falling away of the Orthodox and

Catholic Churches, higher criticism, and formalism), worldwide evangelism, concentration of riches in the hands of the few, and above all the restoration of the Jews to the Holy Land, which he called "God's sun-dial."

The Jews were central in Blackstone's thought. He believed strongly that they could only find salvation in Christ, and as a result, he founded the Chicago Hebrew Mission in 1887, which he superintended for four years. The Jewish tradition—their beliefs, laws, and rituals—had merely kept them waiting for the Messiah and the reestablishment of their national home in Palestine. They would fulfill the role God had intended for human history. On the other hand, Blackstone viewed reformed and liberal or assimilated Jews quite negatively. He maintained that they had turned their back on their role in the divine plan for the endtimes. As most of them did not favor the Zionist program, he assumed they would not participate in the national restoration, and because they were resistant to evangelical missionary efforts, they would surely perish. These individuals would not find salvation now through Christ, nor would they be saved in the land of Israel. He taught that the Jews in Palestine would accept Jesus during the great tribulation. Whereas all deviant Christians and non-Protestant groups would surely be consigned to eternal damnation, Orthodox and Zionist Jews would have a chance because of their place in God's program.

Blackstone believed the United States had a special role in carrying out the divine plan for humanity. America was the modern-day Cyrus who would assist in the Jewish restoration to the Promised Land, and it would be judged according to how it carried out this divine assignment. In 1891 Blackstone single-handedly drew up a petition to President Benjamin Harrison that urged him to gain international consent for the granting of Palestine as a haven for persecuted Russian Jews. He secured signatures from 414 noted Americans, including political officials, clergymen, journalists, and big businessmen, but the federal government did nothing about it. In 1916 he organized a second petition calling for the Jewish restoration to Palestine, this time in conjunction with prominent Zionist leaders including Louis D. Brandeis, the first Jewish Supreme Court justice, who were seeking Christian support for the Zionist cause. The aging Blackstone was able to win endorsements from several mainstream Protestant figures, thereby bridging the widening gap between fundamentalists and modernists. However, it was never formally presented to President Woodrow Wilson, although he was aware of it.

Blackstone is significant because he was the earliest dispensationalist who sought to influence the American government to support Zionism—a tradition that has continued to the present among dispensational supporters of Israel. However, his primary motivation was not the physical and national survival of the Jews but rather the establishment of the Jewish state, which was needed to prepare the way for the coming of the Messiah, Jesus Christ, and the millennial kingdom.

C. I. Scofield

A contemporary of Blackstone's, C. I. (Cyrus Ingerson) Scofield, was the other great popularizer of dispensational premillennialism. Born in Michigan, he moved with his family to Lebanon, Tennessee, where he was raised an Episcopalian. After Civil War service in the Confederate army, he went to St. Louis, studied law, and then moved to Kansas, where he became a lawyer and elected official. He fell victim to alcohol, which wrecked his marriage, but sometime around 1880 while in prison he was converted and became a Congregationalist minister. Although he had no theological training, he took over a Congregational mission church in Dallas, Texas, and was ordained in 1882. He taught himself dispensationalism, began a correspondence Bible study course, and published *Rightly Dividing the Word of Truth* in 1885, a book that established his credentials as a proclaimer of the doctrine.

After building the Dallas congregation into a prospering church, in 1895 he went to Northfield, Massachusetts, to pastor the local Congregational church, work with D. L. Moody, and engage in Bible conference ministry. In 1902 he returned to the Dallas church and labored on a reference Bible project. He later switched his ordination to the Southern Presbyterian Church, moved to New York, where he operated a correspondence Bible school and engaged in conference preaching, and then with Lewis S. Chafer founded the Philadelphia School of the Bible.

His most important endeavor was *The Scofield Reference Bible,* which expounded the dispensationalist distinctives he had been preaching on the Bible conference circuit. It was published in 1909 by Oxford University Press and became the most widely used work that propagated dispensationalism. It was revised and expanded in 1917 and updated in 1967, and over the years more than ten million copies have been sold. Using the King James Version, Scofield embellished it with a system of chain references and footnotes that largely followed the eschatological teaching of John Nelson Darby. Had Scofield presented his explanatory notes in a separate commentary, they would have probably gone unnoticed. As it was, however, the notes were printed in a manner that a person would read them as he or she studied the Bible. Decades before the current fascination with specialty or "niche" study Bibles, Scofield's influential work gave millions of readers a sense of authority as they learned to view the Scriptures through the dispensational system. Simply put, *The Scofield Reference Bible* did more than any other printed work to anchor dispensational premillennialism in American evangelicalism.

The Bible institute movement was also a force in the propagation of dispensationalist ideas in North America. Beginning with the first schools, Moody in Chicago and Nyack in New York, these institutions provided rapid, practical training for laypeople who wished to become "full-time Christian workers." By 1945 over one hundred Bible institutes had been founded, although some were rather ephemeral. They also served the interdenominational fundamentalist movement like the headquarters of a denomination, and by the mid-twentieth century they were the prime source of evangelical Protestant missionary recruits. The heart of the instructional program was the English Bible, and it was almost invariably taught from a dispensationalist perspective.

Billy Graham

The best-known heir of early-twentieth-century dispensationalism is evangelist Billy Graham. Born in 1918 into the family of a dairy farmer in Charlotte, North Carolina, he was converted at an evangelistic meeting at age sixteen. He attended two colleges in the South before enrolling at Wheaton College in 1940. After graduating in 1943 he served a brief pastorate and then became an evangelist for Youth for Christ. He also served as president of Northwestern Schools in Minneapolis (1947–51). In 1949 he was catapulted to national attention through a successful evangelistic campaign in Los Angeles. He formed an organization that spawned a global network of endeavors, and he traveled incessantly throughout the world preaching the gospel. Not only were his books best-sellers, but he also became the confidant of U.S. presidents, heads of state, and powerful people in the realms of business and entertainment.

The second coming has been a consistent theme in Graham's preaching and writing, although in his later years the more dispensationalist aspects of it have been muted. For example, in his book *World Aflame*, he speaks of the "signs of the times" and that they are "converging for the first

---

The Scofield Bible Tradition

The Scofield Reference Bible, first published in 1909 and revised in 1917, was produced by Oxford University Press. Harold Lindsell, the editor of *Christianity Today,* declared in 1967 that Oxford had published several million copies of *The Scofield Reference Bible,* and the firm had sold more copies of it than any other title it had issued in the United States. The impact of this Bible in spreading dispensational teachings is incalculable. It brought these teachings even into churches that otherwise had no historical connection with the movement.

Old Testament scholar Dewey M. Beegle observed that the Scofield notes became so dominant within evangelical circles that many adherents considered the commentary "the true interpretation of the Bible," thus implicitly granting it the status of equal authority with the biblical text itself. In other words, for many evangelicals the Scofield notes possessed what amounted to de facto canonicity. Critics of evangelicalism never tire of pointing out that the very people who say they can read the Bible for themselves all too often end up poring over Scofield's notes to discover what the text really means.

Over time, however, many evangelicals came to believe the reference Bible was outdated, due to the new light that had been thrown on the Scriptures by textual criticism, archeological discoveries, and developments in the area of Bible prophecy. Also, the language of the King James Version, which had not been updated since the late eighteenth ▶

century, had in places become incomprehensible and even inaccurate. Thus, in 1954 Oxford University Press decided that a revision of its famed annotated Bible was needed, and a nine-person committee was appointed to undertake the task. It was a veritable who's who of evangelical scholars: E. Schuyler English, Frank E. Gaebelein, William Culbertson, Charles E. Feinberg, Allan A. MacRae, Clarence E. Mason, Alva J. McClain, Wilbur M. Smith, and John F. Walvoord. The editorial committee met together in Chicago regularly over the next nine years, and the result of their labors was *The New Scofield Reference Bible,* released by Oxford on April 13, 1967, the fiftieth anniversary of the publication of the 1917 edition.

The revisers based *The New Scofield Reference Bible* on the King James text, but they freely changed words that had become archaic, such as changing *prevent* to *precede* in 1 Thessalonians 4:15 and *conversation* to *citizenship* in Philippians 3:20. They sanitized "indelicate words or expressions," such as changing *dung* and *piss* in 2 Kings 18:27 to the more refined *refuse* and *water.* They also dropped the Ussher chronology from the margin and replaced it with more accurate dates. The introductions to all the books of the Bible were completely redone, and many existing notes were rewritten and new ones added to incorporate textual and critical matters and recent archeological findings. The system of seven dispensations was retained, but the name of the sixth was changed from "grace" to "church." The revisers also clarified that salvation in every dispensation was strictly by faith, not good works, even in the period of law, and they even more forthrightly affirmed the verbal inspiration of Scripture.

In short, *The New Scofield Reference Bible* was more irenic and less dogmatic than the earlier edition and contained far more sophisticated notes. How much it would be accepted was another matter. By the time of its release, it had to compete with a growing number of other evangelical commentaries and reference Bibles.

Despite the growing competition, however, the Scofield tradition continues strongly today. A search of the Amazon.com online bookstore reveals 208 Scofield "items" available. These range from *The New Scofield Reference Bible* (the 1967 edition) to *The Scofield Study Bible* (the new name for the original 1909 edition), all available in a variety of bindings and sizes. Further, *The Scofield Reference Bible,* once synonymous with the King James Version, is now available in several formats of the more contemporary New International Version.

Sources: Harold Lindsell, *Christianity Today,* 14 April 1967, 711; Dewey M. Beegle, *Scripture, Tradition, and Infallibility* (Grand Rapids: Eerdmans, 1973), 110.

18 24]   REVELATION.   [19 17

in thee: for thy merchants were the great men of the earth; for by thy *sorceries were all nations deceived.
24 And in her was found *the *blood of prophets, and of saints, and of all that were slain upon the earth.

CHAPTER 19.

(Parenthetical: the four allelu-ias of the glorified saints. Cf. Rev. 17. 1-7; 18. 1-8.)

AND after these things I heard a great *voice of much people in heaven, saying, Alleluia; *Salva-tion, and glory, and *honour, and power, unto the Lord our God:
2 For true and righteous *are his judgments: for he hath judged the great *whore, which did corrupt the earth with her fornication, and hath *avenged the blood of his servants at her hand.
3 And again they said, *Alleluia. And her *smoke rose up for ever and ever.
4 And the four and twenty *elders and the four *beasts fell down and worshipped God that sat on the throne, saying, Amen; Alleluia.
5 And a *voice came out of the throne, saying, *Praise our God, all ye his servants, and ye that fear him, both small and great.
6 And I heard as it were the voice of a great multitude, and as the voice of many waters, and as the voice of mighty *thunderings, say-ing, Alleluia: for the Lord God omnipotent reigneth.

The marriage of the Lamb.

7 Let us be glad and rejoice, and give honour to him: for the mar-riage of the Lamb is come, and his *wife hath made herself ready.
8 And to her *was granted that she should be arrayed in fine linen, clean and white: for the fine linen is the *righteousness of saints.

[right sub-column references:]
A.D. 96.
* Cf. Nah 3.4.
* Rev. 17. 6.
* Rev. 18. 20; 11. 15.
* See salvation. See Rom. 1. 16, note.
* power of our God.
* Rev. 17. 1.
* Cf. Rev. 6. 10; cf. Lk. 18. 7, 8.
a v. 1.
* Cf. Rev. 18. 9, 18; cf. Mk. 9. 48.
* Elders. Tit. 1. 5-9.
* living creatures.
* Cf. Rev. 18. 4.
* Cf. Psa. 134. 1.
* Cf. Re. 20. 18.
* Bride (of Christ). vs. 6-8; Rev. 21. 9; John 3. 29; Rev. 19. 6-8.)
* Cf. 1 Cor. 15. 10.
* righteousness Righteousness (garment). (Gen. 3. 21.)
* Cf. Lk. 14. 15.
* Inspiration. Rev. 21. 5. (Ex. 4. 15; Rev. 22. 19.)
* Cf. Heb. 1. 14.

9 And he saith unto me, Write, *Blessed *are they which are called unto the marriage supper of the Lamb. And he saith unto me, *These are the true sayings of God.
10 And I fell at his feet to worship him. And he said unto me, See thou do it not: I am thy *fellow-servant, and of thy brethren that have the testimony of Jesus: wor-ship God: for the *testimony of Jesus is the spirit of prophecy.

The second coming of Christ in glory. (Cf. Mt. 24. 16-30.)

11 And I *saw heaven opened, and behold a *white horse; and *he that sat upon him was called *Faith-ful and True, and in righteousness he doth judge and make war.
12 His *eyes were as a flame of fire, and on his head were many *crowns; and he had a name written, *that no man knew, but he himself.
13 And he was clothed with a ves-ture *dipped in blood: and his name is called The Word of God.
14 And the armies which were in heaven followed him upon white horses, clothed in fine linen, white and clean.
15 And out of his mouth goeth a *sharp sword, that with it he should smite the nations: and he *he treadeth the winepress of the fierceness and wrath of Al-mighty God.
16 And he hath on his vesture and on his thigh a name written, *KING OF KINGS, AND LORD OF LORDS.

The battle of Armageddon (Rev. 16. 14; 19. 17, note).

17 And I saw an angel standing in the sun; and he cried with a loud voice, saying to all the fowls that fly in the midst of heaven, *Come and

[right sub-column references:]
* Cf. Eph. 1. 9, 10; cf. 1 Pet. 1. 10-12.
* Contra, Rev. 6. 2; cf. Psa. 45. 4; con-tra, Mt. 21. 5.
* Christ (Second Advent). vs. 11-18; Deut. 30. 3; Acts 1. 9-11.
* Cf. Rev. 1. 7.
* Rev. 1. 14.
* diadems.
* Cf. v. 15. 16; cf. Mic. 11. 27; cf. 1 Tim. 6. 16.
* Cf. Isa. 63. 2, 3.
* Rev. 14. 20; Isa. 63. 3, 6; cf. Joel 3. 13.
* Rev. 17. 14; 1. 5.
* mid-heaven.

[footnotes:]
[1] The "Lamb's wife" here is the "bride" (Rev. 21. 9), the Church, identified with the "heavenly Jerusalem" (Heb. 12. 22, 23), and to be distinguished from Israel, the adulterous and repudiated "wife" of Jehovah, yet to be restored (Isa. 54. 1-10; Hos. 2. 1-17), who is identified with the earth (Hos. 2. 23). A forgiven and restored wife could not be called either a virgin (2 Cor. 11. 2, 3), or a bride.
[2] The garment in Scripture is a symbol of righteousness. In the bad ethical sense it symbolizes self-righteousness (e.g. Isa. 64. 6; see Phil. 3. 6-8, the best that a moral and religious man under law could do). In the good ethical sense the garment symbolizes "the righteousness of God . . . upon all them that believe." See Rom. 3. 21, note.
[3] The vision is of the departure from heaven of Christ and the saints and angels preparatory to the catastrophe in which Gentile world-power, headed up in the Beast, is smitten by the "stone cut out without hands" (Dan. 2. 34, 35).
[4] Armageddon (the ancient hill and valley of Megiddo, west of Jordan in the plain of Jezreel) is the appointed place for the beginning of the great battle in which the
1348

19 18]   REVELATION.   [20 4

gather yourselves together unto the *supper of the great God;
18 That ye may *eat the flesh of kings, and the flesh of captains, and the flesh of mighty men, and the flesh of horses, and of them that sit upon them, and the flesh of all men, both free and bond, both small and great.
19 And I saw the *beast, and the kings of the earth, and their armies, gathered together to *make war against him that sat on the horse, and against his army.

(2) Doom of the Beast, (3) and of the False Prophet.

20 And the *beast was taken, and with him the *false prophet that wrought *miracles before him, with which he deceived them that had received the mark of the beast, and *them that worshipped his image. These both *were cast alive into *a lake of fire burning with brimstone.

(4) Doom of the kings.

21 And the remnant were slain with the sword of *him that sat

[right sub-column references:]
A.D. 96.
* great supper of God.
* Cf. Dan. 7. 5; cf. Ezk. 32. 21-31.
* The Beast. vs. 19, 20. (Dan. 7. 8.)
* Armageddon (battle of). Rev. 16. 14; 19. 17, note.
* Antichrist. Rev. 13. 11-17. 1 John 2. 18; Rev. 13. 11-17.)
* signs.
* Rev. 13. 12, 15.
* Day (of destruc-tion). vs. 19, 20; Rev. 20. 11-15.
* the.
* Kingdom. (O. T.) 5. vs. 11-21; Rev. 20. 1-15. Cf. Isa. 1. 31-32; 1 Cor. 15. 24.)
* Cf. Dan. 3. 6.

upon the horse, which sword pro-ceeded out of his mouth: *and all the fowls were filled with their flesh.

CHAPTER 20.

Satan bound in the abyss during the kingdom-age.

AND I saw an angel come down from heaven, having the key of the bottomless pit and a great chain in his hand.
2 And he laid hold on the dragon, that old serpent, which is the Devil, and *Satan, and bound him a *thousand years,
3 And cast him into the bottom-less pit, and shut him up, and set a seal upon him, that he should *deceive the nations no more, till the thousand years should be ful-filled: and after that he must be loosed a little season.

The first resurrection (1 Cor. 15. 52, note), and the kingdom-age.

4 And I saw thrones, and they sat upon them, and judgment was given unto them: and I saw the souls of

[references:]
* Rev. 20. 11-15.
* Job 21. 20; Rev. 20. 11-15.
* Kingdom (O. T.) 5. vs. 11-21; Rev. 20. 1-15. Cf. Isa. 1. 31-32; 1 Cor. 15. 24.)
* Satan. vs. 2, 7, 10. (Gen. 3. 1.)
* v. 8; 2 Cor. 4. 4.

[footnotes:]
Lord, at His coming in glory, will deliver the Jewish remnant besieged by the Gen-tile world-powers under the Beast and False Prophet (Rev. 16. 13-16; Zech. 12. 1-9). Apparently the besieging hosts, whose approach to Jerusalem is described in Isa. 10. 28-32, alarmed by the signs which precede the Lord's coming (Mt. 24. 29, 30), have fallen back to Megiddo, after the events of Zech. 14. 2, where their de-struction begins; a destruction consummated in Moab and the plains of Idumea (Isa. 63. 1-6). This battle is the first event in "the day of Jehovah" (Isa. 2. 12, refs.), and is the fulfilment of the smiting-stone prophecy of Dan. 2. 35.
[1] The day of Jehovah (called, also, "that day," and "the great day") is that lengthened period of time beginning with the return of the Lord in glory, and ending with the purgation of the heavens and the earth by fire preparatory to the new heavens and the new earth (Isa. 65. 17-19; 66. 22; 2 Pet. 3. 13; Rev. 21. 1). The order of events appears to be: (1) The return of the Lord in glory (Mt. 24. 29, 30); (2) the destruction of the Beast and his host, "the kings of the earth and their armies," and the false prophet, which is the "great and terrible" aspect of the day (Rev. 19. 11-21); (3) the judgment of the nations (Zech. 14. 1-9; Mt. 25. 31-46); (4) the thousand years, i.e. the kingdom-age (Rev. 20. 4-6); (5) the Satanic revolt and its end (Rev. 20. 7-10); (6) the second resurrection and final judgment (Rev. 20. 11-15); and (7) the "day of God," earth purged by fire (2 Pet. 3. 10-13).
The day of the LORD is preceded by seven signs: (1) The sending of Elijah (Mal. 4. 5; Rev. 11. 3-6); (2) cosmical disturbances (Joel 2. 1-12; Mt. 24. 29; Acts 2. 19, 20; Rev. 6. 12-17); (3) the insensibility of the professing church (1 Thes. 5. 1-3); (4) the apostasy of the professing church, then become "Laodicea" (2 Thes. 2. 3); (5) the rapture of the true church (1 Thes. 4. 17); (6) the manifestation of the "man of sin," the Beast (2 Thes. 2. 1-8); (7) the apocalyptic judgments (Rev. 11.-18.).
[2] The Beast. Summary: This "Beast" is the "little horn" of Dan. 7. 24-26, and "desolator" of Dan. 9. 27; the "abomination of desolation" of Mt. 24. 15; the "man of sin" of 2 Thes. 2. 4-8; earth's last and most awful tyrant, Satan's fell instrument of wrath and hatred against God and the Jewish saints. He is, perhaps, identical with the rider on the white horse of Rev. 6. 2, who begins by the peaceful conquest of three of the ten kingdoms into which the former Roman empire will then be di-vided, but who soon establishes the ecclesiastical and governmental tyranny de-scribed in Dan. 7. 9., 11.; Rev. 13. To him Satan gives the power which he offered to Christ (Mt. 4. 8, 9; Rev. 13. 4). See "The great tribulation," Psa. 2. 5; Rev. 7. 14, note.
[3] The duration of the kingdom of heaven in its mediatorial form (1 Cor. 15. 24, note).
1349

Fig. 3.11 Scofield's Notes. Generations of readers have read Bible prophecy through the Scofield lens. Here his notes on Revelation 19–20 from *The Scofield Reference Bible* amplify the meaning of this crucial millennial passage.

time since Christ ascended into heaven."[13] He identifies twelve of these signs. The world is in a mental state of bewilderment and psychological breakdown. Bored hu-mans are on a moral binge but yet can find no satisfaction. False prophets have seduced people away from the truth of the Lord. Lawlessness is on the increase. Scoffers deny the coming of Christ. Christians are being persecuted. People lust after wealth, while millions of others are starving. The science of warfare has been perfected, making wars more devastating than ever before. Knowl-edge and travel have increased at an expo-nential rate. Statesmen seek peace, but with-out consulting the Prince of Peace. The possibility of a world dictator coming to power is more realistic today than at any time in history. The evangelization of the world has occurred.[14]

Fig. 3.12 The Bible Says . . . Billy Graham has preached the gospel to more people than any person in history. He has been highly influenced by the premillennial dispensational tradition.

Graham goes on to say that the second coming of Jesus will be "sudden, unexpected, and dramatic," and we must be ready and watch for it.[15] But on the very next page he states that it will be the culmination of "a series of events transpiring over a rather long period," thus revealing how much his thinking has been influenced by dispensationalism.[16] What are these events? They include the rapture, in which living believers will be caught up to meet Christ in the air, the first resurrection, in which believers from all ages will rise from the dead and assemble with the others in heaven, and the marriage supper of the Lamb, the moment when Jesus Christ is crowned as Lord of lords and King of kings. Other events include the great tribulation and the rise of the Antichrist. He notes that some of them are clearly outlined in the Scriptures, and others are mysterious hap-penings about which we can only speculate. The ultimate results of Christ's coming include the establishment of peace on earth, social justice, the restoration of the natural order to its original state, the transformation of human nature and all people made righteous, and finally the creation of the new heaven and new earth.

More recently, Graham portrayed the four horsemen of Revelation 6 as restatements of the signs of the end in Matthew 24. He interprets the symbolic meanings of the riders as counterfeit religion, war and peace, famine and pestilence [epidemic disease], and the trauma of death and the suffering of Hades.[17] He describes them as symbolic warnings for us today and insists we should "put our ears to the ground and hear their hoofbeats growing louder by the day."[18] He also claims a prophetic vision: "With John, I have heard the distant sound of hoofbeats. I have seen the evil riders on the horizons of our lives. . . . [T]here is serious trouble ahead for our world, for all of us who live in it, and in the four horsemen of the Apocalypse there is both a warning and wisdom for those troubled days ahead."[19] Although the book treats current events in an alarmist fashion, Graham holds out as "hope in the holocaust" the triumphant return of Christ and urges his readers to receive Christ now.

The significance of both Scofield and Graham in shaping the eschatological thinking of American evangelicalism is illustrated in Helen Lee Turner's study of Southern Baptist pastors. This scholar of American religion surveyed Southern Baptist associational ministers in 1987 and included the question: "What has had the widest influence on the eschatology of the ministers in your area besides the biblical text itself?" Of the 461 people surveyed, 41 percent said *The Scofield Reference Bible* had the greatest influence, whereas only 33.3 percent cited seminary education as the greatest influence.[20] Billy Graham's sermons about the second com-

Fig. 3.13 Four Horseman of the Apocalypse. The avenging angels of Revelation 9 are brought to life in Albrecht Dürer's vision.

ing and his apocalypic rhetoric also must have had an impact. In 1985–86 Turner polled fifteen hundred Southern Baptist ministers and found he was by far the most favored of the television preachers. Of the respondents, 75 percent said they "agreed

RAPTURE

OCTOBER 28, 1992
JESUS IS COMING IN
THE AIR.

"Fear God, and give Him glory, because the hour of His judgment has come."
(Rev. 14:7)

TIMETABLE OF RAPTURE (OCT. 28, 1992)			
City & Time Zone	Time	City & Time Zone	Time
New York (Eastern)	10:00 am	Jerusalem	17:00 (5 pm)
Rio de Janeiro	13:00 (1 pm)	Moscow	18:00 (6 pm)
London	15:00 (3 pm)	Peking	23:00 (11 pm)
Paris	16:00 (4 pm)	Seoul	24:00 (Midnight)
Rome	16:00 (4 pm)	Tokyo	24:00 (Midnight)
Cairo	17:00 (5 pm)	Sydney Oct. 29, 1992	02:00 am

MISSION FOR THE COMING DAYS
43-08 Main St., 3 Fl. Flushing, N.Y. 11355
• Queens Branch of N.Y.: (718) 463-5042 • 639-8205

Fig. 3.14 Representing the Rapture. Here is a variation on the urban rapture scene seen earlier. Pictured is the cover of a pamphlet distributed by Mission for the Coming Days. Note the date and time originally forecast for the rapture along with a timetable for calculating its occurence in cities and time zones across the world.

with Dr. Graham," and only 1 percent disagreed with him.[21]

Progressive Dispensationalism

Dispensationalism has gone through some noteworthy changes since the heyday of the Bible institutes and prophetic preachers of the immediate post–World War II generation. In the early 1990s some professors at evangelical theological institutions known for their dispensationalist stances sought to redefine the principal categories of the teaching.[22] The progressive dispensationalists, as they call themselves, drew ideas from the covenant theology that informed the thinking of such historic premillennialists as George Ladd and downplayed the sensationalism that is the stock-in-trade of most contemporary prophetic evangelists.

For the progressive dispensationalists the kingdom of God is the unifying theme of biblical history. Christ has initiated the messianic/Davidic reign in heaven as he sits at the right hand of the Father, and he will eventually rule on earth in the millennium. The new covenant is already in force although its blessings will only be fully realized in the millennium. There are not two distinct purposes of God, one for the church and one for Israel. In fact, they play down the importance of ethnic Israel and its future in the land of Palestine and place far more emphasis on the church and its present and future role in the plan of God. They restructure the

Fig. 3.15 A Millennial Breakfast. A moment of levity helps to put things in perspective.

customary dispensational conception of biblical history into four periods: the Patriarchal (Adam to Sinai), Mosaic (Sinai to the ascension of Christ), Ecclesial (the ascension to the second coming), and Zionic (part one: the millennium; part two: the eternal state).

The key millennial view of the progressives is that some of the blessings of the new covenant are being fulfilled now, for example, the forgiveness of sins and the ministry of the Holy Spirit, but its complete fulfillment will take place at the second coming. They affirm that many of the promises classical dispensationists relegate to the millennial kingdom are currently seeing their fulfillment because of Jesus' reign on the Davidic throne in heaven. Redemption begins not in the millennium but in the church, the workshop in which kingdom righteousness is pursued in the name of Christ. A process of holistic redemption occurs through social and political action, and the eschatological kingdom is gradually being realized. Thus, the progressive dispensationalists pay much less attention to such eschatological matters as the pretribulation rapture, a literal tribulation period, and interpreting the difficult imagery in the Book of Revelation.

Conclusion

Christians in our time hold to a variety of positions concerning the second coming and the millennial kingdom. Unfortunately, there seems to be little hope that a consensus will emerge in the foreseeable future.

The coming of the new millennium has only accentuated the debates and the forceful manner in which the exponents of these views propagate them. The propagation of millennial views is not, however, a new phenomenon. Those who feel most strongly about eschatological matters are part of an extensive tradition of people, ranging from cultic to orthodox groups and individuals, who have actively proclaimed a doomsday script to their particular generation.

To fully appreciate the impact of such doomsday millenarian thinking we need to take a closer look at some of the more prominent manifestations. In chapter 4 our travels will take us on a search of what history can teach us about the prophetic perils of date setting.

4

Does Anyone Really Know What Time It Is?

The Doomsday Script

> The verdict of history seems clear. Great spiritual gain comes from living under the expectation of Christ's return. But wisdom and restraint are also in order. At the very least, it would be well for those in our age who predict details and dates for the End to remember how many before them have misread the signs of the times.
>
> Mark A. Noll

Picture this scene: For sixteen hours a day, while middle-aged women clad in white and gold robes pray and sway, singing of the time when they will "dance on streets that are golden," others spiritedly blow into rams' horns proclaiming the second coming. No, this is not an apocalyptic vision from the Book of Revelation, but part of a typical day for those who meet annually for the End-Time Handmaidens' prophecy convention. Gathered together at the Sheraton Washington ballroom, seventy-something matriarch Gwen Shaw announces to the fifteen hundred faithful that Christ's second coming is indeed near: "We're running out of time. We're running out of time."[1]

While the Handmaidens are admittedly a fringe group, their focus on time and date setting is quite typical of many today who look to the skies for the return of Christ. Millennial madness characterizes our day. According to many, the return of Christ will be preceded by terrible judgments and the world as we know it now will be turned completely upside down. But as we have already seen, the soothsayers of doom are not new on the religious scene; they are part and parcel of a timeless obsession with date setting—predicting precisely what is going to happen in the future and exactly when it will occur. The fact that such forecasts have invariably failed to come to pass is no deterrent to the modern-day speculators who feel they know exactly what is about to happen and are not shy about proclaiming when it will take place.

Faced with such a dizzying array of predictions, pilgrims entering the new millennium may rightfully ask the prophetic prognosticators: Does anyone really know what time it is? Are we truly running out of time? Let's take a closer look at what many have said and are saying now about the end of the world.

The Date-Setting Tradition

As we mentioned in the last chapter, as far back as the Middle Ages, Joachim of Fiore set in motion an apocalyptic groundswell that did not easily subside. In 1260 bands of men and boys carrying candles and banners roamed from town to town in Europe, gathering in the square before the town church and beating themselves with whips. These so-called Flagellants identified themselves with Christ and were convinced that their actions would assure the redemption of humankind. Based on Joachim's predictions, they believed 1260 was the predetermined date that marked the final earthly age.

When the great plague—the Black Death—tore at the social fabric of Europe

in the fourteenth century, many felt they were witnessing the end of the world foretold in Revelation. The Taborite sect in Bohemia predicted that in 1420 Christ would appear, cleanse the world of sinners, and bring in the glorious millennium. The radical sectarian Thomas Müntzer preached in the early 1520s that the elect must rise up and annihilate the godless to prepare for Christ's coming and the millennium. The Scottish thinker John Napier (remembered as the inventor of logarithms) predicted in 1593 that Rome, which Protestants regarded as the personification of the Antichrist, would fall by 1639 and the world would end around 1688.

In the seventeenth century Johann Heinrich Alsted in Germany predicted that the last judgment would begin in 1694, the saints would be raised from the dead, and the thousand-year reign of the elect would begin. In England the Fifth Monarchists were the most prominent political-religious sect that expected the imminent establishment of the kingdom of Christ on earth. This would be a theocratic regime in which the saints would exercise godly discipline over the largely unregenerate masses and prepare for the second coming. They believed they had the right and duty to overthrow the existing government and set up the millennial kingdom.

LeRoy Edwin Froom, in his massive compilation entitled *The Prophetic Faith of Our Fathers,* identifies a wide variety of seventeenth- and eighteenth-century date setters. Depending on which particular author one reads, the end of the 1,260-day tribulation period was supposed to occur in 1697 (Thomas Beverly), 1714 (Pierre Jurieu), 1762 (Richard Clarke), 1798 (Edward King and Richard Valpy), 1830 (J. A. Bengel), 1847 (J. P. Petri), or 1866 (Joseph Lathrop, John Gill, and Samuel Hopkins). And these are only selected examples; Froom cites numerous others.[2]

Jewish Mysticism and Messianic Speculation

A messianic movement in Judaism, rooted in Jewish mysticism, paralleled these events in English and American Protestantism. In the late 1100s a traditionalist mysticism arose called the *Cabala* (also spelled Kabalah, Kabbalah, or Qabbalah), a Hebrew word meaning "doctrine received by tradition." Serving as an alternative to the Jewish rationalism exemplified by the Talmud and the scholars who studied this vast collection of teachings from the early centuries of the common era, Cabalism developed into a highly elitist and esoteric school of philosophy that attracted a small and disciplined group of devotees (hence our modern word *cabal*). The Cabala literature focused on the details of Scripture, the spiritual life, and the means of achieving ecstatic experiences with a God who is utterly transcendent. By seeking and understanding God, one could bring about the redemption of the Jewish people. Adherents to Cabalism bypassed the intense legalism of

Fig. 4.1 End-Time Handmaidens. A scene from a recent prophecy convention shows one example of endtime groups.

Talmudic Judaism, which was the prevailing approach to the faith in the medieval world.

The theological and philosophical distinctives of Cabalism, along with its borrowings from occultism and Gnosticism, are far too complex to explain in detail here. However, what is significant for eschatological thinking is the Cabalist approach to the Hebrew Scriptures.

Cabalist adherents believed the Torah was divinely inspired even down to the individual letters used. In ancient languages, such as Greek and especially Hebrew, the letters of the alphabet possessed numerical values. Through the process known as *gematria,* a Cabalist could total up the letters or handle them in a variety of other mathematical ways and arrive at a hidden truth. For instance, the name for God, YHWH or Yahweh, has the value of $1 + 5 + 6 + 5 = 17$. The word translated "good," *tov,* is $9 + 6 + 2 = 17$, while *rishon* ("first") is $2 + 1 + 3 + 6 + 5 = 17$. Therefore, the numerical revelation in Scripture is that God alone is "good," and he is the "first" of all beings in the universe.

Another way of finding hidden meanings, known as *notarikon,* involved arranging the initial or final letters of the words of a phrase in an acrostic system, thus creating a new word that had spiritual significance. Through the system called *temurah,* that is, transposition, one transposed letters in a word or phrase or actually substituted other letters in a coded fashion. One could replace letters on a numerical basis or even according to their shapes. For example, the words for *delight* and *pain* each have the numerical equivalent of 123. By transposing the Hebrew letters, delight is changed to pain. Cabalists used these techniques to find hidden meanings in Scripture placed there by the Creator. These hidden meanings, in turn, validated their belief that the sacred writings were literally inspired of God and an utterly unique book. The Scriptures were not merely words, phrases, and sentences; they were the living incarnation of the divine

wisdom that is constantly sending out new light to humankind.

Nevertheless, Scripture does not make the claim of hidden meanings. We are to pay heed to what its words say and not seek occult revelation. The Cabalistic exegetical technique was imposed on the Bible from without, and it led to all sorts of outlandish conclusions. Unfortunately, this sort of symbolic analysis of biblical words was revived in the twentieth century, and as will be shown later, the eschatological speculation followed very much in the path of the Cabalists.

Cabala was strongly oriented toward the coming of the Messiah, who would redeem the world and bring in a period of utter happiness, one without sin or pain. With the expulsion of the Jews from Spain and Portugal at the end of the fifteenth century, Cabalists saw that a new era of suffering lay ahead, and a wave of messianic speculation resulted. The massacres in the Ukraine at the hands of Bogdan Chmielnicki's Cossacks in 1648, one of the largest mass murders of Jews prior to the twentieth century, further reinforced their hope of a coming Messiah. The Cabalists now focused their religious fervor on the imminent redemption of God's people, and it was not long before a figure arose from their

110

circle who seemed to be that long-awaited personage.

That figure was Shabbetai Zevi (also Tsevi or Zvi), who was born in 1626 into the home of a prosperous merchant in the city of Smyrna in the Ottoman Empire. His family recognized that he was intellectually gifted and enabled him to devote his life to study, which allowed him eventually to become a rabbi. First he mastered the Talmud and then the Cabala. He manifested extreme manic-depressive tendencies, and when he was in the ecstatic stage he would even pronounce the name of God, the unspeakable letters YHWH, an action that violated Jewish law and was reserved only for the Messiah. In his melancholy periods he wrestled with demonic powers who attacked him. He increasingly came to be an embarrassment to the Jewish community in Smyrna, and the rabbis finally expelled him from the city in the early 1650s. After some years of wandering he met a young rabbi in Jerusalem named Nathan of Gaza, who claimed to have had a vision revealing that Shabbetai was the Lord's anointed one, the Messiah.

Now that his fancies had been confirmed, Shabbetai Zevi proclaimed himself the Messiah in 1665, and excitement spread throughout the Jewish communities in Europe as well as the Middle East. He called the people to repentance, and a mass movement began as followers gathered around him. He set the date for redemption as June 18, 1666, and announced he would seize the crown from the Turkish sultan. He returned to Smyrna, where he assigned the kingdoms of the world to his supporters, before setting out for Constantinople. As he neared the capital, he was arrested by the Ottoman authorities, but rather than executing him as a rebel, they placed him in prison.

Shabbetai's claim to be the Messiah also caused a stir in Protestant Europe. Many people in millenarian circles in England, Holland, and Germany believed Christ would return in 1666. Shabbetai's prediction confirmed their belief, and Shabbetean propaganda spread among these groups.

Although the Ottoman authorities had arrested him, his imprisonment was extraordinarily mild. Shabbetai was given many privileges and even had a secretary and received visitors. In fact, he virtually held court as a "king" in the jail. Then on September 15, 1666, he was brought before a royal court with the sultan present. After an interrogation he was given an option: Convert to Islam or be put to death. He accepted Islam. He was released with a substantial pension and spent the last ten years of his life in a never-never land between Judaism and Islam before dying in exile in Albania in 1676.

Many of Shabbetai Zevi's followers rationalized his apostasy and continued to believe in his messianic mission. The apostasy, they said, was part of the mystery of his unique mission to the world, and they explained it in Cabalistic terms as a para-

Fig. 4.2 It's Miller Time. An early proponent of eschatological date setting, William Miller was the founder of Adventism.

dox. He had descended into the abyss of impurity, sin, and evil, and by so doing had vanquished them all. He was the mystical counterpart of the red heifer of Numbers 19. He had purified the unclean but in the process became, as it were, impure himself. As a result, many disciples were convinced that he would come again as a redeemer to lead them to freedom, and a remnant Shabbetean movement continued well into the eighteenth century in Central and Eastern Europe.

The Adventist Date-Setting Tradition

As their predecessors in the previous two centuries, preachers in nineteenth-century America often made rash statements about the imminent return of Christ. For example, the renowned evangelist Charles Finney once told a gathering in New York City in March 1835, "If the church will do all her duty, the millennium may come in this country in three years."[3] But the most noteworthy of all the date setters were the Adventists. The principal twentieth-century survivors of this millennial tradition are the Seventh-day Adventists and Jehovah's Witnesses.

The Millerites

The founder of Adventism was William Miller (1782–1849), a self-educated farmer who originally was a deist and skeptic. His experiences during the War of 1812 caused him to reevaluate his personal faith and the meaning of life in general, and in 1816 he was converted at a revival. He then immersed himself in the Scriptures and after two years of intense study became convinced that within twenty-five years the world would end and Christ would come again. In 1831 he began sharing his prophetic ideas with his neighbors and attracted a sizable following. Although he had no formal theological training, a Baptist group licensed him to preach in 1833, and he spoke in hundreds of communities around the country. In 1836 he published the book *Evidences from Scripture and History of the Second Coming of Christ* in which he predicted that Christ would appear around 1843.

Three years later in 1839 the movement was transformed when Miller won over a well-known Boston minister, Joshua V. Himes. Himes became the publicist par excellence of Miller's views, launching the magazines *Signs of the Times* and *Midnight Cry* and cranking out a steady stream of pamphlets and tracts. His media blitz of over five million pieces of literature gave Adventism worldwide exposure. He also provided a structure for the movement by organizing a general conference of Adventist Christians and holding camp meetings in the Northeast and Midwest. Some of these meetings took place in the spectacular "Great Tent," a mammoth tent fifty-five feet high and three hundred feet in circumference that held three to four thousand people.

Miller did not intend to start another denomination, and his followers worked among the existing churches as they proclaimed Christ's return. They wished only to arouse the church and warn the world that the second advent was at hand. By 1843, however, Millerite sympathizers may have numbered as many as one hundred thousand and they began to be called "Adventists."

Miller believed that Bible prophecy was like a treasure map; one had to decipher the symbolism in order to find the treasure. The key to understanding the hidden truth of Scripture was the 2,300 days mentioned in Daniel 8:14 and the seventy weeks in Daniel 9:24–27. Drawing upon the passages Numbers 14:34 and Ezekiel 4:5–6, he concluded that a prophetic day was equal to a calendar year. He reasoned that the Daniel 8 passage, which spoke of the

Fig. 4.3 It's the End of the World Again. This pictorial explanation shows Miller's understanding of the end of the world.

cleansing of the sanctuary, actually meant the earth and its cleansing by fire in the last days. Thus, Christ would return to the earth around 1843 at the conclusion of the 2,300 days (years) from the time when King Artaxerxes had issued his decree for the rebuilding of Jerusalem in 457 B.C. Miller was reluctant to go public with this theory, however, since his interpretation required a premillennial understanding of Christ's second advent, and, therefore, went against the popular postmillennialism of the day.

The Millerites tried a few times to forecast Christ's return, but in each instance they failed. Finally, they settled on October 22, 1844, which in that year corresponded to the Day of Atonement in the Jewish calendar. Some Adventists were so sure Christ would come that they did not bother to plant crops that spring. Some merchants closed their stores or gave away their goods in anticipation of the event.

However, when Christ failed to appear as expected, the movement fragmented. After the "Great Disappointment," as this miscalculation is called in Adventist history, the majority of the Millerite Adventists continued to believe the second coming was imminent. They eventually became the Advent Christian Church (which still exists today) and a variety of ephemeral Adventist sects. A smaller group, however, accepted the view of Hiram Edson, a Methodist farmer in upstate New York, who argued that it was the nature of the event and not the date per se that had been incorrect. Edson told his friends that he was crossing a field the day after the Great Disappointment and suddenly heaven was opened before him. He looked up and saw distinctly, and clearly, that instead of our High Priest coming out of the Most Holy of the heavenly sanctuary to

come to this earth on the tenth day of the seventh month [the Day of Atonement in the Jewish calendar] at the end of the 2,300 days, that he for the first time entered on that day the second apartment of that sanctuary; and that he had a work to perform in the Most Holy before coming to this earth.[4]

Seventh-day Adventists

This "sanctuary doctrine" became the hallmark of the new Adventism. It was adopted by Ellen G. Harmon; her husband-to-be, James White; Joseph Bates; and a loyal band of followers. Ellen White claimed to have had many visions and soon was accepted as a prophet. To the core beliefs of her Methodist upbringing and Millerite Adventism, she added from the Seventh Day Baptists the idea of honoring the Sabbath. Under her leadership the movement grew rapidly, and with its emphasis on biblicism, legalism, and millenarianism the new body showed itself to be a typical nineteenth-century evangelical sect. For a while the group continued setting dates for the return of Christ but soon acknowledged Edson's view that Jesus was continuing to purge the sanctuary in heaven while they were to be busy spreading his gospel on the earth.

They argued that Christ had not accomplished all his earthly work on the cross. When he ascended to heaven, he

Fig. 4.4 Daniel's Visions. Miller's charts forecasting a failed March 21, 1843, date for the return of Christ were lampooned in such national media as Horace Greeley's *New York Tribune*.

DANIEL'S VISIONS.

NOTED IN THE SCRIPTURES OF TRUTH." "FOR OUR LEARNING."

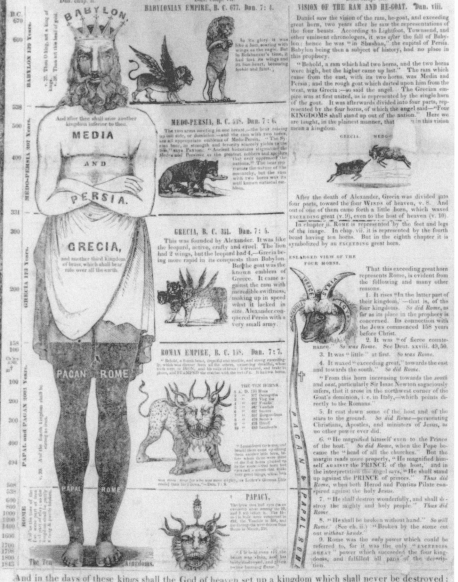

Dan. chap. ii.

Dan. chap. vii.
BABYLONIAN EMPIRE, B. C. 677. Dan. 7: 4.

In its glory it was like a lion, wearing with wings as the eagle. But in Belshazzar's time, it had lost its wings and its lion-heart, becoming feeble and faint.

MEDO-PERSIA, B. C. 538. Dan. 7: 6.

The two arms meeting in one breast,—the bear raising up its side, or dominion,—and the ram with two horns, are all appropriate emblems of Medo-Persia. "The Syrian bear, in strength and ferocity scarcely yields to the lion," says Paxton. "Ancient historians stigmatize the Medes and Persians as the greatest robbers and spoilers that ever oppressed the nations." The bear represents the nature of the monarchy, but the ram with two horns was its well known national emblem.

GRECIA, B. C. 331. Dan. 7: 5.

This was founded by Alexander. It was like the leopard, active, crafty and cruel. The lion had 2 wings, but the leopard had 4,—Grecia being more rapid in its conquests than Babylon. But the goat was the known emblem of Greece. It came against the ram with incredible swiftness, making up in speed what it lacked in size. Alexander conquered Persia with a very small army.

ROMAN EMPIRE, B. C. 158. Dan. 7: 7.

"Behold, a fourth beast, dreadful and terrible, and strong exceeding; which was diverse from all the others, exceeding dreadful, whose teeth were of IRON, and his nails of brass; it devoured, and brake in pieces, and STAMPED the residue with the feet of it. It had ten horns.

THE TEN HORNS.

| A. D. 356 Huns |
| 377 Ostrogoths |
| 376 Visig'ths |
| 407 Franks |
| 407 Vandals |
| 407 Suevi |
| 407 Burgundians |
| 476 Heruli |
| 483 Saxons |
| 483 Lombards |

PAPACY.

VISION OF THE RAM AND HE-GOAT. Dan. viii.

Daniel saw the vision of the ram, he-goat, and exceeding great horn, two years after he saw the representations of the four beasts. According to Lightfoot, Townsend, and other eminent chronologers, it was *after* the fall of Babylon; hence he was "in Shushan," the capital of Persia. Babylon being then a subject of history, had no place in this prophecy.

"Behold, a ram which had two horns, and the two horns were high, but the higher came up last." The ram which came from the east, with its two horns, was Media and Persia; and the rough goat which darted upon him from the west, was Grecia:—so said the angel. The Grecian empire was at first united, as is represented by the single horn of the goat. It was afterwards divided into four parts, represented by the four horns, of which the angel said—"Four KINGDOMS shall stand up out of the nation." Here we are taught, in the plainest manner, that ... in this vision mean a kingdom.

GRECIA.   MEDO-

After the death of Alexander, Grecia was divided into four parts, toward the four WINDS of heaven, v. 8. And out of one of them came forth a little horn, which waxed EXCEEDING great (v. 9), even to the host of heaven (v. 10).

In chapter ii. ROME is represented by the feet and legs of the image. In chap. vii. it is represented by the fourth beast having ten horns. But in the eighth chapter it is symbolized by an EXCEEDING great horn.

ENLARGED VIEW OF THE FOUR HORNS.

That this exceeding great horn represents Rome, is evident from the following and many other reasons.

1. It rises "in the latter part of their kingdom,"—that is, of the four kingdoms. So did Rome, as far as its place in the prophecy is concerned. Its connection with the Jews commenced 158 years before Christ.

2. It was "of fierce countenance." So was Rome. See Deut. xxviii. 43, 50.

3. It was "little" at first. So was Rome.

4. It waxed "exceeding great," towards the east and towards the south." So did Rome.

"From this horn increasing towards the *south* and *east*, particularly Sir Isaac Newton sagaciously infers, that it arose in the northwest corner of the Goat's dominion, i. e. in Italy,—which points directly to the Romans.

5. It cast down some of the host and of the stars to the ground. So did Rome—persecuting Christians, Apostles, and ministers of Jesus, as no other power ever did.

6. "He magnified himself even to the Prince of the host." So did Rome, when the Pope became the "head of all the churches." But the margin reads more properly, "He magnified himself AGAINST the PRINCE of the host," and in the interpretation the angel says, "He shall stand up against the PRINCE of princes." Thus did Rome, when both Herod and Pontius Pilate conspired against the holy Jesus.

7. "He shall destroy wonderfully, and shall destroy the mighty and holy people." Thus did Rome.

8. "He shall be broken without hand." So will Rome." (See ch. ii.) "Broken by the stone cut out without hands."

9. Rome was the only power which could be referred to, for it was the only "EXCEEDING GREAT" power which succeeded the four kingdoms, and fulfilled all parts of the description.

And in the days of these kings shall the God of heaven set up a kingdom which shall never be destroyed: and the kingdom shall not be left to other people, *but* it shall break in pieces and consume all these kingdoms, and it shall stand for ever. *Daniel ii. 44.*

SYNOPSIS OF
MILLER'S VIEWS.

I.—I believe Jesus Christ will come again to this earth.

PROOF.—John xiv. 3. And if I go and prepare a place for you, I will come again, and receive you unto myself; that where I am, there ye may be also. Also, Acts i. 11; 1 Thess. iv. 16; Rev. i. 7.

Also, Col. i. 22. Jude xxiv; 1 Thess. iii. 13; 1 Cor. i. 7, 8.

VII.—I believe when Christ comes the second time, he will come to finish the controversy of Zion, to deliver his children from all bondage, to conquer their last enemy, and to deliver them from the power of the tempter, which is the devil.

PROOF.—Isa. xxxiv. 8, xl. 2, 5, xli. 10—12. For it is the day of the Lord's vengeance, and the year of recompences for the controversy of Zion. Speak ye comfortably to Jerusalem, and cry unto her, ...

XII.—I believe many who are professors and preachers will never believe or know the time until it comes upon them.

PROOF.—Jer. viii. 7. Yea the stork in the heaven knoweth her appointed times; and the turtle, and the crane, and the swallow, observe the time of their coming; but my people know not the judgment of the Lord.

Also Matt. xxiv. 50. Jer. xxv. 34, 37.

XIII.—I believe the wise, they who are to shine as the brightness of the firmament, Dan. xii. 3, will understand the time.

entered the outer sanctuary, not the Holy of Holies, and still had to finish his work as priest by making the great atonement. He first cleansed the outer sanctuary (or apartment) of the heavenly temple, and while there sinners appealed to him for mercy and salvation. After 1844, however, the door to this section of the temple was closed, and he entered the inner sanctuary. There he began the task of making the atonement, which would at last blot out the sins of the believers. The cleansing of Daniel 8:14 was a cleansing from sin that was accomplished by Christ's own blood. According to the group, when Christ's "second apartment ministry" is completed, he will return to the earth as king.

While Christ is preparing for the atonement, they are to preach the message of righteousness to all people. Central to the message is the necessity to observe God's commandments, of which the most important is the keeping of the Sabbath. This is God's last message of mercy to the world prior to the great harvest of souls that will occur at his second advent. Because they felt they were commissioned by God to warn the world of the coming judgment and to call individuals to repentance and righteous living, the Adventists became a dynamic missionary movement. While they no longer set a precise date for Christ's return, they insist that the signs of the times make it clear that the coming of Christ can happen at any moment.

The Jehovah's Witnesses

The other significant offspring of the Millerite movement was the Jehovah's Witnesses. Its founder, a men's clothing merchant named Charles Taze Russell (1852–1916), was a Congregationalist layperson in Pennsylvania who underwent a serious period of doubt as a youth. In 1869 he attended an independent Adventist meeting and was won over to their views about the divine inspiration of the Bible and the last days, including the idea that the world would soon be consumed by fire and only Adventists would survive this judgment.

Within two years Russell and some friends had started a study group to learn about God's plan for humankind and the world. After he met Nelson H. Barbour, an independent Adventist preacher, he began setting dates for Christ's return. Barbour had concluded that Bishop Ussher's chronology of the Bible was in error, and the six thousandth year from Adam's creation was 1873 or 1874. On that date the thousand-year or millennial reign of Christ would begin. However, when nothing happened, Barbour revised his prediction by using other biblical data and recalculated the date of Christ's return as 1878. Further, both Barbour and Russell, who was following his lead from then on, spiritualized the coming of Christ by arguing that the Greek word *parousia* (translated "coming" in the King James Version of the New Testament) actually meant "presence," and thus Christ had made a spiritual return to the "upper air." Russell went on to conclude from his studies of Daniel and Revelation that Christ would set up the millennial kingdom in 1914, but before that time there would be a forty-year time of preparation that would herald the day of the millennium. He called this period the "millennial dawn."

When the rapture of the saints did not occur, Russell and Barbour parted company. Barbour set out to revamp his chronological system, while Russell held that an invisible resurrection of the saints sleeping in death had occurred. Other doctrinal differences had also developed between them. Russell was a master organizer, and aided by the fortune he had gained from his clothing business, he launched a magazine in 1879 called *Zion's Watchtower* with an initial press run of six thousand copies. A century later fifteen million copies were being printed on a regular basis. In every sense of the word Russell was a remarkable success story. He made extensive lecture tours in America and abroad, and for many years a sermon of his was printed each week in fifteen hundred newspapers in America and Canada, reaching the homes of millions. His major book sold fifteen million copies.

He spelled out his doctrines in *Divine Plan of the Ages* (1886) and *The Time Is at Hand* (1889), the first two volumes of what would be the six-volume set *Studies in the Scriptures*. As mentioned above, he drew his eschatology from Daniel and Revelation and buttressed it with the mathe-matical measurements of the Great Pyramid of Giza in Egypt. (A popular belief of the time was that God had laid out there in stone the details of his plan for the ages.)

Russell linked biblical prophecies to events in his own day in an extraordinarily complex and creative fashion. Thus, he located the beginning of Christ's invisible presence and the onset of the "harvest," a forty-year process of winning believers to Christ, in 1874. Further, he claimed that in 1878 Christ had come and a spiritual resurrection had occurred. The year 1881 marked the fall of Babylon the Great (the end of false religious influence over the church) and the end of the general call to join the special flock of 144,000 saints. Russell believed Christ was choosing a church of 144,000 "spiritual Israelites" (Rev. 7; 14:1) who would reign with him during the millennium. The rest of humanity would be resurrected during the thousand years, allowed to learn God's will, and given the opportunity to accept his teachings. Those who did would pass through the final battle of Armageddon and live on the new earth, a restored Garden of Eden. Those who rejected Christ would be destroyed with Satan in the rebellion he will unleash at Armageddon.

In 1914 the times of the Gentiles would come to an end. This would be followed by the battle of Armageddon, the cleansing of the earth, and the restoration of the natural Jews to Palestine. Then Christ's active rulership would begin and the saints would be taken up into heaven to reign

Fig. 4.5 All along the Watchtower. Charles Taze Russell's religious movement claims three million members in more than two hundred countries today.

with him over the earth. However, the only conflict that took place in 1914 was the outbreak of World War I, and Russell accordingly adjusted his timetable to 1918. The year 1914 marked Russell's third major prophetic failure, and he died two years later.

The non-fulfillment of the central prophecies and the death of the founder should have meant the demise of the sect.

However, Russell had found an Elisha, Joseph F. Rutherford (1869–1942), a lawyer from Missouri who for a short time (four days) had served as a judge in a lower court and thereafter called himself "Judge." In 1906 he joined the Russellite organization as its lawyer, and in 1917 he took over as president of the moribund society. He adjusted the eschatology, developed a new organizational structure, and provided the sect with more practical methods for propagating the faith.

Rutherford explained that Russell really had not been wrong. The world had come to an end in a legal sense. Christ was enthroned and the kingdom had begun, but in heaven. After a transitional period the full millennial reign would begin on earth. The faithful were to continue witnessing and bringing as many people to a knowledge of God as possible. Judge Rutherford proceeded to turn the society into a well-oiled machine with world assemblies, massive outpourings of literature from the Watchtower Press in Brooklyn, New York, door-to-door solicitation, and even a new name—Jehovah's Witnesses, which he bestowed on them in 1931.

His most memorable work, *Millions Now Living Will Never Die!,* appeared in 1920. In it he calculated from the Old Testament jubilee years that the millennium would begin in 1925. As he stated in one of his works, the "full restoration" of humankind would occur then. "We may expect 1925 to witness that return of those

118

faithful men of Israel [Abraham, Isaac, and Jacob] from the condition of death, being resurrected and fully restored to perfect humanity and made the visible, legal representatives of the new order of things on earth."[5] At the same time, those millions of people living on the earth would gain eternal life. When 1925 came and nothing occurred, Rutherford shied away from firm date setting and redefined his followers as part of the great multitude mentioned in Revelation 7.

Although 1925 witnessed no resurrection of the men of old and most of the millions who were alive at the time eventually died, Rutherford did not admit failure. In 1929 he built a spacious mansion in San Diego, California, called the "House of Princes," which would be a residence for the ancient worthies when they did come back. In reality, it was set aside for his own use in his declining years. Eventually in 1948 the Witnesses sold the house because the princes had failed to appear, while at the same time they claimed that the current leaders were the ancient worthies, and they would be the elders who would survive Armageddon, which lay just around the corner.

Jehovah's Witness beliefs continued to center on the 144,000 who comprised the nucleus of God's new nation: those who would rule with Christ in the millennium. A much larger number, the "great multitude" (Rev. 7:9) or "other sheep" (John 10:16), will enjoy a blessed life on earth, although they will not be part of the millennial ruling class. The United Nations and the world's religious leaders will line up on Satan's side in the battle of Armageddon, and against them will be arrayed both the 144,000 and the other sheep. Christ's army will triumph, but the only survivors will be the Jehovah's Witnesses.

Because this view of the future was so central to Witness theory, they had to choose other dates—1941, 1954, and above all, 1975. They revamped the earlier chronology, discarded the idea that Christ had returned invisibly in 1874, and redefined 1914 as the beginning of his invisible presence. This event marked the end of Gentile rule, although it was not obvious to anyone outside the Watchtower group. Now, when one of the elect remnant died, he or she was immediately and invisibly resurrected from the dead and taken to his or her reward in the heavens. Using the six thousand years from the creation of Adam and Eve as the new chronological benchmark (defined as 4026 B.C.), the Witnesses pinpointed 1975 as the year of destiny and the end of human existence on the earth.

Students of social movements, however, recognized the real reason for these ongoing adjustments of the date of Christ's return. The leaders of the Watchtower Society had noted a growing apathy among the Witnesses and began reemphasizing a definite date for Christ's return in order to rekindle zeal and devotion among the rank and file. Thus, when 1975 arrived and the millennial rule did not begin, the leaders once again hedged on the figures and downplayed the precision of their calculations. "Short-term millenarianism" was essential to reconfirm the sect's worldview, and even though each new vision was little more than recycled endtime prophecy, it served to sustain cult excitement and activity.

The irony was that the failure of prophecy actually separated the chaff from the wheat, the true believers from the "hangers-on," and thereby reinforced in-group cohesion. As one disillusioned former Jehovah's Witness said about the massive eschatological revisionism of the sect: "Ours has been one of the greatest 'Chicken Little' religions in modern history. For over a hundred years the sky had been going to fall shortly. Yet apparently Jehovah hasn't been listening."[6] Melvin D. Curry accurately summed up the approach of all the Adventist date setters in words of wisdom that remain as valid today as they ever were: "Biblical chronology is the play dough of millenarians. They stretch it to fit whatever timetable they need, or reduce it to a meaningless mass of dates and figures so that future predictions can be molded out of the original lump."[7]

Date Setting in the Interwar Years

The Jehovah's Witnesses may have been the most forthright in making statements about the immediate future, but as millennial trends shifted in the early twentieth century, some evangelical writers went

Fig. 4.6 Who's That Knocking at My Door? The Jehovah's Witnesses are known for their aggressive door-to-door evangelistic campaigns. Here is one possible antidote.

pretty far out on the limb of their own prophetic speculation. Revival preachers increasingly espoused pretribulational premillennialism (see chap. 3), as it proved to be a powerful evangelistic weapon. They equated being left behind at the rapture and having to go through the horrors of the great tribulation with dying without Christ and going to hell.

Many who observed the signs of the times began to make rash predictions about the meaning of contemporary happenings. Above all, they saw the Great War of 1914–18 as the precursor to the revival of the Roman Empire and the return of Israel. In other words, the end of the time of the Gentiles was at hand, and events were rushing toward the climax of history. The war, however, was only the beginning. The formation of the League of Nations was one more step toward the realization of the new Rome and the appearance of the last dictator, the Antichrist. Eventually the powers of the world would gather in Palestine to do battle against God's chosen people at Armageddon, but Jesus Christ would come quickly, bring a speedy end to the last war, and set up his kingdom on earth.

A Millennial Suffragette

One person who ventured out on the thin ice of specifics was Christabel Pankhurst (1880–1958), best known for her activities in Britain to secure voting rights for women. She had enthusiastically supported the war effort and was a candidate for Parliament in the first election following the adoption of women's suffrage, but her failure to win the election combined with the growing disillusionment surrounding women's suffrage led her to look for another outlet for her seemingly inexhaustible personal energy. Toward the end of the war she happened to pick up a volume dealing with biblical prophecy at a bookstore, and in it she discovered the concept of the second coming of Christ. It became a beckoning vision, the ultimate and only answer to the problems of the day, and the gateway to a new age. She could put human striving into a heavenly perspective by setting forth the promise of the reign of the Son of God on earth.

She saw the signs of Armageddon multiplying rapidly—wars and rumors of war, the return of the Jews to Palestine, the blasphemous actions of the Soviet dictators, the arrogance of science, the decay of faith and moral standards, and the worship of money and pleasure. In *The Lord Cometh*

she insisted that the Zionist plan for re-settling Jews in the Holy Land was one of the signs that was now heralding the end of the age. Two years later in 1925 she told a New York audience that the return of the Jews to Palestine was the supremely important factor in world affairs because it was the decisive, practical guarantee that the Son of God was soon to appear. But in another talk a few days later she went even further to say:

> The year 1925 will see a big advance toward the final crisis of the closing age. A last effort to save the world situation by human means will be made. A number of nations will confederate and will

Fig. 4.7 A Woman's Word. Christabel Pankhurst was one of the few women to gain prominence for her writing on prophetic matters.

121

accept the headship of a dictator, who will be the Anti-christ of prophecy.[8]

Over the next years she continued to identify current events—the onset of the depression, catastrophic unemployment, an earthquake in England, and new discoveries in science—as signs of the imminent return of Christ. She said the Bible was the one sure guide to world affairs. She predicted a victory for Franco in the Spanish civil war, since Spain was destined to be part of the Roman Empire that Mussolini and Hitler were reviving. In fact, she even developed a friendship with British Prime Minister Winston Churchill. He shared her pessimistic view of historical development and was fascinated by her idea that the great power blocs of the world would clash in the struggle to determine who would emerge as the true and ultimate Antichrist, the one who would challenge God himself and provoke the battle of Armageddon.

Leonard Sale-Harrison

An evangelical preacher whose use of specifics came perilously close to outright date setting was the Australian-born Bible teacher Leonard Sale-Harrison (1875–1956). He held prophetic conferences at churches in Britain and North America, especially during the 1920s and 1930s, and published over a dozen books and pamphlets including *The Remarkable Jew: His Wonderful Future, God's Great Timepiece, The Resurrection of the Old Roman Empire, or the Future of Europe, The Coming Great Northern Confederacy: or the Future of Russia and Germany,* and *Palestine: God's Monument of Prophecy, The Wonders of the Great Unveiling.* Some of his books went through several editions and were updated in light of current events.

In *The Resurrection of the Old Roman Empire* he matched Scriptures with events in the life and times of Benito Mussolini. Sale-Harrison based his interpretation on the image in King Nebuchadnezzar's dream (Daniel 2), which had feet of clay and iron. He believed this described the Roman Empire in the last days. The clay represented extremely democratic elements, such as the socialists, while the iron depicted that strong body of men who would stand and support law and order.[9] The latter group, identified with the Fascists, would call for a superman or strong ruler (Antichrist) to bring order out of chaos. Mussolini, who may or may not have been the final Antichrist, was certainly preparing the way for him.

He then explained how the Italian dictator, in conformity with biblical prophecy, was reviving the Roman Empire. His territorial conquests were designed at converting the Mediterranean Sea into an Italian lake, like the *mare nostrum* of ancient Rome. The Duce was even trying to establish a state cult with himself at the center. As the Italian dictator put it: "I am the State. I, because of God, I am called. I, because I am the superman incarnate . . . was the heaven-sent. . . . I am a law-giver as well as war lord."[10] Like the Caesars, he took control of all the major offices of state and restored the ancient buildings of the city of Rome. He even planned to erect a huge statue in his own honor, thus fulfilling Revelation 13:14–15.

Sale-Harrison cited the involvement of Italy in Austria, the Balkans, the Middle East, and Spain as examples of Italian efforts to take control of the old Roman lands. Mussolini's agreement with the papacy in 1929 brought it under his domination. At the same time he had a favorable attitude toward Protestantism. He encouraged Bible societies in their distribution of the Scriptures, prohibited the sale of indecent literature, regulated the liquor trade, and discouraged swearing and drunkenness. According to Sale-Harrison, this fairness in religion fulfilled Revelation 17, which indicated that the real power during the endtime would be political rather than ecclesiastical Rome. Other evidence of the resurgence of Roman power in preparation for the coming of the Antichrist included the introduction of Roman characters in place of the traditional alphabet in Turkey, the Bank of America becoming an international organization (it originally was the Bank of Italy), the use of the fascist emblem on the U.S. dime, and the spread of fascism to the Americas. Further signs of the coming of the Antichrist were the founding of a company called The British Monomarks, Ltd., which would provide customers with an identity mark that could be used in commerce (a fulfill-ment of Rev. 13:16–18, the mark of the Beast), the advance of science through such things as robotics and television, the first worldwide radio broadcast by the pope in 1931, the spread of spiritualism, and the growth of anti-Semitism.

Sale-Harrison did admit that date setting was a tricky business and that he personally did not believe in the dates that had been set for future events, though some remarkable predictions had been made that were based on biblical mathematical calculation.[11] Yet he was extremely inconsistent. If there are no signs required before the coming of the Lord to rapture his church, then why did he spend so much time in reading biblical prophecy into current events? Also, although he hesitated to set a precise year, by identifying Mussolini with the prophecies of the Antichrist, Sale-Harrison in essence set the date within his own generation.

The New Evangelical Date Setters

As much as evangelical Christians have decried the practice of making specific predictions based on the apocalyptic scriptural passages, there are those who just cannot resist the temptation to do so. The historical record of failure is there for all to see, yet some seem to believe they have received divine revelation that enables them to speak with precision about the future. Since an unsophisticated reading public eagerly snatches up books about such predictions and some televangelists and publishers alike see an opportunity to get a leg up on the competition, all too much of this sort of naive speculation continues to take place.

Apart from plain human curiosity and greed there are additional factors that have contributed to the current eschatological ethos. Three major developments in the post–World War II era helped to feed the date-setting frenzy. The first was the development of atomic weapons with incomprehensible destructive power together with delivery systems that left no place on earth safe from the threat of thermonuclear annihilation. The second was the establishment of the Jewish state of Israel in 1948 and the successful defense of its territory in conflicts with its neighbors during the ensuing decades. The third was the emergence of the Cold War, the conflict between the United States and the Soviet Union. Particularly in evangelical circles it was portrayed as an ideological struggle—capitalism versus communism, democracy versus dictatorship, freedom versus slavery—rather than a geopolitical conflict for hegemony in the areas of the world that the two protagonists regarded as their spheres of interest. These themes pervaded the prophetic and apocalyptic literature that rolled off the evangelical presses.

While there are scores of contemporary examples of sensationalist prophetic teachers, we wish to focus on two of the better known proponents. The Scripture passages cited, issues raised, and attitudes promulgated are remarkably similar whether proclaimed from a national TV ministry or local pulpit.

The Reign of Hal Lindsey

The most successful author of prophetic materials in the last half of the twentieth century is without a doubt Hal Lindsey. Born in Houston, Texas, in 1929, Harold L. Lindsey studied business at the University of Houston for two years and then dropped out to serve in the coast guard during the Korean War. Next he worked as a Mississippi River tugboat captain in New Orleans. As a result of the breakup of his first marriage and his increasing anxiety about the world, he contemplated committing suicide, but at this critical point in life he happened to read a Gideon New Testament and was converted. For a time he had doubts about his newly found faith because some of his Christian friends said the Bible contained errors, but then in 1956 he heard a lecture on biblical prophecy by a young preacher in "Colonel" Robert Thieme's Berachah Church in his hometown of Houston. He knew instantly that he had found a basis for his faith.

Following this, Lindsey became an avid reader of the Scriptures, particularly its prophetic sections, which convinced him that the Bible was truly the Word of God. During that time he also seems to have had ecstatic experiences of the Holy Spirit and felt the love of God moving over him. Thieme arranged for the young convert to

124

CHARISMA & CHRISTIAN LIFE. OCTOBER 1988

Fig. 4.8 Prophetic Comics. Cartoonist Wayne Stayskal's 1988 reference to Whisenant is prophetic and amazingly versatile in that it's applicable with a simple change in date to a whole host of failed date setters.

Will 88 Turn to 99?

Edgar Whisenant created a major prophetic stir in 1988 with his *88 Reasons Why the Rapture Will Be in 1988*. Acknowledging that according to Scripture the day and hour of Christ's return could not be known, he, nonetheless, felt it was possible to predict the month and year. In fact, while he would not set an exact date for the return, he was willing to calculate Christ's calendar to a September 11–13 return "estimate." Whisenant became a sensational seer as his best-seller sold over a reported two million copies. Many readers were eager to examine the eighty-eight reasons that pointed to the rapture. As a testimony to the impact of Whisenant's work, consider this: Rather than stage their nightly Trinity Broadcasting Network TV show on September 11–13, 1988, Paul and Jan Crouch's "Praise the Lord" series ran prerecorded broadcasts on the topic of the rapture those evenings. The message was directed to those left behind. One can only wonder what new work Whisenant might have on the prophetic drawing boards for 1999.

enter Dallas Theological Seminary in 1958, although Lindsey was not a college graduate. He spent the next four years there and graduated with a degree in theology with an emphasis on the New Testament and early Greek literature and a minor in Hebrew—studies that proved to be helpful in his later career. He met his second wife, Jan, at Dallas (they eventually had three daughters but were divorced two decades later), and they became domestic missionaries for Campus Crusade, lecturing to college students throughout North America. In this period he learned how to communicate with university youth by discarding traditional theological language and making the faith accessible through the lan-guage of the day. In the early 1970s he left Campus Crusade and started his own ministry at the University of California at Los Angeles under the banner of "The Jesus Christ Light and Power Company."

In the late 1960s he began gathering his Dallas Seminary and Campus Crusade lecture notes into a book that would make

Fig. 4.9 A Prophecy Blockbuster. Sales of Lindsey's *The Late Great Planet Earth* firmly entrenched him as the best-selling prophecy writer of all time, aside from the biblical apocalyptists.

It soon became the best-selling nonfiction book of the 1970s (so the *New York Times* said) and was translated into over fifty languages with sales in excess of thirty-five million copies. In 1978, there was even a film version of the book with narrations by Orson Welles, Lindsey, and others.

Over the next three decades more volumes flowed (or were, some might say, recycled) from his fertile imagination, including *Satan Is Alive and Well on Planet Earth* (1972), *There's a New World Coming* (1973), *The Liberation of Planet Earth* (1974), *The Terminal Generation* (1976), *The 1980s: Countdown to Armageddon* (1980), *The Rapture: Truth or Consequences* (1983), *Combat Faith* (1986), *The Road to Holocaust* (1989), *The Final Battle* (1995), *The Messiah* (1996), *Planet Earth Two Thousand A.D.: Will Mankind Survive?* (1996), *Apocalypse Code* (1997), and most recently *Planet Earth: The Final Chapter* (1998). Lindsey claims he has sold over forty million copies of *The Late Great Planet Earth* and its various sequels. Along with his writing endeavors, he has also produced tapes of his works, operated Holy Land tours, and even pastored a church. Eventually he founded his own publishing firm called Western Front, Ltd., which now produces his books.

his name a household word around the world. Assisted by the freelance writer Carole C. Carlson (she had worked with Corrie ten Boom and Billy Graham), he published his seminal book in 1970 with the novel title of *The Late Great Planet Earth*. Some readers undoubtedly thought the volume dealt with ecology, a subject that was just beginning to attract attention in the evangelical Christian community, but in fact it was pure dispensational premillennialism dressed up for the modern age.

By 1977 he had become very wealthy and was living in a luxurious home in the Palos Verdes area of Los Angeles. An interview conducted the same year for *Publishers Weekly* revealed that Lindsey drove a luxurious Mercedes sports car, had a taste for fine food and wine, and employed a personal management firm that was channeling his royalties into long-term real estate investments. Although to the ordinary Christian observer these actions would seem to contradict his belief that Jesus would come in his own generation, Lindsey defended his sumptuous standard of living as part of his life-affirming style.[12] Some twenty years later he claimed, "I just try to live each day as if it's the last one I've got."[13] By this time he had also married for the third time.

Basic to Lindsey's eschatology is his identification of various signs that prove we are now living at the end of the age, or as he put it, in the "terminal generation." Satan is behind the miracles and wonders that Scripture predicts will accompany the collapse of our civilization in the end times. They include famines, earthquakes, unusual weather, increasing crime rates, and the appearance of false religions. In fact, in *Satan Is Alive and Well on Planet Earth* Lindsey credits the entire intellectual foundation of modern thought to satanic genius. He "took their concepts and wired the underlying frame of reference for our present historical, educational, philosophical, sociological, psychological, religious, economic, and political outlook."[14] Among the "thought bombs" dropped by the devil on our civilization are those of Kant, Hegel, Kierkegaard, Marx, Darwin, and Freud. Contemporary art, music, education, the mass media, and television all reflect the despair emanating from a world infected by these satanic influences.

In *The Late Great Planet Earth* Lindsey dealt specifically with the signs of the times that made up the prophetic jigsaw puzzle of endtimes events. The key pieces in this puzzle were the creation of the Jewish state of Israel in 1948; the recovery of the ancient capital city of Jerusalem in 1967; the emergence of Russia as a powerful nation and enemy of Israel; the Arab confederation arrayed against the state of Israel; the rise of a great military power in East Asia that can field untold millions of soldiers; the movement toward European integration; the revival of the dark occultic practices of ancient Babylon; the increase of wars, earthquakes, famines, and pollution; the apostasy of Christian churches from historic Christianity; the move toward one-world religion and government; and the decline of the United States as a world power.

Other pieces of the puzzle that had yet to fall into place included the secret rapture of the church (which he expected to occur in 1981), the seven-year tribulation period following this event, and the visible return of Christ in 1988. The sequence of events that would occur during the tribulation were those that many dispensationalist prophecy preachers identified (see chap. 2). Among them were the appearance of the Antichrist who would head up a revived Roman Empire comprised of the European Community (the United States would have faded from the scene because of its spiritual, political, economic, moral, and military decline), the rebuilding of the Jewish temple, the assault on Palestine by

Fig. 4.10 The Lindsey Look. Hal Lindsey is pictured first from the 1970 cover of *The Late Great Planet Earth* and second in a more recent photo after the book had amassed sales of over thirty-five million copies.

the Arab-African confederacy followed by the even larger invasion of the region by Russia (the Gog of Ezek. 38:16), and the showdown battle of Armageddon in which the European alliance, after having defeated the Russians, would be attacked by an army of two hundred million Asiatics. A nuclear exchange would ensue that would kill a third of the world's population, but just as the battle reached its peak, Christ would suddenly appear to halt the hostilities and protect believers from total destruction.

The critical point in this scenario was Lindsey's concept of the generation. Citing Matthew 24:34, "This generation will not pass away until all these things take place" (NASB), he defined a generation in the Bible as forty years and concluded that all these things would take place within forty years after the founding of Israel.[15] Thus, he predicted the return of Christ in 1988 and the rapture of the church seven years earlier, but like all the other date setters, he had to do some swift backpedaling when Jesus did not show up as expected.

Also central to his thinking was the appeal to what is "clear" or "plainly true" in the biblical text. He rejected modern scholars who used critical methodologies to explain away the simple truth of God's Word. Since for centuries interpreters had vigorously debated what the plain and literal meanings of the prophetic and apocalyptic Scripture passages actually meant, Lindsey ended up claiming special powers of interpretation for himself.

Today, Christians who have diligently studied prophecy, trusting the Spirit of God for illumination, have a greater insight into its meaning than ever before.

128

The prophetic word definitely has been "unsealed" [a reference to Dan. 12:9] in our generation as God predicted it would be.[16]

This writer [Lindsey] doesn't believe that we have prophets today who are getting direct revelations from God, but we do have prophets today who are being given special insight into the prophetic word. God is opening the book of the prophets to many men.[17]

Although Lindsey insisted that the meanings of the biblical materials are plainly evident, in fact he often clouded his writings with statements such as "the symbolism [of this passage] may seem very strange to modern ears."[18] He urged readers not to believe scholars who explain away the clear and evident meaning of a given text, but at the same time he used his own "special insight" to mold the biblical materials into his own interpretive scheme.

An excellent example of how he can squeeze concrete details out of obscure texts is a comment made in his 1997 book, *Apocalypse Code,* about the Book of Revelation, which he labeled "John's Time Travel Experience." By now Lindsey had conveniently shelved his 1988 prediction of Christ's return, but he portrayed the writer of Revelation as "an 'eyewitness' to events of the twentieth and twenty-first centuries." He was a "first century time traveler" who was shown the beginning of the twenty-first century and the phenomena of a global war fought with weapons of unimaginable power, speed, and lethality. As Lindsey put it, John "testified and God bore witness" that he actually saw and heard things such as:

- supersonic jet aircraft with missiles, hyperspeed cannons, and guided bombs
- advanced attack helicopters
- modern main battle tanks
- intercontinental ballistic missiles with Multiple Independently Targeted Reentry
- vehicles tipped with thermonuclear warheads (ICBMs that are MIRVed)
- battlefield artillery and missiles with neutron-nuclear warheads
- biological and chemical weapons
- aircraft carriers, missile cruisers, nuclear submarines
- laser weapons
- space stations and satellites
- the new supersecret HAARP weapon system (High-frequency Active Auroral Research Program) that can change weather patterns over whole continents, jam global communications systems, disrupt human mental processes, manipulate the earth's upper atmosphere, etc.[19]

Lindsey then says John was brought back to the first century and told to write an accurate eyewitness account of this terrifying future time. He was to do this in "encoded symbols." Now the time has come for these prophecies to be "uncoded," and "a Christian guided by the Spirit of God" is required to interpret them. The question is, what happened to all the plain, clear statements Lindsey continually talked about? He, in fact, has become as imaginative an interpreter as the liberals he so often criticized.

The decline and fall of communism presented Lindsey and his many imitators with a monumental problem. Almost without exception they had identified Russia with Gog and Magog, and especially the "Rosh" mentioned in Ezekiel 38:2–3. (This term is used untranslated in several of the modern translations; the King James and New International Versions, however, translate it as "chief prince.") They also associated the place-name Meshech in the passage with Moscow. Associating the Soviet Union with the monolithic fountainhead of all wickedness in the world allowed them to view America as the land of virtue, albeit one that was under constant threat from the insidious forces of evil, both within and without. The prophecy preachers' use of Daniel and Revelation compelled believers to think in terms of a grand conspiratorial drama, and the idea of a communist bloc, an evil empire engaged in a Manichaean struggle with the free world, made this an easy task.

Pat Robertson

The collapse of the Soviet Union sent the prognosticators scurrying for a new conspiracy in which to fit their preconceived prophetic notions, and they found it in the "New World Order." The idea of a new order is as old as America itself. It is enshrined in the great seal of the United States and can be found on the back of the one dollar bill. The New World Order as a replacement for the failed communist world conspiracy, however, is of recent origins. While even President Bush unwittingly used the phrase to characterize the kind of international cooperation he hoped to see come out of the Gulf War in 1991, no one exemplifies the switch to the new paradigm as well as America's leading televangelist, Marion G. "Pat" Robertson.

Born in Lexington, Virginia, in 1930, the son of a U.S. senator, Pat Robertson came from a background of privilege. He attended elite educational institutions, Washington and Lee University and Yale Law School, and served as a lieutenant in the Marine Corps during the Korean War. After graduating with a law degree, he failed the New York bar exam and dabbled in the business world. Although he had forged a successful marriage with a Yale nursing student, Adelia "Dede" Elmer, he was quite unhappy. Then in 1956 the nominal Baptist was converted, enrolled in the ministerial course at Biblical Seminary in New York, and came under the influence of Pentecostals. After graduating in 1959, he returned home to Virginia, where he became an associate minister in a Southern Baptist church in Norfolk and in spite of his charismatic tendencies was

Harold Camping: Forecasts from Another Front

While the majority of endtime date setters are premillennialist in theology, specifically dispensationalist, radio preacher Harold Camping stands out in the doomsday crowd as a Reformed amillennialist. A civil engineer by training, Camping is president of Family Radio Inc., a network of Christian radio stations and shortwave transmitters. Camping came into the prophetic spotlight in 1992 with the publication of his *1994?*, which boldly predicted that the world would end on September 6, 1994. There was a willing and ready audience waiting for his sequel on doom

deciphering, *Are You Ready?*, which covered much the same territory—again setting a September 1994 date for the second coming. However, when September 7 arrived and no end had occurred, he subsequently set other dates—September 29, October 2, and finally March 31, 1995—each time backpedaling because of a prophetic miscalculation.

Camping's failed forecasts were based on a chronological blueprint that combined sophisticated systems of dating and numerology. Despite his miscalculations, his radio ministry prospered in the years following his best-selling book's publication.

ordained. At the same time, he purchased a small defunct UHF television station and founded the Christian Broadcasting Network (CBN). He developed the concept of "faith partners" to raise money for the struggling enterprise, and in 1963 he asked for seven hundred people to pledge ten dollars per month to help him meet his budget. Thus was born the "700 Club," his flagship program. Two years later Jim and Tammy Bakker came to work for him, and the ministry prospered. In 1975 he bought 680 acres of land in Virginia Beach, and two years later CBN University (now Regent University) was founded on the sprawling campus that houses all his enterprises. By 1987 the annual budget of CBN exceeded two hundred million dol-

lars, and it was the most prosperous evangelical media operation in the world.

Robertson soon ventured into politics. He organized a "Washington for Jesus" rally in 1980 that allegedly drew two hundred thousand people to the nation's capital, and he was a central figure in the New Christian Right, which helped elect Ronald Reagan to the presidency. He sponsored a variety of political and legal organizations to mobilize evangelicals for conservative causes, the best known of which are the Christian Coalition and American Center for Law and Justice. In September 1986 he announced that he would run for president on the Republican ticket if he could secure the signatures of three million registered voters on petitions supporting his candidacy. As expected, he did enter the race but faded early in the 1988 campaign. Through his Christian Coalition, however, he continued to be a major force in Republican politics throughout the 1990s.

In his early years on television and in his many books and speeches Robertson sounded a line close to that of Lindsey's. He spoke repeatedly of the loss of Gentile world power that came with the rebirth of Israel, and the rising power of Russia as fulfillment of Ezekiel 38–39. In 1982 he even told his "700 Club" supporters that the end of the world may come by the fall of that year. When that did not happen he said it was because God was giving him more time to spread the gospel message. Still he remained a staunch supporter of Israel, even urging the United States to subordinate its national interests to those of Israel because Israel is the nation that will be glorified in the millennium. He vigorously opposed any kind of disarmament negotiations with the Soviet Union, the nation he saw as an ideological monster bent on the destruction of all free peoples.[20]

But then Robertson set forth a revised understanding of endtimes events in the 1991 best-seller *The New World Order,* which can best be described as post-communist eschatology. He argued that men of goodwill such as Woodrow Wilson, Jimmy Carter, and George Bush unknowingly and unwittingly carried out the mission and mouthed the phrases "of a tightly knit cabal whose goal is nothing less than a new order for the human race under the domination of Lucifer and his followers."[21] In this long, rambling account of two hundred years of conspiracy, Robertson showed how "monopoly bankers" have controlled the course of history. He began with the small secret society known as the Illuminati, founded in 1776, and showed how this occultic group (with the help of Jewish bankers) infiltrated and took over the Freemasons and then launched the French Revolution and the reign of terror.[22]

The movement next surfaced in nineteenth-century Germany and France under Karl Marx and Friedrich Engels, who were guided by a radical Jew named Moses Hess. They set out to create a new world order that would be characterized by the elimination of private property, national governments and national sovereignty, traditional Judeo-Christian theism, and the establishment of a world government controlled by the elite.[23] The conspiracy was comprised of secret Illuminists and Jewish bankers, and it not only gained control of the United States through the founding of the Federal Reserve System but also financed the Bolshevik Revolution of 1917 in Russia. These money barons of Europe incited the world wars and the Cold War to funnel money from taxpayers to themselves.[24] In fact, he insisted that the secret cabal that ran the United States through the Council on Foreign Relations[25] had convinced the American people that the enemy lived behind the iron and bamboo curtains and thus constant massive ex-

Fig. 4.11 Not a President but a Prophet. Pat Robertson, one of the leading right wing religious leaders of our day, has not shied from prophetic speculation.

penditures for arms, maintenance of large ground forces in Europe and Asia, and the stockpiling of an ever-growing arsenal of thermonuclear weapons was necessary. Then after we had spent our money to develop these weapons, our leaders negotiated with the Soviets to destroy them. As a result, the United States and other countries had to keep going to the international moneylenders for more funds to pay for weapons. Both the American taxpayers and the Russian people suffered for generations to enrich a small number of bankers.[26]

Robertson also contends there is a grand design in the events of our times. He predicts the unfolding of a giant plan, with everything perfectly on cue. Europe is about to unite. Communism has collapsed. A popular war was fought in the Middle East that rescued the United Nations from public scorn. The U.S. president announced a new world order. Christianity has been battered in the public arena; New Age religions are in place in the schools and corporations and among the elite. A financial collapse accelerates the move to a world money system. The United States will no longer be able to afford a strong defense, and so it will turn its defense requirements over to the United Nations, along with its sovereignty. The U.N. in turn will severely limit property rights and will clamp down on all Christian evangelism and Christian distinctives. The New Age religion of humanity will become official, and the new world leaders will embrace it. Then they will elect a world president with plenary powers, a man who is totally given to the religion of humanity.[27]

Computer technology will make it possible for the one-world government to control all people. It will be impossible to escape from its tyranny to a land of freedom or to carry out a revolt against it with outside help. Every citizen will be given a number, coded with his or her nation, region, and personal identity. Supercomputers will contain and be able to recall, in microseconds, the complete vital statistics and life record of every person in the world. Through a world currency and a cashless society it will be possible to monitor and control all wealth. Under such a system it will be possible to limit the types of purchases that certain people are allowed to make or to prohibit all purchases. Monitoring mechanisms, linked by global satellites, will keep tabs on the physical movement of every person in the world.

Some day in the future a "demonized madman" will seize power in a "worldwide, homogenized government and then employ currently existing technology to turn the entire world into a giant prison."[28] He will coerce life and thought into the mold of the New World Order, and the new order will inevitably become what communism has been. At no place on earth will freedom flourish.[29] Thus, the horrors of the rule of the Beast as portrayed in the Book of Revelation will come to pass. Bible prophecy will be fulfilled.[30]

Apocalyptic Prophecy: A Fiction Franchise

In 1990 Pat Robertson published a novel, *The New Millennium,* which speculated on circumstances surrounding the second coming of Christ. Using the vehicle of fiction to prophesy about future events is not a new phenomenon. An early pioneer of the genre was Forrest Loman Oilar whose 1937 novel *Be Thou Prepared, for Jesus Is Coming Soon* described life for those left behind after the rapture. Akron, Ohio–based televangelist Ernest Angley followed a similar line in his 1950 work, *Raptured: A Novel*—a work still available through Armageddon Books. But within the last few decades as we've headed toward the new millennium there has been an explosion of this category.

Another noteworthy purveyor of this style of apocalyptic fiction was Salem Kirban. Although he was largely unknown at the time of its writing, *666,* his "exciting novel on THE TRIBULATION PERIOD"—according to the book's spine copy—made Kirban a prophecy fixture. Complete with sinister photographs illustrating events of the future (e.g., see p. 184 below), Kirban offers an admittedly fictionalized account of how the Antichrist may come into power. First published in 1970, the novel—as well as its sequel, *1000: A Novel*—remains available from the web site of Kirban's Second Coming ministry based in Lancaster, Pennsylvania.

Recently, the apocalyptic genre has been given more of a prophecy celebrity twist. Well-known evangelists, including Pat Robertson, and nonfiction authors ▶

Fig. 4:12 Left Behind . . . Again. Popular prophecy preacher and author Tim La-Haye's rapture series dominated Christian fiction as well as *Publishers Weekly* religion best-seller's lists in the late 1990s. At one point, the series held the top three positions on the paperback list while claiming the number one spot on the hardcover list—a first-time publishing feat according to *Publishers Weekly*.

have begun to pen novels about the endtimes. Mr. Prophecy, Hal Lindsey, joined the parade with the 1996 publication of *Blood Moon: A New World*. But perhaps the most interesting, as well as most successful, example is that of conservative activist and evangelist Tim LaHaye, who teamed up with veteran author Jerry Jenkins to write a series of best-selling endtime novels in the 1990s. The first book, *Left Behind,* centers on the life of folks left behind on planet earth after the rapture. (Sounds amazingly similar to the story line of Oilar's work!) As of late 1998 four books of a similar ilk in a planned series of seven have been released, including *Tribulation Force, Nicolae,* and *Soul Harvest.*

Explaining the phenomenal success of the series, LaHaye, the prophecy celebrity of the writing tandem, commented, "There's a keen interest in prophecy, especially as the millennium approaches. Second, the writing is superb and the

characters are real." After releasing the first four titles, the publisher claimed sales in excess of three million units, including books and audiobooks, and a "Left Behind" series for kids was released.

For fans of apocalyptic novels, the Left Behind series—succinctly described by *Christianity Today* as a "seven-volume post-Rapture, dispensational soap opera"—promised endtime sequels to take readers into the new millennium. A fiction franchise for the enterprising authors and publisher, the series continued a long-time fascination, particularly among those influenced by dispensationalism, with speculation on the events surrounding and timing of the second coming.

Sources: Paul Boyer, *When Time Shall Be No More: Prophecy Belief in Modern American Culture* (Cambridge: Harvard University Press/Belknap Press, 1992), 106, 370; "'Left Behind' Series Now Online," *CBA Marketplace,* August 1998, 56; Michael G. Maudlin, "Inside CT," *Christianity Today,* 5 October 1998, 6.

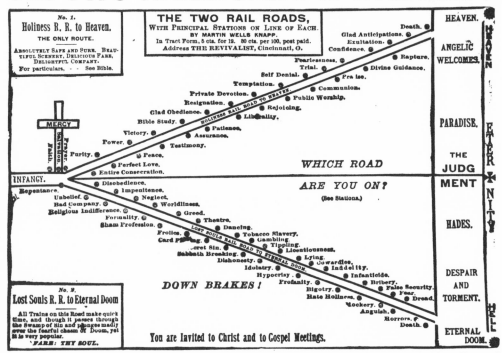

The TWO RAILROADS to ETERNITY

Fig. 4.13 A Slow Train Coming. Regardless of one's millennial position, this early twentieth-century invitation to a revival meeting is a detailed reminder of the virtues that pave the road to heaven and the sins that mark the road to hell.

However, unlike many of the other evangelical prophets of apocalypticism, Robertson is not a fatalist, even though he ties the New World Order to the prophecies of Revelation. Although this completely contradicts his entire system, he insists that it is possible to turn things around now. If the American people, and especially Christians, are informed about the machinations of the humanistic-occultic leaders of the New World Order, they can take steps to counter them. They must work to rebuild the foundation of a free, sovereign America from the bottom up and to defeat the Council on Foreign Relations's program of a one-world collectivist government and a drastically diminished role for United States sovereignty. According to Robertson, "There

136

is an epic struggle for the future. If it were not important, the Establishment would not have committed the better part of a hundred years of labor and billions of dollars of their resources to bring it about."[31] He contends, "The time has come to mount an all-out assault on the ultimate power of the Establishment—the ability to elect or destroy political leaders through the control of the money supply"—in other words, abolish the Federal Reserve System.[32]

What Robertson in effect does is vacillate between a traditional apocalyptic premillennialism and a sort of postmillennialism based on Christians working to bring in the kingdom now. If they would turn back to God, seek his help in thwarting the liberal advocates of the New World Order, and usher in a kingdom of righteousness, then all people would recognize the Lord as their God and live according to his ways. They would honor his holy Scriptures and adhere to his moral values. We can have a better world, because "the triumph of God's world order is certain."[33] This is the "decade of opportunity for the church," because at least one billion people will come to faith in Christ. Also, concerted, believing prayer has the miraculous power to alter world events. There will be a struggle between people of faith and those of the humanistic-occultic sphere, but Jesus has promised us that "in the world you have tribulation; but be of good cheer, I have overcome the world" (John 16:33 RSV).

Conclusion

The date setters examined in this chapter extracted all sorts of fanciful ideas from vague and obscure biblical passages, and their ideas of the future mirrored the events taking place in their own particular lifetimes. In fact, as one writer observed, the centuries of envisioning and predicting the millennium perhaps reveal more about the dreams, hopes, and fears of people in the past than about the Apocalypse itself.[34]

As we have seen, the desire to experience the Lord's return in these prophets' own times often led to hasty and rash predictions. The inevitable failure of such specific predicted events resulted in a variety of responses, ranging from embarrassment at best to disillusionment at worst and inevitably to new predictions for the future. Regardless of the scriptural warning that no one will know the day nor hour of Christ's coming (Matt. 24:36), the temptation to set specific dates was and continues to be just too much for many earnest believers.

While the date-setting tradition is largely a conservative Christian—and North American—phenomenon, millenarianism has had a much wider impact on the international social, political, and cultural landscape. In the following chapter we will explore some of these broader phenomena, further mapping out the terrain for pilgrims entering the new millennium.

5

Apocalyptic Bebop

Millennialism as a Worldwide Phenomenon

> And what rough beast, its hour come
>   round at last,
> Slouches toward Bethlehem to be
>   born?
>
> William Butler Yeats

On January 11, 1992, tens of thousands of participants worldwide, dressed only in white, performed dances at 11:11 A.M., 11:11 P.M., and 11:11 Greenwich Mean Time. This "11:11 event," orchestrated by New Age leader Solara was designed to open a "doorway" to a higher consciousness. Apparently it succeeded, for according to Solara's forecast, inhabitants of planet earth have until December 31, 2011 (actually a longer period of time than many of the year-2000 doomsayers are allowing) to attain a higher dimension. Otherwise, cataclysmic destruction may result.[1]

Solara's fantastic vision is but one of many millenarian movements on the scene today as we approach the twenty-first century. In fact, Ted Daniels, editor of the Philadelphia-based *Millennial Prophecy Report,* follows the activities of over eleven hundred such groups and individuals in America alone, largely through Internet research. In a similar vein, Boston University history professor Richard Landes has created the Center for Millennial Studies for scholars to, among other things, "gather and archive the vast 'harvest' of apocalyptic literature that is appearing at the turn of the second Christian millennium."[2]

Most Christians in the West regard millennialism as a tenet peculiar to their faith. As we have seen, the hope of the second coming infuses all branches of Christianity, regardless of denominational or con-

139

fessional stance. Thus, the advent of the new millennium has taken on theological significance for Christians, especially the more conservative and bibliocentric ones. However, millennialism and millenarian ideas are elements of many other belief systems that often utilize what we have always regarded as distinctly Christian concepts. Millennial travelers who desire to be accurately informed about the world around them and wish to avoid making ill-advised judgments about beliefs divergent from theirs need to be aware of this situation. This chapter will call attention to a number of less familiar and esoteric millennial manifestations that have played varied roles of importance in the modern world.

Civil Millennialism in the United States

In the 1930s theologian H. Richard Niebuhr called attention to the fascination Americans had with the idea of the kingdom of God, especially with regard to social gospel thought, but he did not apply the relationship of the millennialist idea to American history and thought in any meaningful way.[3] By the 1960s, however, scholars had begun to pay attention to the millennial theme as a central idea in American thought and life. The seminal work on the subject was Ernest Lee Tuveson's *Redeemer Nation: The Idea of America's Millennial Role*,[4] which traced the development of American political and moral destiny within a religious framework. He revealed the arguments of prominent nineteenth-century writers that the nation was ordained by God to occupy the North American continent and to carry the blessings of democracy to all the peoples of the world. Quickly other historians began to look more closely at the writings and sermons of nineteenth-century preachers and intellectuals, and they discovered how deeply rooted this sense of American uniqueness was.

Advocates of the view held that God had a plan for this nation, which he had chosen to be a special people, just as he had ancient Israel. By placing America beyond the broad ocean and separating it from Europe with its age-old tensions and despotisms, God had created a natural environment for the growth of civil and religious freedom. The new nation was founded on the political and religious principles that made this freedom possible. The boundless resources of the country—land, population, learning, the spirit of enterprise, and the English language—were given by God to enable Americans to preach the Word and teach native peoples the rudiments of culture. Then the development of the railroad and steamship helped them carry enlightenment and the gospel to the ends of the earth. American democracy, free enterprise capitalism, and the application of technology to human problems would be the means by which America would save the world.

As the idea of American uniqueness became more and more secularized, Christians and non-Christians alike saw the nation as the primary agent of God's meaningful activity in history. This nation of heroic, self-reliant, freedom-loving people stood as a beacon to the world of the inestimable benefits of a society that was governed by consent and in which the free individual could live in peace and happiness. Over the passage of time other ideas flowed from this belief. According to "manifest destiny," Americans were destined to spread across the entire continent. They were to make the world safe for democracy and achieve the ultimate victory of freedom over godless communism. Since the breakup of the Soviet Union, America, the only superpower, stands poised on the brink of the twenty-first century ready to lead humankind into the New World Order, a millennium of peace, prosperity, and happiness.

The major secular exponent of civil millennialism in our time was President Ronald Reagan, and his optimistic affirmation of America's happy future was a major reason for his great popularity. As he said, America "was set apart in a special way," and men and women from every corner of the world "came not for gold but mainly in search of God. They would be free people, living under the law, with faith in their Maker and in their future." On another occasion he affirmed his belief "in the goodness of the American people" and suggested that they were

Fig. 5.1 Ronald Reagan's Kingdom. President Reagan's vision of the United States as God's New Israel is a view still shared by many today.

"blessed in so many ways [because] we're a nation under God, a living and loving God." In 1987 he told a gathering, "The guiding hand of providence did not create this new nation of America for ourselves alone, but for a higher cause: the preservation and extension of the sacred fire of human life. This is America's solemn duty." Moreover, in a world wracked by tension, "America remains mankind's best hope."[5] Evangelicals, who voted for Reagan in droves, widely accepted this sort of civil millennialism, as did those who were strong advocates of pessimistic premillennialism.

The books by Peter Marshall and David Manuel, *The Light and the Glory* (1977) and *From Sea to Shining Sea* (1986), which explain God's providential plan for America, were offerings of a major evangelical publisher, Fleming H. Revell, and were runaway best-sellers in the evangelical

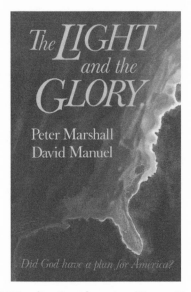

Fig. 5.2 Reading Providence into History. Marshall's and Manuel's *The Light and the Glory,* though roundly dismissed by serious Christian historians, has sold over 530,000 copies in twenty years (a children's edition has sold over an additional 125,000 copies) and spawned an ongoing series perpetuating a subtle civil millennialism among the faithful masses, particularly homeschoolers.

community. A host of similar books and videos have flooded the market during the last few decades, and they are even used as American history textbooks in Christian schools around the country and as discussion guides in churches. These works maintain that America was founded as a Christian nation, and the continuing national and spiritual blessings that God bestows on America testify to the special place it has in the divine purpose. As the well-known evangelist Tim LaHaye put it, "America is the human hope of the world,

and Jesus Christ is the hope of America. . . . [It is] the greatest nation under God that the world has ever known."[6]

Of course, God will judge his people for their sins, and the preachers are constantly calling the nation to repentance on the basis of Old Testament texts, but the United States still has its special place in God's program for humankind. That this glorification of America as God's last, best hope for the world contradicts much of their prophetic preaching and is something that strikes Christians in other countries as ethnocentric at best and arrogant at worst does not seem to bother the modern-day advocates of civil millennialism.

American Blacks and Their Alternative to Civil Millennialism

At the same time white Americans were developing their conception of the nation as God's "new Israel," blacks in the late nineteenth century were developing their own unique forms of cultural millenarianism. One variety emphasized the role of the church, evangelism, missions, and reform in bringing forth a millennial age marked by racial equality, harmony, and brotherhood. It would be a time in which there would be no wars, militarism, saloons, opium traffic, slavery of any form, or heathen religions. America would be reconstructed into a nation in which there would be happiness for all.

Another vision, more African in character, looked to a future golden age that was continuous with the glorious African past and would involve God's judgment on white society. Drawing from the proof-text "Ethiopia shall soon stretch out her hands unto God" (Ps. 68:31 KJV), these African Americans felt that the important role of Africa in biblical history confirmed its future glory. Bringing Christianity to Africa would enable its redemption, and thus many black churches enthusiastically supported foreign missions. However, they would carry the message of Christ to their ancestral homelands, not the "white man's religion." The white nations spread the gospel, but they did not place enough emphasis on the peace that is crucial to the millennial reign of Christ. The black race, however, is morally unique and has the task or mission to bring about human brotherhood.

African Methodist James T. Holly insisted that the African race will experience a reversal from curse to blessing, from being the servants to having "the post of honor under the heavenly government of God." Another African Methodist, T. G. Steward, insisted that white Christians will soon experience judgment because of their Anglo-Saxon pride, militarism, and betrayal of Christianity into a clan religion. Christ will inaugurate the millennium, but blacks will have a special role in spreading its influence and benefits. This "millennial Ethiopianism" stressed the supernatural intervention of God, Western civilization as only a stage in history and not its fulfillment, the importance of biblical prophecy (especially Ps. 68:31), and the moral leadership and prophetic insight of black peoples.[7]

Black Islam, a twentieth-century phenomenon, went much farther in providing a millennial vision for African Americans. It became a protest movement that drew on the wellsprings of traditional millennialism, with its identification of a devil or evil force and the ultimate victory of the good people. Thus, they called for separation from white civilization because it was by nature evil and doomed to destruction. They looked to Allah and especially his messengers, such as Elijah Muhammad and Louis Farrakhan, to unite black people and lead them to freedom. They believed roles would be reversed, the "first shall be last," and the black Nation of Islam would be the redeemer people of the world. In short, black Muslims became a redeemer nation, a chosen people, a redemptive force in the world.

The Millenarian Vision of the German Nazis

The development of National Socialist Germany under Adolf Hitler is one of the most thoroughly studied and intensely debated historical events of our day. Space does not allow a discussion of this remarkable period in world history, except to point out that Nazism possessed a distinctly millenarian character.

Historians tend to mention this character only in passing, but James M. Rhodes has examined it in detail in his provocative book, *The Hitler Movement: A Modern Millenarian Revolution*.[8] Rhodes follows the lead of Norman Cohn, whose *The Pursuit of the Millennium: Revolutionary Millenarians and Mystical Anarchists of the Middle Ages* is a well-known work in the comparative history of millennialism.[9] In this book Cohn identifies six features that characterize millennial movements. They are:

- a disaster syndrome
- some sort of supernatural revelation or visions
- an identification of the primary cause of evil
- a sense of divine election or choice
- the expectation of an apocalyptic conflict or final war
- the hope of a new order of eternal goodness and happiness in which evil will no longer exist

All these features are present in Christian eschatology—the horrors of the tribulation period; the visions and direct revelations to Daniel, John, and other prophets; Satan in the form of the Antichrist; God's saints chosen to be redeemed from the tribulation; the all-out final battle of Armageddon; and the establishment of the millennial reign of Christ on earth. Thus, Nazism with its millenarian quality can be regarded as a substitute faith, a counterfeit belief system that gripped the souls of millions of unthinking Germans, including practicing Christians. In fact, pastors and laypeople alike were attracted by the National Socialist political program, which promised the restoration of traditional values and the renewal of national greatness. Once again Germany would be standing tall and would command respect in the world.

Following World War I, the situation in Germany could be characterized as a "disaster syndrome." It was a time of bewilderment, loss of discipline, and absolute disorientation. The traditional world that Germans knew had vanished. The old authorities of state, church, and family had lost their hold on the populace. New ideas and ideologies now prevailed—liberalism, Marxist socialism, communism, internationalism, democracy, feminism, modern art, sexual license—or so the Nazi propaganda machine claimed. Radical agitators decried Germany's loss of the war as due to treason. The hated Versailles peace treaty of 1919 intended to keep Germany in perpetual slavery, and the victorious Allies were bent on Germany's annihilation. The German *volk* (people) had been humiliated and faced a grim future of pain and misery. Racial pollution on the part of the Jews and foreign elements threatened the integrity of the *volk*. While many of these ideas were imaginary, Hitler and his minions convinced millions of Germans that they were true.

The Nazis also had their visions of what could be done about the situation and how a better world could be built. These ideas came from mystical stirrings within their own beings and not from without. Hitler said on various occasions that he had been "called" by the racial "origin" of his existence. The Nazis were led by the voices of "personality," "instinct," "feeling," and "magic insight." They seemed to know truths by looking at their situations; ideas came into their heads as if from nowhere. Nazi knowledge did not come from unaided reason or intellectual effort. On one occasion Hitler declared: "The understanding [intellect] alone achieves very little. The correct feeling does more than all understanding. . . . The certain feeling never betrays you." Other Nazi figures talked about "blood," "inner voices," "spirit," "will," and even "a demon" as sources of truth. They were clearly all of one accord in rejecting rationalism and the intellect as sources of guidance.[10]

As for the source of the disasters facing Germany, the Nazis did not find it in the generally accepted historical causes of post–World War I problems, that is, Allied uneasiness about a German revival, the threat of the Soviet Union, and economic practices that caused the onset of the world depression. For the Nazis, the devil, the all-encompassing source of evil, was a secular force, the Jewish "race." Jews were seen as parasites living off other people; they poisoned the healthy races of the world. Because they had gained world fi-

Fig. 5.3 Hitler's History. Adolf Hitler's Nazis were propelled by a distinct secular millennial vision.

nancial power, they were responsible for Germany's defeat in World War I. And through the Western international stock exchange capitalist system they were currently strangling Germany with war reparations payments and enormous high interest loans. Another even more ominous tentacle of the international Jewish octopus was Marxism. The socialists and communists were working with the monopoly financiers to destroy Germany by fomenting class warfare.

In Germany proper the main source of Jewish power was the Weimar Republic, formed after the collapse of the imperial government at the end of the war. The republic was allegedly run by Jews who stabbed the brave German army in the back in 1918 by surrendering to the Allies and then delivering up the country to the slavery of the Versailles treaty. The parliamentary government and multiparty system that were the hallmarks of Weimar democracy were only devices to keep Germany weak. Other Jewish enemies included bankers, department store owners, and the mass media. Jews had perverted Germany with their charms and corrupted the *volk*.

Hitler believed that fate or the German *volk* had called him to lead the struggle for national rebirth. He told his inner circle in 1932 that "we are chosen. . . . Whoever proclaims his allegiance to me is, by this very proclamation and by the manner in which it is made, one of the chosen."[11] Many Nazis talked about being "renewed," "reborn," and "awakened"; others felt "bright enthusiasm" (as if they were glowing with "the spirit") and "inner power." They had a clear sense of calling to lead the *volk* and the nation in its redemption. They were chosen not by God but by mysterious, intangible secular powers.

Millenarians throughout history have believed a war is necessary to defeat the forces of evil, and the Nazis were no exception. Hitler insisted repeatedly that a titanic struggle between Jews and Aryans (his term for the culture-creating races of the world) was now going on, and in the ultimate war that would eventually take place, Jewish power would forever be wiped from the face of the earth. Repeatedly Hitler talked of war, and once he had gained power in Germany he began full-scale preparations for it. In his famous speech to the German parliament on January 30, 1939, he spoke as a self-proclaimed prophet:

> If international financial Jewry, in Europe and beyond, should succeed in plunging the nations into another world war, the result will not be the Bolshevization of the world and thus the victory of Jewry, but the destruction of the Jewish race in Europe.[12]

The Führer's associate Joseph Goebbels had no doubts that "world Jewry" had started World War II and that it would suffer the same "process of destruction that it had planned for us."[13] The Nazis had countered the power of the Jewish demons who were getting ready to deliver the final blow to the German people. Hitler, the modern-day messiah, would draw the true fighters to his side and destroy the forces of evil gathering to wipe out the *volk*. The earth would be redeemed from the power of Jewry.

With the final victory in the climactic struggle against international Jewish power, the Nazi millennium would begin. Known as the new Reich, the new Germany, the Germany of the future, or most dramatically, the thousand-year Reich, it would be a totally secular equivalent of the kingdom of God on earth. Nazi thought never made clear what this new heaven and earth would be like. Some saw it as a paradise for Aryan people, a new world in which all members of the *volk* would live happily ever after. They could deify both themselves and their descendants through scientific racial breeding (re-creation of the pure Aryan stock), awakening of minds to the consciousness of participation in the soul of the *volk,* creation of culture, and heroic deeds. A few saw it as a more mundane kind of utopia in which they would be able to exercise power and enjoy a pleasurable existence.

In Hitler's mind, however, the classless society of the new Reich would be a much more austere sort of community. The Nazi New Jerusalem would be characterized by a sort of sinless perfection as all extinguished within themselves the vices of hatred, envy, jealousy, avarice, lust, greed, egoism, strife, and discord. The new Nazi man would have a "boundless, all-encompassing love for the *volk,*" would act solely for the welfare of the *volk,* and possess the "self-sacrificing will to give one's personal labor and if necessary one's life" to the community.[14] With no transcendent base on which to construct the Nazi millennium, it is no wonder that the vision was so vague. And the method that Hitler chose to bring this about, a general European war, guaranteed in advance that he would fail.

Marxism as a Millenarian Movement

It seems like only yesterday Marxism was the unstoppable force in the world, the wave of the future that was washing away the antiquated values of the present. Marxist governments held sway over a large portion of the earth's population, and oppressed peoples everywhere were lured by their promises of a better life. Then came 1989 and Marxism itself was swept away as regimes crumbled one by one and people sought material wealth in the free market economy and spiritual refuge in traditional religions. Now Marxism barely rules but in a few backward countries and on the campuses of some elite educational institutions. Marxism's basic appeal lay in its millennialist character, and when it failed to deliver on the promised hope, the movement was doomed.

Karl Marx and his alter ego, Friedrich Engels, set forth a millenarian vision in their famous tract published in 1848, *The Communist Manifesto,* and further expounded their ideas in various other works. As many social radicals of the day, they were concerned about the toll the Industrial Revolution was taking on the masses of Europe. The conditions of life in the new industrial cities were terrible, to say the least, and several humanitarian and radical thinkers offered possible solutions to the situation that apparently had little impact. Some intellectuals called for the restructuring of society or the estab-

147

lishment of utopian communities in which workers themselves would control their productive activities. Others sought to obtain factory and social reform legislation that would address the worst evils of the new industrial order.

Marx and Engels rejected these approaches as mere utopianism. They claimed to have found the "laws" underlying the social order, and they believed that by understanding the ongoing processes of these laws the laboring class could eventually achieve liberation through socialism. They labeled their doctrine scientific, because it was supposedly based on careful research and analysis of the forces at work in the real world. In actuality, it was a kind of romantic apocalypticism, and Marx was essentially a prophet. It is with good reason that some have labeled Marxism a Christian heresy, because in spite of his emphasis on materialism and atheism, Marx offered a secularized millennial hope modeled on the pattern of the ancients who preceded him.

The central argument of Marxism is that the economic forces of production comprise the foundation of society, and power is exercised by the social class who controls or owns the productive assets. The ones who are actually doing the work, that is, producing the necessary goods of life, are excluded from power and thus are oppressed. However, the latter try to gain control over their destiny and the ownership of the means of production. Thus, *The Communist Manifesto* opens with the

stirring line: "The history of all hitherto existing society is the history of class struggles," and goes on to say:

> Freeman and slave, patrician and plebeian, lord and serf, guildmaster and journeyman, in a word, oppressor and oppressed, stood in constant opposition to one another, carried on an uninterrupted, now hidden, now open fight, a fight that each time ended, either in a revolutionary reconstruction of society at large, or in the common ruin of the contending classes.[15]

The class struggle took place in the form of the dialectic. In other words, each class grew out of an earlier one, sought liberation within the productive process, and challenged the current ruling class for power. Once the newly liberated class had gained victory, it became the ruling class and restructured the society in accordance with its own class interests. However, as the productive process expanded, sooner or later the new ruling class would in turn be challenged by another class growing out of the totality of the productive enterprise.

In the nineteenth and twentieth century the bourgeoisie (middle class, in the European sense of the word) emerged as the ruling group. It owned the land, factories, machines, banks, transportation systems, and all the other significant means of production. It controlled the state as well. As the *Manifesto* put it, "Each step in the development of the bourgeoisie was accompanied by a corresponding political advance of that class."[16] The bourgeois state and its institutions dominated the world, and they extended their tentacles through the all-encompassing corruption known as free trade. However, the actual productive work was being done by the proletariat, that is, the working class. It was now the oppressed class in the Marxist scheme. In millenarian terms, the bourgeoisie personified radical evil. It was Babylon and Rome all rolled into one, while the proletariat was Israel, the chosen people, the innocents longing to become free. It was the pure class because it had been excluded from the corruption of the ruling order of society.

The proletariat took on a messianic character, and the leadership of the class was provided by the communists, which in the *Manifesto* were described as "practically, the most advanced and resolute section of the working-class parties of every country, that section which pushed forward all others."[17] This party would lead, inspire, and sustain the masses in their struggle to overthrow bourgeois rule. It would see the workers through the revolution, the Armageddon that would destroy the ruling powers, and usher in the Marxist millennium. The bourgeoisie would not voluntarily give

up power or yield to reform; it would have to be destroyed through violent upheaval. Only in such a revolution could the proletariat "succeed in ridding itself of all the muck of ages and become fitted to found society anew."[18] Although the bourgeoisie possessed superior power of all kinds, the proletariat as the chosen people would triumph over their enemies—the rich, the mighty, the proud. Thus, the revolution had the irresistible power of destiny that goes far beyond ordinary idealism.

Here we have the key ideas of millennialism—redemption and restoration. The righteous people would at last rule. Guided by the communists they would set up a virtuous dictatorship—the democratic rule of the great majority of the people over the tiny bourgeois minority, who then would need to be reeducated if they were to have any place in the new order. Those who refused to do so, the enemies of righteousness, or the enemies of the people, would simply be eliminated or purged. In millennial terms, the historical process decreed the destruction of Babylon. The world would be inhabited by an entirely new race of people, all of whom would have an altered consciousness in which the deepest drives in human nature have been transformed. During the proletarian dictatorship, in which the institutions of bourgeois society would be dismantled and the new order brought into being, the desire to gain wealth and power and dominate others would be eliminated. Education would create a new humanity, a new generation of people who would endeavor to improve the condition of every member of society.

Then at last would begin the classless society, the millennium and the New Jerusalem all rolled into one. Humankind would return to the primeval, egalitarian, harmonious society that existed before the corrupting original sin of a different and corrupt consciousness invaded human existence. In the hunting and gathering, pastoral, and early agricultural stages of culture, ownership of productive assets had been tribal—held by the entire community. But then the emergence of patriarchal monogamy, characterized by exclusive marriage and possession of women, had dramatically altered human relations. This had induced in the child a sense of "possessive consciousness," and following that had come such evils as private property, state ownership of goods, and slavery. Now greed and aggressiveness were the hallmarks of human society and class relations among people had begun.

The classless society would be marked by great material abundance because the all-around development of the individual productive forces would have increased. As Marx put it in *The Critique of the Gotha Program* (1875), with the abolition of private property "all the springs of cooperative wealth flow more abundantly." People would be free to exercise the truly humane treatment of one another. Then would "society inscribe on its banners: from each according to his ability, to each

according to his needs."[19] Or as Marx stated in *The Communist Manifesto*:

> When, in the course of development, class distinctions have disappeared, and all production has been concentrated in the hands of a vast association of the whole nation, the public power will lose its political character. Political power, properly so called, is merely the organized power of one class for oppressing another.[20]

In the purified utopia of the classless society, the state would have withered away. Since the state was the executive committee of the ruling class and there would be no more classes, any purpose for the state would have vanished. During the dictatorship of the proletariat humans would be transformed into rational people, and so in the classless society they would govern their townships by consensus. Democracy would occur as naturally and instinctively as breathing itself.

Also, religion would wither away. Marxists believed religion was a product of the social environment and accordingly an instrument of the ruling class. It provided a way for people to project their desires into the distant supernatural realm without threatening the power of the rulers. Christianity, in particular, directed people's attention toward the hereafter and away from the real problems of the time. Christians were not interested in the social transformation of this world, and they promoted the principles of cowardice, self-contempt, abasement, and dejection. Since the proletariat needed courage, self-esteem, pride, and a sense of independence to engage in the struggle against the bourgeoisie, religion stood in the way of the revolution. Moreover, for Marxists man must not be viewed as an abased creature, enslaved to sin and in need of redemption by a Savior who had died for him.

Marxists argued that religion justifies the exploitation of the working class by promising them a better future in heaven. The working class needed to abandon this illusion and face reality on earth. They needed to realize that the meaning of life and history was to be found in the work of people in the here and now. They had to create the future themselves, and there they would find the increase of humanness. Marxism provided the strategies for action whereby they could build a better world and find the future golden age. Humanizing humanity was an achievable goal. The incomplete world could be completed. In the classless society people would achieve perfect identity between their true humanness and their present condition. Therefore, in the new earthly kingdom the place of God and religion would no longer exist. The human community would have reached perfection, but only on a material basis. There was no spiritual dimension to this, and Marxists saw no need for it.

The theologians of liberation have attempted to link the prophetic texts of Scripture to the Marxist strategies against oppression and for the revolutionary transformation of bourgeois society. They can only go so far with this, however, because the Marxist materialist vision of the future is quite different from the Judeo-Christian one. Both groups share the utopian hope of a realm of freedom beyond nature and society's production and exchange process, but Marxism ignores totally the concept of original sin and the possibility that humankind by its own efforts might not be able to achieve perfection. The idea of the proletariat as the elect and perfect people has given Marxist millenarianism a powerful dynamic, but the realities of Marxist transitional regimes have revealed that spiritually it is a broken reed. It simply leads to even more oppressive situations than those that existed before the revolutions.

In addition, although Marxism claims not to be a religion, it functions precisely as one. For all practical purposes it adapted the Judeo-Christian messianic pattern of history to socialism. Moreover, comparing it more closely to Christianity per se, one finds that the materialistic dialectic that governs historical development corresponds to the biblical God, the proletariat to the saints, the communist party to the church, the revolution to the second coming, and the classless society to the millennium. However, the substitute faith possesses, to cite the title of a famous book written by former Marxists in 1949, a "God that failed." Despite its somewhat useful analysis of laissez-faire capitalism,

The following was written by the Rev. JOHN WESLEY, of London, in 1774; and a copy of it was sent to the King of England, which has ever since put a stop to the play, called "*The Day of Judgment*," which was about that time performing in the London Theatres.

BY COMMAND OF THE KING OF KINGS,

And at the desire of all those who love His appearing.

SEARCH THE SCRIPTURES.
John v. 39.

a) Rev. 19. 16. — 1 Tim. vi. 15.
b) 2 Tim. iv. 1. — Tit. ii. 13.

At the Theatre of the UNIVERSE, *c)* on the Eve of Time, *d)* will be performed,

THE GREAT ASSIZE, or
DAY OF JUDGMENT. *e)*

THE SCENERY,

WHICH is now actually preparing, will not only surpass every thing that has yet been seen, but will infinitely exceed the utmost stretch of human conception. *f)* There will be a just representation of all the inhabitants of the world, in their various and proper colours; and their customs and manners will be so exactly and minutely delineated, that the most secret thought will be discovered. *g)* "For God will bring every work into judgment, with every secret thing, whether it be good, or whether it be evil." Ecc. xii. 14.

This Theatre will be laid out after a new plan, and will consist of PIT and GALLERY, only; and, contrary to all others, the Gallery is fitted up for the reception of people of high (or heavenly) birth; *h)* and the Pit for those of low (or earthly) rank. *i)* N. B. The Gallery is very spacious, *k)* and the Pit without bottom. *l)*

To prevent inconveniency, there are separate doors for admitting the company; and they are so different, that none can mistake that are not wilfully blind. The door which opens into the Gallery is very narrow, and the steps up to it are somewhat difficult; for which reason there are seldom many people about it. *m)* But the door that gives entrance into the Pit, is very wide and commodious, which causes such numbers to flock to it, that it is generally crowded. *n)* N. B. The straight door leads toward the right hand, and the broad one to the left. *o)*

It will be in vain for one with a tinselled coat, and borrowed language, to persuade one of High Birth, in order to get admittance into the Upper Places, *p)* for there is One of wonderful and deep penetration, who will search and examine every individual; *q)* and all who cannot pronounce Shibboleth, *r)* in the language of Canaan, *s)* or has not received a White Stone and a new name, *t)* or cannot prove a clear title to a certain portion of the Land of Promise, *u)* must be turned in at the left hand door. *x)*

c) Rev. 20, 11.—Math. 24, 30.
d) Rev. 10, 6, 7.—Dan. 12, 13.

e) Heb. 9, 27.—Ps. 9, 7, 8.—Rev. 6, 17.
2 Cor. 5, 10.—Zeph. 1, 14 to 17.

f) 1 Cor. 2, 9.—Isa. 64, 4.—Ps. 31, 19.
g) Math. 12, 36.—1 Cor. 4, 5.—Rom. 2, 12, 16.
h) John 3, 3, 5.—1 Pet. 1, 23.—Rom. 8, 14.
i) James 3, 14, 15.—Rom. 8, 6, 7, 8.—Gal. 4, 19 to 31.
k) Luke 14, 22.—John 14, 2.
l) Rev. 9, 16.—19, 20.

m) Math. 7, 14.
n) " 7, 13.
o) " 25, 33.
p) " 7, 21 to 23.
q) Ps. 44, 20, 21.—Jer. 17, 10.—Zeph. 1, 12.—3 Tim. 2, 19.—John 10, 14.
r) Judges 12, 6.
s) Isa. 19, 18.—Zeph. 3, 9.
t) Rev. 2, 17.—Heb. 11, 1, 3, 9.—Gal. 3, 9, 29.—2 Cor. 13, 5.
u) Ps. 9, 17.—Heb. 3, 17 to 19.

THE PRINCIPAL PERFORMERS

Are described in 1Thes. 4, 19. 2 Thes. 1, 7, 8, 9. Math. 24, 30, 31.—25, 31, 32. Dan. 7, 9, 10. Judg. 14, 4. Rev. 20, 12 to 15. &c. But as there are some people much better acquainted with the contents of a *Play Bill* than the *Word of God*, it may not be amiss to transcribe a verse or two for their perusal. "The Lord Jesus will be revealed from Heaven with his mighty angels in flaming fire, taking vengeance on them that obey not the gospel, but to be glorified in his saints. A fiery stream issued and came forth from before him. A thousand thousands ministered unto him, and ten thousand times ten thousand stood before him: The Judgment was set, and the Books were opened, and whosoever was not found written in the Book of Life, was cast into the Lake of Fire."

Act First of this Grand and Solemn Piece,

Will be opened by an Arch-Angel with the Trump of God. *z)* "For the trumpet shall sound and the dead shall be raised." 1 Cor. 15, 52.
ACT SECOND—will be a PROCESSION of SAINTS, in white, *y)* with Golden Harps, accompanied with shouts of joy and songs of praise. *z)*
ACT THIRD—WILL BE AN ASSEMBLAGE OF THE UNREGENERATE. *a)*
The Music will consist chiefly of Cries, *b)* accompanied with Weeping, Wailing, Lamentation and Woe. *c)*

To conclude with an Oration by the Son of God.

It is written in the 25th chapter of Matthew, from the 34th verse to the end of the chapter; but for the sake of those who seldom read the Scriptures, I shall here transcribe two verses:— Then shall the King say unto them on his right hand, 'Come ye blessed of my Father, inherit the Kingdom prepared for you from the foundation of the world.' Then shall he say unto them on his left hand, 'Depart from me, ye cursed, into everlasting fire, prepared for the Devil and his angels."

x) 1 Thes. 4, 16.—Math. 24, 31.
y) Rev. 7, 14.—19, 14.
— 14, 2, 3.—15, 2, 3, 4.
z) 1 Cor. 6, 9, 10.—Math. 13, 41.
a) Luke 23, 3.—Rev. 6, 16.
c) Luke 13, 28.—Math. 19, 49, 50.—Rev. 1, 7.—Ezekiel 7, 16.

AFTER WHICH THE CURTAIN WILL DROP!

Then! O to tell!

John 5, 28, 29. Stone raised on high, and others doom'd to hell!	Luke 9, 14, 27. While those who trampled under foot his grace,
Rev. 5, 8, 9. These praise the Lamb, and sing redeeming love,	Math. 25, 30. Are banish'd now forever from his face.
Luke 16, 22, 23. Lodg'd in his bosom, all his goodness prove:	Luke 16, 29. Divided thus, a gulph is fixed between,
	Math. 25, 46. And [everlasting] closes up the scene.

Thus will I do unto thee, O Israel; and because I will do thus unto thee, prepare to meet thy God. Amos 4, 12.

Tickets for the PIT at the easy purchase of following the pomps and vanities of the fashionable world, and the desires and amusements of the flesh *d)* to be had at every flesh-pleasing assembly. "*If ye live after the flesh, ye shall die.*" Rom. 8, 13.
Tickets for the GALLERY, at no less rate than being converted, *e)* forsaking all, *f)* denying self, taking up the cross, *g)* and following Christ in the regeneration : *h)* To be had nowhere but in the *Word of God*, and where that word appoints. "He that hath ears to hear, let him hear, and be not deceived; God is not mocked; for whatsoever a man soweth, that shall he also reap." Math. 11, 15. Gal. 6, 7.
N. B. No money will be taken at the door; *i)* nor will any tickets give admittance into the Gallery, but those sealed by the Holy Ghost, *k)* with Immanuel's signet: *l)* Watch therefore; be ye also ready, for in such an hour, as ye think not, the Son of Man cometh. Math. 24, 42, 44.

d) James 4, 4.—1, 15, 16, 17.—Col. 3, 5, 6.
1 Pet. 4, 2.—Ephes. 5, 5 to 7.
e) Math. 18, 3.—Acts 3, 19.
f) Luke 14, 33.—18, 22, 30.
g) " 9, 23 to 26.—14, 27.
h) Math. 19, 28, 29.—Galater 5, 24. 25. Eph. 5, 1, 2.
i) Acts 4, 31 to 37.—Zeph. 1, 18.
k) Eph. 1, 13, 14.—4, 30.—Eph. 1, 13.
l) Rev. 7, 2.—14, 1.—Ezek. 9, 4.

Printed and for Sale by G. S. Peters, Harrisburg, Pa.

Marxism offers Christians only an empty hope, not the blessed hope.

Varieties of Non-Western Millennialism

Speculation about a future that is millenarian in character occurs in many religious faiths. Some of this thought reflects Judeo-Christian influences, while in other cases the millennial ideas have arisen completely within indigenous belief systems. We must not try to reduce messianic-millennial movements to a common denominator. In fact, many movements that have a messianic quality—that is, they are led by a dynamic personality who challenges the existing order and tries to introduce a better one—are not necessarily millennialist as such. Although a millenarian movement usually has some charismatic or messianic figure as its head, it is also consciously oriented toward some sort of an eschatological kingdom or golden age in the future.

Keeping this warning in mind, we should recognize that some commonalities do exist among the literally hundreds of groups that manifest millenarian traits. To be sure, this is a matter of heated debate among anthropologists and religious studies scholars, but few of them would disagree with the following four points:

1. The movements are found among peoples who are on the margins or periphery of society. They feel deprived in some way, whether socially or economically, in comparison with those who have power in the society.

2. The members of a millenarian movement belong to well-defined groups with common beliefs, perspectives, goals, and sometimes allegiance to a single leader. At the same time, they are a corporate body capable of carrying on actions in a unified way, and others perceive them that way.

3. Some sort of catalytic agent enables the group members to articulate their feelings. This is usually an intermediary or charismatic figure who is in touch with the spirits or other supernatural body, and he or she sets up the short-term goals for the group, thereby giving the members a feeling of success and accomplishment.

4. The movement provides its adherents with some practical means of reaching the group's objectives, either by direct action or by waiting for its goals to be achieved through supernatural means.

To deal with these many millennial manifestations adequately would require

Fig. 5.4 Here Comes the Judge. This eighteenth-century depiction reminds us that God's judgment falls on all people and systems that fail to bow to the Lord of lords.

another book. We will attempt, however, to cite several examples that illustrate the variety of movements that have existed.

Malawian Millenarianism

One of the most interesting millennialist movements occurred in the Southeast African territory of Nyasaland, the present-day country of Malawi. A major influence in this movement was a British-born missionary, Joseph Booth, who began working in the area in 1892. He not only had extensive contacts within evangelical circles in Britain, Australia, South Africa, and the United States, but also with Charles T. Russell and his Watchtower movement (see chap. 4). Booth preached such radical doctrines that the British colonial authorities decided to expel him from Nyasaland. He relocated in South Africa but traveled to other countries as well. After visiting Russell at his headquarters, which at the time were in Pennsylvania, he brought the exhilarating new idea of the "millennial dawn" back to Africa. In 1907 a Malawian Christian named Elliott Kamwana met Booth in Cape Town and became convinced that the prophetic message of Christ's impending return was just what his people needed.

Between 1908 and 1909 Kamwana preached to vast crowds in his homeland, proclaiming that the new age was at hand. Christ would come in October 1914, abolish the existing forms of government, and put an end to the bitterly hated taxes that the colonial authorities imposed on the people. The white population would have to leave Nyasaland, and the Africans would thereafter govern themselves. It was estimated that he baptized at least ten thousand people into the new Watchtower faith before the British deported him as a dangerous radical. The grassroots movement spread rapidly through the territory and into the neighboring colonies, and its adherents saw the outbreak of war in 1914 as evidence that Christ was coming and they should start working for liberation. However, the Watchtower leaders did not support the use of direct action to overthrow colonial rule; rather they told their followers to wait patiently for divine intervention.

Some of the Watchtower people became affiliated with the Jehovah's Witnesses, as the movement would eventually be called, and submitted to its discipline, while others formed independent churches. The latter were much less willing to wait passively for the end to come and engaged in more overt forms of resistance to the colonial regimes. This sort of millennialist discontent spread widely through the African-initiated churches in Central Africa. There, followers longed for the new age in which they could adapt for their own purposes those aspects of European society that attracted them most, while exercising full control over their own homelands.

Rastafarians: From Babylon to Zion

The Rastafarian movement arose in the early 1930s in Jamaica as an indigenous black protest against capitalism and the economic woes of the depression. In recent years it has spread widely through the Caribbean, urban black communities in North America and Britain, and even into Africa proper. It takes its cue from Psalm 68:31, "Princes shall come out of Egypt; Ethiopia shall soon stretch out her hands unto God" (KJV), a passage that also had a strong impact on the development of independent churches in Africa. The key mythic event in its belief system was the ascension of Prince Ras Tafari, from whom the sect took its name "Rastafarian," to the throne of Ethiopia in the form of Emperor Haile Selassie on November 2, 1930.

The sect's adherents are best known for their unique dress and hair styles (their religiously unkempt dreadlocks), the sacramental use of marijuana in their rituals, refusal to eat pork or drink anything made from grapes, and reggae music.[21] More important, however, are their beliefs: Black people were exiled to the West Indies because of their moral transgressions; they are now sojourning in "Babylon," the evil, destructive force in the world that oppresses black people; the wicked white man is inferior to black people; and Haile Selassie is Jah, the true and living God who is the eternal life force of love and goodness.

The Ethiopian emperor, known as His Imperial Majesty (H.I.M.), is the personification of Christ the Messiah, the king who arose out of the house of David, the fulfillment of the prophecies of Daniel and Revelation. In accordance with Jeremiah 8:21 ("For the hurt of the daughter of my people am I hurt; I am black; astonishment hath taken hold on me" [KJV]), Rastafarians believe that God is black. The god of the whites is the devil, the instigator of all evils that have come upon the world. The white god is one of hate, blood, oppression, and war, while the black god is one of peace and love. The fact that H.I.M. died physically in 1975 changed nothing. Selassie lives eternally, and his spiritual presence is with them in all that they do. They have a vague millennial vision that their god-figure will return from the dead, arrange for Africans to return to their homeland, and set up a new order in which white people will serve blacks.

Babylon has been responsible for the suffering in the world, but through the power of Jah and resistance by the Rastafari, freedom may be obtained through a sort of spiritual/physical repatriation. With the destruction of Babylon, black humanity will attain unity in Zion. However, Rastas are extremely vague as to what this Zion really means. Is it a heaven on earth to which blacks will come in a physical exodus, or is it transcendent/spiritual reality? We cannot be sure. Rastafarianism is a widespread form of social protest, and because of the diversity within the movement itself, some scholars question whether it should even be regarded as a millenarian sect any longer.

Fig. 5.5 Bridges to Babylon. Haile Selassie, the Rastafarian prophet, messiah, God, is pictured late in his regal career.

A Not So Shining Path

A totally secular millenarian sect is the Shining Path (*Sendero Luminoso*), an extremely violent Maoist communist movement in Peru. It is a peasant-based movement (but led by urban intellectuals) that seeks to mobilize the ethnic and racial hostility of the majority Indian population against the white-controlled political system. The *Sendero* ideology is that of Marxism, the inevitable march forward

to the goal of communism. In the holy war against the established European elite, destruction, suffering, and death are a cleansing process that will permit building anew. The new order will reverse the system that has only brought false promises and suffering to the marginalized majority of Peruvians. The apocalyptic destruction will turn back five hundred years of conquest and bring in a primeval rule of bliss.

The idea of restoring pre-European social relationships in the Andes seems to fly in the face of Marxist ideology, but the group's ideology reflects how Marxian millennial concepts can be used selectively to try to bring back an egalitarian golden age that in fact never existed.

Islamic Millennial Elements

Islam, particularly the Shi'ite branch that wields power in present-day Iran, exhibits a very potent millenarian thrust. One element in this is the institution of the Mahdi, "the rightly guided one," who would restore true religion and redress injustice. This figure entered the history of Islam in the 680s and became a distinct feature of radical Shi'ite sects. Many believed that a hidden leader, or Imam, would eventually return as the Mahdi and bring justice to the world. He then would preside over the end of the world and the last judgment.

The leader of the Safavid movement in early sixteenth-century Persia, Shah Ismail, claimed to be the lieutenant of the

156

Hidden Imam, and the dynasty's reign was to continue until his reappearance as the Mahdi. Eventually the doctrine ossified as a support for the Iranian dynasty, and from time to time new persons appeared claiming to be the Mahdi and challenging the power of the ruler. One of these, Ali Muhammad of Shiraz, also known as the Bab because he claimed to be the Bab, or the gateway, to the Hidden Imam, proclaimed in Mecca in 1844 that he was the Mahdi. His followers even utilized Islamic cabalistic-type numerology to prove that he was foreseen in the Koran. He led a millenarian uprising against the Iranian government and preached the common ownership of property, but he was captured and executed in 1850 and his movement was brutally repressed. He would later be venerated by the Bahai faith as one of its forerunners.

Other Mahdis appeared in the Islamic world from time to time, perhaps the most noteworthy being Muhammad Ahmed, who led a resistance movement against the British who were trying to take over the upper Nile region. His victory at Khartoum in 1885 (which resulted in the death of the colorful General Charles Gordon) was a major setback for European imperialism, although a few years later with modern weaponry the British were able to gain the upper hand.

In Iran the idea of the Mahdi was a motivating factor in the constitutional revolution of 1906 to 1911, but much more important was the revival of the idea in the 1960s. The modernization and secularization of the Iranian educational and political system had undermined the plausibility of the literal reappearance of the Hidden Imam as the Mahdi, but Islamic traditionalists used the idea to challenge the educated intellectuals in charge of the country. The idea was taken over by the radicals, the People's Mujahedin, as the struggle to restore a classless, egalitarian society that had been perverted by exploitation, oppression, and monopolistic power by the dominant classes who possessed wealth. The radicals would combat the great idol of their times, imperialism, and bring about the victory of the masses.

The Ayatollah Ruhollah Khomeini exploited these kinds of feelings by encouraging his acceptance as the Imam. He was able to draw upon the millennialistic expectations of his followers to oust the Shah, Mohammed Reza Pahlavi, from power, which occurred in the last year of the fourteenth century according to the Islamic calendar (1979 in the Western calendar). He was welcomed back to Iran by millions of enthusiastic supporters who saw him as the Imam of the Age, the Mahdi himself. Some enthusiasts were prepared to declare him officially as the Hidden Imam and march on Jerusalem to proclaim his reappearance as the Mahdi and to witness the reappearance of Jesus Christ and his final conversion to Islam. However, the humiliating defeat in the war with Iraq, the inability to dislodge the Jewish state from Palestine, and Khomeini's own death in 1989 took much of the steam out of the millenarian immediacy of the Iranian revolution.

Cargo Millenarianism

Melanesia, the region in the Southwestern Pacific that includes New Guinea and other nearby archipelagos, is the site of a millenarianism based on the idea that a messianic figure would arrive bringing material riches (European goods) and would liberate the people from colonial rule. Adherents looked for the individual to come with the "cargo," first by water (the "Great White Ship") and later by airplane, and when the cargo arrived they would surely have a happier life. They felt they had a right to these goods because in a way they were the product of the entire society. The movement also functioned as a form of moral renewal, promoting a rededication to the values of the community.

Some adherents were influenced by Christian missionary work, particularly the Seventh-day Adventists, whose Melanesia field is one of its most important. Christian millennialism was quite attractive because it seemed to be the way to unlock the door to the white man's cargo. "But seek first his kingdom and his righteousness, and all these things will be given to you as well" (Matt. 6:33) was a widely used prooftext. The acquisition of material goods would follow the acceptance of Christ.

Most of the sects that fit under the heading cargo millenarianism had a hodgepodge of traditional and Christian beliefs, and it is impossible to generalize satisfactorily about them. The groups, diverse in nature from the beginning, were also heavily affected by the changes that have resulted from the introduction of Western culture into Melanesia since World War II.

There is such a variety of messianic movements in non-Christian religious traditions that it is difficult to categorize all of them as millenarian. A significant difference exists between the concept of *revitalization,* the term coined by anthropologist Anthony Wallace that means a "conscious, organized effort by members of a society to construct a more satisfying culture," and a genuinely millenarian movement.[22] The terms *millennial* and *millenarian* are used interchangeably in the literature to characterize a wide variety of primary resistance movements to the influences of Western culture and political and economic power. Thus, such complex upheavals as the Tai-ping movement in China in the 1850s, Maji-Maji in East Africa (1905–6), Saya San in Burma (1930–32), and Mataram in Java (1825–30) have been characterized as millenarian protest movements. The same has been true for such African independent church movements as the Lenshina and other Ethiopian churches in southern Africa and the Kimbanguists in the Belgian Congo and Zaire.

Millenarian Speculation about the Blessed Virgin Mary

The veneration of Mary, the mother of Jesus, has always been a troubling matter for the Roman Catholic Church. In medieval times it represented a people's religion that was more or less forced upon the hierarchy of the church from the bottom up. Although the official church has taken an amillennial view of the return of Christ, devotion to the Virgin Mary represents a route by which apocalyptic speculation has entered by the back door.

According to one writer on Marian "cults" (a technical term used by scholars to categorize organized divergent subgroups in a major religion), there have been hundreds if not thousands of "documented" visitations by the Virgin since the time of Christ, and, in fact, they have substantially increased in number since the Protestant Reformation.[23] Most of these incidents were visions to groups of small, deeply devout children. Commonly labeled as "apparitions," they involved the physical presence of Mary. Several favored people could see her and communicate with her at one time. Prior to the Second Vatican Council (1962–65) seeing and speaking with the Virgin were key elements of Catholic spirituality. In fact, throughout the history of the Roman Catholic Church, mystics and seers from Nostradamus to Anna-Katarina Emmerick to Lucia dos Santos were upheld as the true authorities of faith, the ones who were given prophetic insight into the final drama of world history.

The most significant of the more recent encounters with the Virgin took place at La Salette (1846), Lourdes (1858), Fatima (1917), Garabandal (1961), and Medjugorje (1981). The vision at Lourdes, France, was seen by a fourteen-year-old girl named Bernadette Subirious and had only to do with her personal future. The others dealt with messages for the endtime that involved all humanity. The appearance to two shepherd children at La Salette, France, involved a prophecy of horrible catastrophes that would beset the church and the world because of their sinfulness. One of the children, Melanie Calvat, later wrote a small book outlining the content of the Virgin's message. The apparition at San Sebastian de Garabandal, Spain, began with four small children and involved over two thousand appearances over a two-year period. The secrets revealed to Conchita Gonzáles are the first modern source of information about the chastisement, a popular endtime theme of contemporary Catholic apocalypticism.

One set of apparitions, those at Medjugorje in Herzegovina in the former Yugoslavia, seems to be ongoing. In 1981 Mary appeared to six peasant children, and within days crowds of thousands gathered at the place to pray to the Virgin. Before long this became an international sensation, and pilgrims flocked by the busload and even planeload to the tiny village, searching for some contact with the supernatural. The revelations at Medjugorje

Fig. 5.6 Our Lady of Lourdes. The Procession of the Blessed Sacrament is a daily occurrence at Lourdes, a shrine to Mary that two million pilgrims visit each year in search of miracles.

a matter of intense conflict among theologians and church figures in the area.

The most famous encounter with Mary involved three illiterate young shepherds, Lucia dos Santos and her cousins Francisco and Jacinta, at Fatima, Portugal, in May 1917. The Virgin promised the children a miracle if they would come to the same place and pray on the thirteenth of each month. Five months later, on October 13, as she promised, a miracle was performed before a crowd of fifty thousand people when the sun seemed to dance in the sky, tremble, and fall. An official Roman Catholic commission declared the revelation to the children to be authentic and authorized the establishment of a formal cult (a group that pays special devotion to a saint) of Our Lady of Fatima. Although Francisco and Jacinta died within three years of the event, Lucia entered a convent and, with approval of the bishop in August 1941, wrote her recollection of the vision. She stated that she had received three major prophecies. The first was a vision of hell in all its horrors, which awaited all those who did not follow Mary's words. The second revelation showed that a conflict worse than World War I (just then ending) would sweep over the earth during the pontificate of Pius XI (1922–39) if Russia was not consecrated to Mary's Immaculate Heart, that is, to Roman Catholicism. Since Hitler had seized the Sudetenland region of Czechoslovakia through the Munich agreement in 1938, the event that set Eu-

concerned not only personal matters for the seers and details of the Virgin's life not known before, but also ten secrets. The precise details were not spelled out to the public, but these secrets seem to indicate that the end of the age is near and that the severity of the coming judgment might be moderated if people would repent and be converted (to Catholicism). Interpretation of the events at Medjugorje are currently rope on the road to World War II, many believed the prophecy was fulfilled.

As a result, many felt Lucia's third prophecy or secret would also come to pass. The story of the third secret reads like a detective novel. Because of mounting pressure on her to relate the third secret, in 1944 she wrote it out and sent it in a sealed envelope to the Bishop of Fatima-Leira. Fearing to open it himself, the bishop in 1957 persuaded the pope to accept it. In 1960 John XXIII apparently read the letter but said nothing about its contents. His successors, Paul VI and John Paul II, also read the letter and decided not to divulge its contents. As far as we know, it is still being kept under lock and key in the Vatican. Dozens of books have appeared about the grim forebodings of this third secret of Fatima.

In 1954 and 1957 Lucia dos Santos gave some hints to interviewers about this third secret. On the first occasion she indicated that world conditions were so bad that the end was near. In the second interview she let slip the idea that a monumental struggle was about to occur for the souls of the world. If Russia were left unconsecrated, it would become God's instrument of judgment. It would spread errors throughout the world, start wars, annihilate nations, and persecute the church. It was clear that the Fatima myth was linked to the Cold War, giving it power among the grassroots of the church.

For example, the popular American bishop Fulton J. Sheen went to Fatima on October 31, 1951, where the end of a holy year was being celebrated. One hundred thousand people had gathered at the vision site and were waving white handkerchiefs. Sheen, an outspoken anticommunist, reported that the faithful had turned the place into a "white square." He said that the Bolshevik Revolution and the apparitions at Fatima had both begun in 1917. Thirty-four years had passed since then, and in another thirty-four years one of the two phenomena would cease to exist. "What will disappear will be a dictator reviewing his troops in the Red Square; what will survive will be a Lady reviewing her children in the White Square."[24] He foresaw a future day when, as the result of the sacrifices and prayers of the "millions in the White Square," the symbol of the hammer on the red flag would look like a cross and the sickle would look like the moon under Mary's feet. A Marian date setter might venture to say Sheen's prophecy was fulfilled, since Mikhail Gorbachev came to power thirty-four years later.

As interpreted by apocalyptic Marianists, Pius XII and John Paul II, the two popes who went even further and consecrated the entire world to Mary, had fallen short of what the Virgin at Fatima had demanded. The popes were supposed to carry out this consecration in unison with all the bishops of the world, and Russia was to be specifically mentioned in their action. However, since the Second Vatican Council many bishops and church bu-

161

reaucrats had become communist sympathizers and so it was unlikely they would ever follow Mary's orders.

Catholic apocalypticists represent a premillennial current within the Roman church, and they believe they are getting their directions from the Virgin Mary through a variety of sources. Although they do not agree on the details of the prophetic utterances, most of them accept a three-stage analysis of the last days. First, there will be a great collapse of faith or apostasy when Catholics abandon their religion and turn to secularism. An anti-pope will seize power in Rome, and the true church will be reduced to a persecuted remnant. Communism or something equivalent to it, such as secular humanism or the New World Order, will assume totalitarian control over the entire world. A "Great Pontiff" and a "Great Monarch" (Great Pope and Great King), however, will, through God's empowering hand, lead the true church in a counterattack against the forces of evil. In the course of this chastisement the world will be ravaged by floods, earthquakes, droughts, and plagues, many of which will result from comets striking the earth.

This leads to the second stage in which the Great Pope and the Great King conquer evil and establish peace and prosperity on the earth. The church will be renewed and millions converted as the spiritual and temporal powers cooperate in doing God's work. The Catholic utopia, however, will not last forever.

A third and final stage will occur in which people will turn once again away from the truth, and history will end with a final battle and the last judgment. There are some variations on this fundamental theme. For example, some Marians teach that in the first stage true Catholics will be raptured and thereby escape the chastisement. They will be carried off into a supernatural realm of the eternal Father where they will await the return of Mary's son to earth.

The demise of communism put a heavy strain on the Marianists who followed the Fatima interpretation, just as it did on those Protestant fundamentalists who had declared that Russia and communism were foretold in the Scriptures. Thus, they replaced communism with a new hit list of evils—drug addiction, family breakdown, abortion, war, political corruption, the United Nations, and the New World Order. Some Marian groups even believe that the pope is an imposter and that the Vatican is run by the Freemasons, Jews, and communists.

Catholic sociologist Michael W. Cuneo, who has closely studied Marian movements, explains why this sort of apocalypticism continues to find so many adherents in the church, from the Baysiders of Queens, New York (followers of the seeress Veronica Lueken who had apparitions of the Virgin), to the masses who gazed at a supposed image of Mary on the glass side of a building in Clearwater, Florida. The Second Vatican Council, which introduced the most far-reaching changes in the history of church, was the catalytic event. Before the council, popular devotionalism in the church contained a strong component of magic. Holy pictures and statues, votive candles, relics, and medals all seemed to possess supernatural power. If these were approached properly and with the right sort of piety, they could assist in bringing about miraculous healings and other benefits. But the modernization and rationalization of the church that had been in process for some time, and which came to its final fruition at Vatican II, left people with a church that was much less mysterious and enchanted than before and considerably more distant from the concerns of everyday life.

Thus, the reaction to Vatican II and its transformation of the church varied widely. Some, the separatists, simply rejected the council's decrees and refused to have anything to do with the new order. Others, conservatives, remained in the church but criticized the changes. The Marianists, however, made up a third group that turned to a realm of miraculous apparitions and mystical prophecy.

The separatists retreated into isolation by emphasizing traditionalism of all kinds (such as the Latin mass), while the conservatives stressed moral purification through activities such as fighting abortion and maintaining male dominance in the clergy. The Marianists saw the Virgin as taking an active role in history by delivering messages of hope and warning to the suffering faithful. In their view she transmits these to especially appointed seers, spells out the exact steps Catholics must take in order to gain salvation, and lays out the punishments for those who refuse to heed her instructions. However, these are not just a form of spiritual consolation. They reveal that in an age in which any expression of religious passion is greeted with scorn, here is direct evidence that miracles continue to take place and that forces greater than nature and the human will still rule the world. And the vengeful Virgin is ready to move against scoffers who deny this.[25]

It is clear that millions of Catholics believe the new millennium will bring in the era of peace and prosperity that the Virgin has prophesied. Numbered among them may be none other than Pope John Paul II, as he has advanced Marian devotion to new heights in the church and, in the opinion of some, may be about to declare Mary co-redemptrix with Christ. In addition, the pope has fueled Catholic apocalyptic expectations by declaring 2000 a jubilee year in Rome. This is likely to lead to an increase in millennial pilgrimages to Jerusalem and other religiously significant cities.[26]

Catholic Apocalyptic Streams

While there is much disagreement on interpretation, the following passage is typical of various strains of Catholic apocalyptic thought.

Precisions on the Great Disaster

These "precisions," that is, specific levels that will take place in the future, run from 12 to 75. Since they are repeated in many different prophecies, it is not possible to treat them separately. Each of the paragraphs, therefore, may contain one or more of these predictions.

General Events

- Not a two-camp war, but only a multi-sided war.
- Not a war only, but a world-wide revolution as well.
- Not simply a man-made holocaust, but also a God-sent chastisement, accompanied by cosmic disturbances.
- To last about four years.

Particular Events

The whole world will be involved in the fighting. A unique feature is the internal disintegration of the Western democracies and the invasion of Western Europe by Arab forces.

The roles of the U.S.A. and U.S.S.R. are not clear in the beginning. The U.S.A. may be involved in the Far-East or at home or both. The U.S.S.R. may want to keep out of the fray at first, while abetting the Arab world, or may be involved in Siberia.

Civil wars rage in Western Europe. The Church is persecuted; the Pope leaves Rome and dies in exile; an anti-pope is installed in Rome; the Catholic Church is split, leaderless and completely disorganized. Communism is victorious. The Mohammedans invade Europe and commit innumerable atrocities.

In the West, however, Christians rally around an unexpected leader, an army officer of royal blood, but their chances seem very slim.

The natural disturbances begin: floods, droughts, famines.

A comet approaches the earth: Whole mountains split open; huge tidal waves swallow up low-lying lands; stones fall from the sky; a deadly fog or gas poisons the atmosphere; a prolonged darkness envelops the earth. Two-thirds or three-fourths of the human race is wiped out.

The powers of evil are shattered. The Christian Prince leads his growing army to battle and wins victory upon victory. In West Germany he crushes a Germano-Russian Army. Communism collapses everywhere. The Mohammedans are thrown back to the sea. The war is carried to Africa and the Middle East, where the Arab Power is dealt a deadly blow. At this stage, if not earlier, U.S. troops come to the assistance of Western Europe.

Russia and China are converted to Catholicism, as also are the Moham- ▶

medans. All non-Catholics return to the Mother Church. A holy Pope is elected; he shows great firmness; and he restores all the former disciplines in the Church.

All the nations of Western Europe unite and form a new Roman Empire, and accept as their emperor the great Christian Prince, chosen by God, who works hand-in-hand with the holy Pope. The triumph of the Catholic Church is universal.

The whole world enjoys a period of complete peace and unprecedented prosperity in mutual love and respect among people and nations.

This great peace will last until the coming of Antichrist.

Source: Yves Dupont, *Catholic Prophecy: The Coming Chastisement* (Rockford, Ill.: Tan Books and Publishers, Inc., 1970, 1973), 90–91. No changes have been made in the original wording. Used by permission.

Prophetic Perils

Despite the importance of the doctrine of the return of Christ, it should be approached with a good deal of modesty and caution. We have seen myriad examples of those who have not heeded this warning. However, some glaring abuses of prophetic interpretation have recently reemerged that need to be carefully evaluated. They demonstrate the promise and peril of prophetic speculation. And if we haven't learned already, they confirm the truth in regard to prophetic predictions that "there is nothing new under the sun" (Eccl. 1:9).

Occultic Prophecy

Evangelical Protestantism is plagued with apocalyptic extremism. Some evangelical prophecy buffs are not content with simply extracting their conceptions of the future from the words of Scripture alone.

Rejecting the historic understanding of the sufficiency of Scripture, they have turned to extrabiblical or "occultic" sources to find information. The word *occult* conjures up all sorts of ideas about black magic, incense-filled rooms, and crystal balls, but in fact it simply means "hidden." It refers to something not obvious to the normal viewer. One needs another to reveal these hidden truths. In fact, many sincere Christians have engaged in the questionable practice of going outside the Scriptures to find concealed truths about God and his plan for the ages.

Some have looked to the stars for hidden messages from God and turned to the ancient study known as astrology. The best-known works on the topic were published in the nineteenth century—*The Gospel in the Stars* (1884) by Joseph A. Seiss and *The Witness of the Stars* (1893) by E. W. Bullinger—and they are still read today by prophecy enthusiasts. The approach is justified by reference to various prooftexts: Psalm 19:1: "The heavens de-

Nostradamus: The Man Who Saw Tomorrow

Michel de Nostredame—Nostradamus—(1503–66) was born in France to Jewish parents who converted to Christianity. A physician who served as a plague doctor in rural France, he became interested in astrology and prophecy. As he approached his fiftieth birthday he began to compose prophetic four-line verses (quatrains) that he arranged in groups of one hundred. Ten books of verses were eventually written and published as *Centuries,* a book which, according to devotees of the seer, has prophesied an amazing number of future world events. His vague, cryptic predictions have fascinated the gullible for centuries.

Equally obscure and random interpretation of Nostradamus's verses by his followers have allowed them to attribute such forecasts to him as the following:

"August 15, 1769: The birth of Napoleon Bonaparte. Nostradamus's first anti-christ.

"An emperor will be born near Italy. / He will cost his empire dearly; they / will say that from the sort of people / who surround him that he is less a / prince than a butcher. C1 Q60*

"1889: The birth of Hitler. Nostradamus saw Hitler as the second anti-christ and possibly the greatest demagogue in our history. The prophet's belief was that each of the three anti-christs named would, in escalating degree, bring humanity closer to the final holocaust. Hitler, named as 'Hister,' was responsible for the death of fifty million people during a six-year war costing the world billions of dollars. He set standards of horror that even modern statesman would find hard to equal.

"From the deepest part of Western Europe, / A young child will be born to poor people: / Who by his speech will seduce a great multitude, / His reputation will increase in the / Kingdom of the East. C3 Q35

"The 20th century: Nostradamus saw the 20th century as an evil and mechanized time in which every one would be numbered, recorded, categorized, and organized.

"Before long everything will be organized / We wait a very evil century: / The lot of the masked and solitary / ones (clergy) greatly changed, / Few will be found who wish to stay in their places. C2 Q10

"The 1980s: The third anti-christ was named directly by Nostradamus, as were the first and the second. If we are to accept his 'system' of warning us of future trends, then it is possible that this third 'demagogue' lives today and is named 'Mabus.'

"Mabus will soon die, then will come / A horrible slaughter of people and animals, / At once vengeance is revealed coming / from a hundred hands / Thirst, and famine when the comet will pass. ▶

"September 1993: The great pestilence—AIDS. The prophet spoke in some detail about another vast plague which would strike man and he alludes to it being a plague of the blood and of semen. The references are difficult to dispute in many cases and seem most closely to apply to the relatively new disease—Acquired Immune Deficiency Syndrome. According to Nostradamus's estimates, this plague, in any event, will infect half of the world by the mid-1990s.

"A horrible war which is being / prepared for the West, / The following year the pestilence will come, / So very horrible that young nor old, nor animal (may survive). / Blood, fire, Mercury, Mars, Jupiter in France. (September 1993) C9 Q55

"July 1999: The last conflagration. Nostradamus dates the holocaust at '1999 and seven months.' This will be the culmination of the twenty-seven years of war and the final destruction of the civilized world.

"In the year 1999 and seven months / The great King of Terror will come / from the sky / He will resurrect Ghengis Khan / Before and after war rules happily. C10 Q72

"2026–3000: A thousand years of peace. The prophet predicts one thousand years of peace in which a galactic community becomes a reality and man enters a period where science and religion merge into a higher consciousness. In this period, toward its

MICHEL NOSTRADAMUS.
Médecin,
Né à S.¹ Remy, en Provence, le 14 Décemb 1503.
Mort le 2 juillet 1566.

Fig. 5.7 I Predict. Nostradamus, the so-called prophet, is pictured here.

end he warns of too much knowledge turning us toward selfishness and the manipulation of others.

"When the seventh millennium has come (2000 A.D.) / There will then be a hecatomb which / will occur close to the millennnium / end. Then those who entered the tomb / will leave. C10 Q74"

Source: John Hogue, *Nostradamus and the Millennium*, 198ff. Copyright © 1987 by John Hogue. Used by permission of Doubleday, a division of Bantam Doubleday Dell Publishing Group, Inc.

*C=Centuries
Q=Quatrains

clare the glory of God"; Job 38:32: "Can you bring forth the constellations in their seasons?"; Romans 1:20: "For since the creation of the world God's invisible qualities—his eternal power and divine nature—have been clearly seen, being understood from what has been made, so that men are without excuse"; and Luke 21:25: "There will be signs in the sun, moon and stars."

The Christian stargazers set out to decode the messages that allegedly are to be found in the group of constellations that comprise the zodiac, a concept which of course is anything but biblical in origin. (Generally the Babylonians or Egyptians are credited with creating the zodiac.) They begin with Virgo because the Christian era began with the virgin birth. Then they move to Libra (the Scales), which contains constellations portraying the cross and the crown. Scorpio contains a serpent struggling with a man. Constellations in Sagittarius (the Archer) portray the harp, the altar, and the dragon. The zodiac continues across the sky with Aquarius (the Water Bringer), which symbolizes Christ pouring out the waters of blessing, and Taurus (the Bull), containing the constellation Orion, which shows light breaking forth in the person of the Redeemer. Finally, Leo (the Lion) represents Christ returning as the lion. Some mark Aries (the Ram or Lamb) as the second coming constellation, while others identify Cancer the Crab as the one. In the latter, Ursa Minor (the Little Bear) represents the church

safely ensconced in heaven when the dragon is cast down to the earth and, thus, is the rapture constellation.

To put the matter in simple terms, these stargazers no longer need the Bible. The source of truth has shifted from the text to the twilight; one need only gaze into the sky on a clear night to receive God's message.

Pyramid Numerology

If the hidden message in the stars seems unusual, the infatuation with the Great Pyramid of Giza, briefly touched on in the previous chapter, is even more so. This study, labeled by its enthusiasts as "pyramidology," draws its biblical support from Revelation 11:1, where the seer was instructed to "go and measure the temple." According to them, the statement really means the divine model of the spiritual temple, which is the Great Pyramid.

The most widely used prooftext is Isaiah 19:19: "In that day there will be an altar to the LORD in the heart of Egypt, and a monument to the LORD at its border." Other passages refer to Jesus as the stone the builders rejected (e.g., Matt. 21:42; Acts 4:11; or 1 Peter 2:7). The Greek term here is literally "chief stone of the corner," and some Bible versions translate it as "cornerstone," while others (such as the NIV) render it as "capstone." Pyramidologists point out that the capstone is missing from the Giza Pyramid, and they draw a variety of parallelisms and allegories with biblical events from the measurements of the

Pyramid and its inner chambers and passageways. They call it a "Bible in stone," the "Lord's pillar," or the "stone of witness" and claim it is a chronological chart of the history of Israel. Moreover, they say it indicates that we are now at the end of the church age, and the battle of Armageddon and the beginning of Christ's reign on earth are at hand.

In the nineteenth century various biblical scholars became intrigued with this massive pile of stone, the largest structure to survive from the ancient world. Erected by the ruler of the Fourth Dynasty, Pharaoh Khufu (or Cheops, the Greek form of his name) around 2500 B.C., the Great Pyramid is one of many pyramids located on the edge of the desert west of the Nile River between Cairo and Memphis. It is the only one, however, that has been regarded as a source of occult knowledge.

The origins of pyramidology can be traced back to British writer John Taylor's 1859 book *The Great Pyramid,* which suggested the Pyramid's various features made up a prophetic record that harmonized with biblical revelation. Soon after, Charles Piazzi Smyth and Robert Menzies popularized Taylor's ideas, and Seiss and Bullinger published their substantial works. The body of literature has continued to grow in the twentieth century.

Interestingly, many of the present-day adherents to pyramidology also accept the British-Israel theory, discussed in chapter 1. According to this theory Britain and America are the linear descendants of the Ten Lost Tribes who were taken into captivity by Assyria in the eighth century B.C., migrated across Western Asia and Europe in unbelief, and eventually settled in the British Isles. They are the true heirs to the Old Testament promises made to Israel, while modern-day Jews make up the false Israel who rejected Christ as their Messiah and in turn were rejected by God. As noted above, the theory's most fervent exponents are found in the virulently racist and anti-Semitic Christian Identity movement. In spite of this, British-Israelism has some following among evangelical prophecy buffs, while pyramidology has found its way into contemporary evangelical prophetic works, including Hal Lindsey's *The Late Great Planet Earth* and Edgar Whisenant's *88 Reasons Why the Rapture Will Be in 1988.*

The pyramidologists measure the exterior dimensions and the interior corridors, passageways, and rooms in the Pyramid and then match them with various things mentioned in Scripture. Thus, the small shaft leading upward from the entrance represents the Old Testament period of the law and the prophets. It then turns into a twenty-eight-foot-high passage called the Grand (or Great) Gallery, which signifies the age of grace. A smaller Queen's Chamber, which represents the church, has access to this through a separate corridor. At the top of the Grand Gallery is a low doorway, which signifies the great tribulation. Then one enters the King's Chamber, thirty-four by seventeen feet and nineteen feet high, which symbolizes

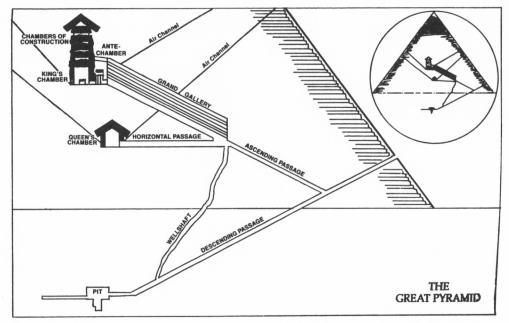

Fig. 5.8 Pyramid Power. This line drawing shows some of the interior elements of the Great Pyramid of Giza.

the second coming of Christ and the millennial kingdom. Beneath the Pyramid is a chamber called the pit, which means hell, and the large descending passage to it indicates that the path to hell is broad. A small shaft leading from this passage to the Grand Gallery symbolizes the narrow way of escape.

The pyramidologists calculate the various distances and dimensions and translate them into different units of time. They use a measure called the "pyramid inch," which is one millimeter longer than an English inch. The argument is that it takes 10,011 standard inches to make up a "divine cubit." The inches are converted into years (or months or days, as the case may be), and then significant historical dates—past and future—are plugged into them. Since these project into the future as well, prophecies can be made. One early pyramidologist concluded from his measurements that the tribulation would begin in 1914. William Alnor cites other pyramid experts who set such varying dates for the Lord's return as 1908, 1928, 1944, and 1953.[27] When the predictions failed, pyramidologists simply redefined their units of measurement and suggested new dates. It is thus no surprise that a second coming date popular with current pyramidologists is September 17, 2001.

170

Christians have good reason to reject the Great Pyramid as a source of hidden revelation, as the noted evangelical Bible teacher Wilbur M. Smith so ably pointed out. For one thing, why would God conceal his message for humankind only in this pyramid and not in any of the others along the Nile? Second, Egyptologists who studied the Pyramid found that alterations were made in its interior structure at various times in history. This is not God's way; he does not change. He gave specific directions for constructing the tabernacle in the wilderness and the temple in Jerusalem, and these were never altered. Third, the idea of some pyramidologists that a godly Old Testament character such as Enoch, Melchizedek, or Job built the Pyramid has no basis in fact. It simply is a pagan structure erected by Egyptian architects.[28] In addition, date setting using Pyramid measurements has always ended in failure. The dates of predicted events developed according to "arithmetic of time" have passed by unfulfilled, and the pyramidologists have had to keep going back to their measuring tapes.

The foolishness of using numerology for any prophetic purpose should be patently obvious to any thinking person, and the ludicrousness has often been demonstrated. For example, a French scholar announced, tongue in cheek, that he had discovered that if one were to subtract the number of people who took part in the Last Supper (13) from the number of steps and landings in the Eiffel Tower (1,927), the result would be the prediction of the date of the First World War's beginning.[29] To give another illustration, literary scholar Kathryn Lindskoog sent to her friends on the Internet the following "revelation" that shows the limitless potentialities of numerology:

Given: Barney is a cute purple dinosaur
Prove: Barney is really the Antichrist in disguise

1. Start with the given:
   C U T E P U R P L E
   D I N O S A U R

2. Change all U's to V's
   (which is proper Latin anyway):
   C V T E P V R P L E
   D I N O S A V R

3. Extract all Roman numerals in the phrase:
   C V V L D I V

4. Convert these into Arabic values:
   100 5 5 50 500 1 5

5. Add all the numbers:
   666

There you have it. Is this just a coincidence?

The bottom line is that every attempt to find hidden revelations in the stars, the Great Pyramid, or through number games results in absurdity. To put it bluntly, occultic revelation does not take place, whether in the sky, stones, or numbers.

The Bible Code

However, Christians looking for hidden revelations do not give up easily. This became clear in 1997 when a book by journalist Michael Drosnin entitled *The Bible Code* vaulted on to the best-seller lists. It was also reviewed in major newspapers and magazines and widely discussed on national television. Its publisher, Simon & Schuster, ran full-page newspaper ads containing the extravagant claim: "In all of history, few books have completely changed the way we view the world. The Bible was one. *The Bible Code* is another."

Regardless of the fact that both mathematicians and serious Bible scholars maintained the book's line of argumentation was lacking in scholarly substance—some even labeled it a literary con job—both the author and publisher made a lot of money from the sales generated by all the attention it attracted. It is safe to say that Drosnin himself was an opportunist who had stumbled on to a good deal. As a self-acknowledged agnostic Jew, he cared little about the deeper religious meaning of the material that he had presented. Nevertheless, many Jews and evangelical Protestants, and those in the general public as well, were deceived by his facile and sensational assertions.

The book is based on the premise that hidden messages are contained in the Hebrew text of the Bible, the Old Testament. They can be discovered by using a mathematical procedure called "Equidistant Letter Sequence" or "Equal Letter Skip" (ELS for short) to analyze the physical structure of a text. The idea is to start with a letter in the text and then skip ahead a predetermined number of letters. For example, if you start with the first letter *t* in Genesis and skip forty-nine letters, the fiftieth is an *o*, the next fiftieth after that is an *r*, and the fiftieth after that is an *h*, thus spelling out the word *Torh*, the Hebrew word for the law or Scripture. The reader who takes seriously the divine inspiration of the Bible would naturally be impressed by this apparent testimony to God's handiwork. Then he or she will be even more overwhelmed with joy to learn that there are many more words and prophetic messages encoded in the Hebrew text.

Actually, the idea of looking for such hidden revelations in Scripture is nothing new. The cabalists, mentioned in chapter 4, developed a rudimentary procedure for doing so hundreds of years ago. More recently, Ivan Panin (d. 1942), an essentially unknown Russian mathematician who emigrated to Canada, spent fifty years studying "biblical numerics" to prove that the text of the Bible was genuinely the Word of God. He produced some forty thousand pages of numerical data analyzing the words of both the Old and New Testaments, and he was particularly interested in finding usages of the number seven, which is the number of divine perfection.

In the last few years a Jewish-Christian scholar, Jacov Rambsel, has been working on Isaiah 53 and other Old Testament texts and claims to have found the "Messiah codes," which reveal much detail about Jesus. Most importantly, a Canadian evangelist and Bible teacher named Grant R. Jeffrey has written about biblical numerics in such best-selling books as *Armageddon: Appointment with Destiny* (1988; 2d ed., 1997), *The Signature of God: Astonishing Biblical Discoveries* (1996), *The Handwriting of God: Sacred Mysteries of the Bible* (1997), and *The Mysterious Bible Codes* (1998). Jeffrey publishes his works and those of Rambsel through his own firm, Frontier Research Publications in Toronto. Although he is a relatively new face on the prophecy scene, his books and videos have attracted considerable attention in evangelical circles.

Jeffrey and other Bible code enthusiasts welcomed Drosnin's book, and their assertions went much farther than the journalist's relatively modest ones. Among the things they claim to have found hidden in the Hebrew text are the names of thirty-four prominent rabbis from the ninth to the eighteenth centuries; words associated with the twentieth-century Holocaust (including Hitler, Nazis, Auschwitz, Eichmann, *Mein Kampf,* genocide, and Holocaust); the assassination of Israeli Prime Minister Yitzhak Rabin; the Persian Gulf War of 1991 (including George Bush, Saddam, Schwarzkopf, Scud-B, and other names); the bombing of the Murrah Federal Building in Oklahoma City in 1995; and two recent massacres by Palestinian

---

It's All in the Numbers

Revelation 13:18 makes the following connection with the Antichrist: "If anyone has insight, let him calculate the number of the beast, for it is man's number. His number is 666."

Just as the number 13 is viewed by the superstitious as one to avoid, some people feel even more strongly about the number found in Revelation 13:18. A 1997 newspaper story reported that five men who contended their Social Security numbers were the "mark of the beast" were allowed to use other forms of identification to apply for their California driver's license. A Superior Court judge ruled in their favor, commenting that the men "sincerely held religous convictions . . . that anyone who uses his or her Social Security number is in danger of not receiving eternal life." The number in question was 666.

Source: Grand Rapids Press, 1 November 1997, p. B4.

---

terrorists. Even the names of Jesus and his disciples, the women followers, the high priests, and the crucifixion itself are encoded in Isaiah 53. The list keeps growing as the industrious Bible code devotees, working overtime with their computers, continue to search the text. As they would put it, the Bible is truly a wondrous book, for God has hidden so much information even within the structures of its words and letters.

Jeffrey, in particular, is impressed by the respectful manner in which Orthodox Jews approach the sacred text of Scripture, and he enthusiastically quotes the words of the eighteenth-century Lithuanian Jewish rabbi and scholar Elijah ben-Solomon Zalman (the Vilna *Gaon*):

> All that all was, is, and will be unto the end of time is included in Torah from first word to the last word. And not merely in a general sense, but including the details of every species and of each person individually, and the most minute details of everything that happened to him from the day of his birth until his death; likewise of every kind of animal and beast and living thing that exists, and of herbage, and of all that grows or is inert.[30]

Jeffrey unabashedly insists that God had hidden a vast amount of information in the Hebrew letters of his holy Word, and the complex nature of the codes was such that they would not be understood until a later generation. "In a sense, God secretly hid these incredible codes within the text of the Bible thousands of years ago with a time lock that could not be opened until the arrival of our generation and the development of sophisticated computers." God foreknew that our time would be characterized by an unrelenting attack on the authority of the Scriptures. Thus, the additional scientific evidence of these codes was needed to prove that God truly inspired the writers of the Bible to record his message to humankind.[31]

Moreover, the discovery of the Bible codes is a striking example of the enormous advance of knowledge that is occurring in our time. Jeffrey sees this as a direct fulfillment of the prophecy in Daniel 12:4, 10:

> But you, Daniel, close up and seal the words of the scroll until the time of the end. Many will go here and there to increase knowledge. . . . Many will be purified, made spotless and refined, but the wicked will continue to be wicked. None of the wicked will understand, but those who are wise will understand.

His point is that only in that time period just before the eschaton will believers understand the things Daniel had prophesied. While unbelievers will never understand the prophetic visions being "unsealed," believers will realize what is happening. They now know Jesus may return at any minute.

Although many Christians (and Jews as well) believe that the codes overwhelmingly demonstrate the Bible is of divine origin, critics categorically reject the idea that they prove anything at all. The problem is that people are very impressed by coincidences. Statisticians warn, however, that we can be fooled in this way. For example, it is a statistical probability that if twenty-three people are together in one room, two of them will share the same birthday, even though there are actually 365 days in the year. The Bible code is a classic example of building a case on the sand of statistical coincidences. As Rabbi Paul Tucher of Terre Haute, Indiana, commented to one of the authors about Drosnin's seemingly remarkable discovery: "If you allow a monkey to touch the keys of a typewriter, every so often he will come up with a word."

Furthermore, one can apply the ELS method to other works of literature beside the Bible and produce the same sort of findings. Australian mathematician Brendan McKay utilized the approach with Herman Melville's classic novel *Moby Dick* and learned that it revealed the assassinations of Rabin as well as John Kennedy, Martin Luther King, and Leon Trotsky. He also applied a coding system to Leo Tolstoy's *War and Peace,* a book about the same length as the Old Testament, and found hidden in that text the names and dates of the great rabbis. The bottom line is that coincidences are just that—coincidences.

Moreover, experts in historical Hebrew linguistics maintain that the Hebrews of the Old Testament did not use the letters of their alphabet as numerals, even though they possessed numerical values. In the Hebrew text numbers were always writ-

Fig. 5.9 He Is Risen. Albrecht Dürer's depiction of the resurrection answers Christ's eternal question: "Who do you say that I am?"

ten out (e.g., "Abraham was ninety and nine years old"). The same thing is true with the New Testament. With the sole exception of the mysterious 666 in Revelation 13:18, numbers are spelled out. The linguistic and numeric uses of the Greek alphabet were two distinct functions quite independent of each other. The fact that a Greek alpha may represent both *a* and *1* does not prove that it means or can mean both at the same time.

Moreover, the Bible code numerologists use the ELS system only when it works; in the far more numerous cases in which it does not work, it is ignored. It is a sort of have-your-cake-and-eat-it-too system of biblical interpretation. Also, there are so many ways one can count letters, words, occurrences of a name, and classes of a specific word until some sort of a pattern emerges that one must question if this is not designed only to evoke predetermined results. Simply stated, the attempt to find mysterious word and numerical patterns in the biblical writings is extremely misguided. The procedure rests on principles that have dubious validity, to say the least, and distracts students from searching out the real meanings of Scripture that are to be found in the words themselves.

As it has so often been said, "It is not the things I don't understand in the Bible that trouble me, but the things in it that I do understand." Historically the church has spoken about the "verbal inspiration" of Scripture. Christians must continue to focus on the meanings found in the words of Scripture and let them speak authoritatively.

Conclusion

In this chapter our millennial tour has been able to touch on but a select few additional religious and secular millenarian endeavors. We have shown, however, that millennialism has been and continues to be a potent force today. It is not merely a Protestant or evangelical concern but one that is found in many traditions. And it is truly a matter of global proportions.

But what are we to make of the new millennium? Should we note it simply as a historic, some would say, climactic date on our calendars, or should we use the Big Calendar Turn as an excuse to think more soberly about the meaning of the Christian millennium—a time unfettered by human calendars? We would like to suggest the latter. And so in our final chapter we offer pilgrims some suggestions for living in the new millennium and beyond.

6

The Final Chapter

The Meaning of the Millennium

> He who loves the coming of the Lord is not he who affirms it is far off, nor is it he who says it is near. It is he who, whether it be far or near, awaits it with sincere faith, steadfast hope, and fervent love.
>
> St. Augustine

Fig. 6.1 Time Is on Our Side, or Is It? Those who predict the future are gambling with time.

This is a book about time. Or perhaps more correctly, according to the title (alluding to Rev. 10:6) of Paul Boyer's comprehensive study of prophecy belief, it is a book about "when time shall be no more."[1] As we have seen, the prospect of the second coming of Jesus Christ has fascinated believers and unbelievers alike throughout history. Implicit to his return is the end of time (as we know it), the future, a new beginning, and a millennium (however one interprets it).

Our pilgrim's progress through the millennial maze has naturally focused on time. The impending beginning of the third Christian millennium has provided an opportunity to reflect carefully on the cares and concerns of those who have gone before us. As we have witnessed, while traveling in such eschatological territory one encounters calculators (the human type)

Fig. 6.2 Ten, Nine, Eight, Seven . . . What better way to prepare for the new millennium than by owning the *Countdown to the Millennium 1998–1999 Calendar?* Included in the countdown are daily listings of events and facts—some millennial, some not. For example, on November 6, 1998, we learned that the predictions of a Millennium Watch time capsule will be posted every six months until January 1, 2001 (at least they have the new millennium date right even if the calendar doesn't) at http://ftp.wdc.com/new/millennium.html.

and prognosticators at every turn. Such is the history of endtime speculation.

However, faced with the task of defining the meaning of the millennium—both the historic Christian hope as promised in Revelation 20 as well as the Big Calendar Turn—we desire to speak as wise evangelical owls (see introduction). Thus our focus will not be on forecast or prediction but simply on living faithfully between the times—the comings of Christ—between the already and the not yet. As we stated in chapter 1, something big is going to happen, but the purpose of eschatology is not so much to tell us the details of what will happen in the future as to call us to holy living in the present. As one theologian has observed, it provides "insight into the significance of the present age in light of God's action in Christ and in light of the future."[2] Simply put, the meaning of the millennium lies as much in the present as in the future. Now that we are prepared for the final chapter,

let's take a closer look at the implications of the millennium.

The Promises of Eschatology

The biblical teaching of eschatology, involving a belief in history as directed toward the restoration of Israel, the millennium, and the new earth, is necessary to give meaning and purpose to the great Christian doctrines of creation, the fall of humankind, the incarnation of Christ, the work of the Holy Spirit, and the mission of the church. There is a purpose behind the great events of the last days, toward which God is moving history, that makes them meaningful at the present time. Yet, as we have emphasized, one must be careful not to draw ecclesiastical diagrams of the future that follow over-simplified prophecy charts in marking out events of the last times. Whatever the perspective portrayed, these represent nothing more than human speculation.

Historian Timothy Weber warns of the grave dangers of such human plotting:

As Christian history makes clear, in the wrong hands the doctrines of providence, divine sovereignty, and eschatology become fatalism; and fatalism takes the significance out of human action. If the future is fixed, people are merely playing out their assigned roles, with no ability to alter the direction or outcome of the divine drama. If one is privy to the process, one can identify the players, evaluate their performance, and make judgments about them. When one knows how the drama is going to end, there are no surprises.[3]

The great Christians of history have felt satisfied to believe that one day they shall experience Christ in a closer way, whether it be by his return or their death. Thus, Paul in a Roman prison, facing execution, could write: "For to me, to live is Christ and to die is gain" (Phil. 1:21), and Peter could state:

Fig. 6.3 The Adoration of the Lamb. Albrecht Dürer's workmanlike woodcut reveals his craftmanship as well as his devotion to Christ.

In this you greatly rejoice, though now for a little while you may have had to suffer grief in all kinds of trials. These have come so that your faith—of greater worth than gold, which perishes even though refined by fire—may be proved genuine and may result in praise, glory and honor when Jesus Christ is revealed. Though you have not seen him, you love him; and even though you do not see him now, you believe in him and are filled with an inexpressible and glorious joy.

1 Peter 1:6–8

We rejoice because we have hope that beyond the present age we shall be with him, and nothing shall ever separate us from him again.

Apocalypse Now and Later

At the same time, we must recognize that endtime speculation is extraordinarily ambiguous in its character and flexible in its specific predictions. Richard Kyle has aptly depicted this as "the elastic apocalypse" and shows that in spite of its failures it quickly takes on new forms and directions.[4] Although millennialist predictions have had a 100 percent failure record, people continue to make them. The very obscurity of the prophetic passages opens the way for a continuing reinterpretation of their meaning and further speculation about the future. James West Davidson suggests that the explanations of the prophecies bear a remarkable resemblance to the modern-day Rorschach inkblot test, a type of psychological test in which a person reads his or her feelings and concerns into the shapes of ink blots on pieces of paper. Since there are so many prophetic symbols to work with, there are innumerable ways writers can come up with a finished product, a logical and consistent view of what could happen in the future.[5]

However, the goal of genuinely meaningful eschatological thinking through the ages was not so much setting forth some specific structure of God's plan for the future as it was assuring Christians that such a plan existed in the first place. Such thinking was designed to provide comfort to believers in troubled times. The promise of redemption is sure; the wicked and unfaithful will not always triumph. The injuries suffered by the innocent and the righteous will not forever go unnoticed and unpunished. God will ultimately deliver his church.

Because millennial perspectives throughout history explained existing social realities, they bent these realities into line with predictions about the future. The agents of Satan and fleshly humans would oppose the gospel in all ages, but God's sure hand of judgment would fall on these evildoers. The result has been a sort of "redemptive history," which seems to be at last finding fulfillment in the events of our times. Yet the final peace predicted in Revelation may not come as soon as one expects. We must continually look to the future reign of Christ. Millennialists have given us a once and future history, from the time of John, the writer of the Book of Revelation, to the current crop of apocalyptic writers and preachers who explain the meaning of current events at the dawn of the third Christian millennium.[6]

Fig. 6.4 Apocalyptic Art. Octogenarian Georgia preacher turned folk artist Howard Finster has made a career of selling his unique artwork. His works are typically littered with eschatological messages calling his audience to turn to Jesus.

The Myths of Progress

The remarkable thing about the doctrine of the second coming of Jesus Christ is that Christians tend to either make nothing of it or they make everything of it. Certainly if we wish to retain a relationship with the historical Jesus who lived and died on this earth, we must acknowledge that he often spoke of his return to establish his kingdom. Moreover, his followers, whose witness is recorded in the pages of the New Testament, were convinced that Christ would return to inaugurate his rule. Thus, according to the Bible, history is moving toward an end—the triumph of Jesus Christ.

It is especially important to reaffirm this Christian belief as we embark on a new millennium. For the past two centuries progress has been a central idea in Western European thought. Indeed, as Carl Becker indicated, the eighteenth-century

Enlightenment writers called on posterity to abandon the belief or hope in a far-distant golden age to be ushered in by Christ. They opted, instead, for hope in progress. The future would surely be better than the world we live in today and science would inevitably solve the age-old moral and physical problems that plague humankind.

Certainly civilization has made great progress, but even here catch-22s reign. For instance, nuclear energy, which offers such great possibilities for power generation and disease treatment, can just as easily bring about the destruction of human life on earth. Or the amazing medical achievements that have contributed to the lengthening of people's lives does not necessarily ensure that the elderly will enjoy a desirable quality of life in their last years. And computers, which simplify so many human activities, have contributed to an increasingly depersonalized and regimented society.

There are several reasons why progress is an illusion. One is the mistaken idea that progress in the material realm leads to progress in all areas of life. The teacher of Ecclesiastes offers a contrary view by suggesting that no progress or evolutionary development is really possible in the world. To him all things move in a circle from one person or one generation to another, as he states: "What has been will be again, what has been done will be done again; there is nothing new under the sun" (Eccl. 1:9).

It is noteworthy that this what-goes-around-comes-around approach to history has fascinated people throughout the intervening centuries, and such scholars as Giambattista Vico, Oswald Spengler, and Arnold Toynbee have built their literary reputations on portraying the historical process in cyclical terms. Nothing really changes, they warn us. Everything has happened before.

In fact, one can see this idea in the Book of Revelation. Time and again the earth is swept by judgment. Fire, disease, voracious insects, and war decimate the populace, and yet "the rest of the people that were not killed by these plagues still did not repent of the work of their hands; they did not stop worshiping demons, and idols of gold, silver, bronze, stone and wood—idols that cannot see or hear or walk. Nor did they repent of their murders, their magic arts, their sexual immorality or their

thefts" (Rev. 9:20–21 NIVILE). The catastrophes of history seem to teach us nothing. As the ultimate cynic would put it, the only lesson we learn from history is that we learn nothing from history. The evils that have plagued humankind from time immemorial—war, poverty, racism, egotism, sexism, just to mention the worst—continue unabated.

Those who put their faith in progress believe one can learn nothing from the past. In reality, we do learn a great deal from those who have gone on before. One great scientist put it quite well: "We are dwarfs standing on the shoulders of giants."[7] Writer G. K. Chesterton referred to "tradition" as "giving the vote to that most obscure of all classes, our ancestors" and as refusing "to submit to the small and arrogant oligarchy of those who merely happen to be walking about."[8] In other words, the wise person acknowledges that in such varied fields as science, theology, morality, literature, and the arts one can learn much from the past.

A pastor once preached a sermon entitled "Which Way Is Progress?" Later a parishioner who had not been present asked, "What did you say? Which way is progress?" The pastor replied: "Sometimes it is backward." Preaching from the Hebrew prophets, he had shown his congregation that there is a time to blaze new trails and discard outworn traditions as well as a time to continue in the old ways. Quite well he had illustrated the truth that technological and scientific progress has a way of blinding people—what C. S. Lewis referred to as "chronological snobbery"—to the wisdom of the past. Such progress conceals the reality that contemporary people are often unable to improve morally and ethically on the teachings of individuals who lived thousands of years ago.

The uncritical acceptance of the idea of progress fosters another illusion: Nothing is permanent; nothing truly lasting can survive in the face of change. To the contrary, the apostle Paul set forth three truths that he was certain would last: faith, hope, and love (1 Cor. 13:13).

As St. Augustine emphasized, a truly Christian understanding of history enables us to see that we are citizens of two worlds, a world of computers and a world of cathedrals, if you will. The one is a visible, constantly changing world, while the other is invisible, consistent, and imperishable. The human realm is one of unrest, anxiety, and revolution; while God's realm is marked by quietness, stability, and revelation. However, both worlds are under the rule of Christ. The time of rapid change in which we live today helps us refocus our attention on the values that will outlast the present age. It forces us to rely on God's promises even more.

The writer of the Book of Hebrews lived in such a dynamic age and realized that despite all the upheaval and confusion in life, God was working out his purpose. Referring to the prophecy of Haggai 2:6, he boldly affirmed God's utterance: "I will once more shake the heavens and the earth." He went on to explain: "The words 'once more' indicate the removing of what can be shaken—that is, created things—so what cannot be shaken may remain" (Heb. 12:27). There is a permanent, enduring dimension to life under God's control that will never pass away.

Eschatological Excesses

As we have discovered, extremist views that overshadow a more holistic vision of the Christian faith are often inherent in millennial teachings. The very gospel that we seek to proclaim is given short shrift when its fullness is compromised through a presentation that majors in the minors. With an eye on the new millennium and the potential abuses abroad, we can profit from a remedial examination of common eschatological excesses to avoid.

Most-Favored-Nation Status

One danger of millennial teaching is the excessive emphasis placed on the creation of the state of Israel. Related to this is the larger matter of the use of force in settling international disputes. Hal Lindsey is typical of the many writers who suggest that the logical fulfillment of Bible prophecy in the endtimes, particularly in the tribulation period, will be in the form of a nuclear holocaust. Citing Ezekiel 38:18–22 and 39:3–5, he assures his readers:

Fig. 6.5 The Mark of the Beast. The difficulties of illustrating an apocalyptic novel are witnessed here in a photo taken from Salem Kirban's horrific 1970 vision of a woman being branded with the devil's number. Somehow the idea of computer chips being inserted under the skin seems more relevant to today.

The description of torrents of fire and brimstone raining down upon the Red Army, coupled with an unprecedented shaking of the land of Israel could well be describing the use of tactical nuclear weapons against them by the Romans. It explicitly says that this force would fall "in the open field," so apparently this position enables the use of nuclear weapons. God consigns this whole barbarous army, which will seek to annihilate the Jewish race, to an utter and complete decimation. Ezekiel speaks of the Russians and ". . . all your hosts and the people who are with you . . ." being destroyed in Israel.[9]

Other popular preachers add their testimony to Lindsey's. For example, Pat Robertson states: "The whole thing [the battle of Armageddon] is now in place. It can happen any time [to] fulfill Ezekiel. It is ready to happen. . . . The United States is in that Ezekiel passage and . . . we are standing by."[10] And televangelist James Robison assures his listeners, "Any preaching of peace prior to [the return of Christ] is heresy. It's against the word of God."[11]

In fact, a scholarly study of evangelical Christians who worked in the main assembly plant for nuclear weapons in Amarillo, Texas, during the Cold War found that a majority of them believed the second coming of Christ would rescue them from the final nuclear holocaust. They were convinced of the divine necessity of their grim work of building up America's nuclear arsenal.[12]

Those who hold this view give modern Israel a sort of theological most-favored-nation status and uncritically support the political objectives of Zionism. Of course, this puts them completely at odds with Palestinian Christians in the ongoing struggle over land rights in the Holy Land. The political leaders of Israel gladly welcome such enthusiastic support of the Jewish state in its resistance to the Palestinian claim for a separate and independent political entity, even if this backing is (in their minds) for the wrong reasons. What exists here is a classic example of an "enemy-of-my-enemy-is-my-friend" policy. At the same time, Orthodox and right-wing extremist Jews do everything possible to prohibit the preaching of the gospel and the winning of Christian converts in Israel. Evangelical prophecy enthusiasts, however, usually look the other way because they regard Israel's return to the Promised Land in unbelief a vital element in the end-times scenario.

Looking at this remarkable event—the restoration of Israel to the Holy Land and formation of a viable Jewish state in an environment of hostile nations—from an eschatological perspective, one can say that it is the fulfillment of biblical prophecy. But then perhaps it may not be so. Israel might be dispersed once again before it is restored in faith as the Bible seems to indicate will happen in the last days. Moreover, many theologians do not feel that prophetic writings of the Old Testament refer to ethnic Israel at all but rather to the church. This body, which is drawn from all tongues and peoples instead of a specific ethnic group, is the New Israel portrayed in the New Testament. In other words, wide differences exist within Christian thought as to what precise role Israel plays in God's overall plan. Again, Weber, assessing the contemporary situation, offers some wise words of caution:

> Part of the problem is the overconfidence evangelicals have about their prophetic views. Bible teachers are not inerrant; and they have changed their minds often. The history of prophetic interpretation shows that the Devil is in the details. Premillennialist prophecy pundits have been wrong over and over again about identifying Antichrist, setting dates for the Rapture, and a host of other things. Nobody anticipated the demise of the Soviet empire or most aspects of the Gulf War. When history takes unexpected turns, the experts have to make adjustments, redraw their maps, and come out with new editions. History is still full of surprises—so why make categorical statements about what cannot happen between Israel and her neighbors?[13]

God's American Israel

Another endtime scenario that goes to extremes is a sort of religious nationalism that sees the United States of America occupying a favored place in God's eyes. As pointed out in the previous chapter, the idea of America as God's chosen people, as God's New Israel, predominated nineteenth-century Protestant thought. This view of America as an exceptional nation is still widely held, especially among evangelicals. Even prophecy enthusiasts who welcome the restoration of Israel find ways to include the United States in God's plan.

Naturally, this view caters to chauvinistic American patriotism and demonizes nations that oppose the United States. First it was the Soviet Union, the "evil empire" as President Ronald Reagan called it in 1983. With the fall of communism the main international enemy has now become certain Islamic nations or the vague New World Order feared by adherents to the militia movement and other patriotic organizations on the far right. In the early 1990s many believed Saddam Hussein, the Iraqi dictator, was the Antichrist. With the end of the Persian Gulf War and the subsequent standoff in the region, other potential Antichrists who oppose American policy will have to be found.

Signs of the Times

Another troubling aspect of millennialism is the effort to identify the "signs of the times" (Matt. 16:3) found in such biblical passages as Matthew 24, Mark 13, and Luke 21. Earthquakes, persecutions, famines, false messiahs, apostasy in the churches, technological advances, and the rise of authoritarian political leaders are cited as examples that the end is near and the second coming of Christ is at hand or imminent. The problem is that such occurrences have always taken place and are, therefore, uncertain indicators that the end of the world is at hand. Recognizing this problem, some say that a multiplication factor is at work, that is, there are far more famines, persecutions, or natural disasters at the present time than in the past. This is also inadequate because we do not have complete and accurate records as to what happened in the past, nor do we know what will happen in the future. Indeed, great disasters such as the Lisbon earthquake of 1755 caused Christians in earlier ages to speculate that the end of the world was near.

The hard reality is that prophecies come and go. Date setters and forecasters have plugged various historical events and personalities into their unfolding endtimes dramas. But then they had to face the embarrassing task of explaining away their failed prophecies, as has been repeatedly shown in the preceding pages. Armageddon did not occur in 1914, and Mussolini did not prove to be the Antichrist. The Red Magog, the Soviet Union, the fountainhead of all evil in the modern world, as well as the future tribulation era, has passed from the scene. A few years ago when the membership of the European Common Market (as it was known then) reached ten states, prophecy experts pronounced that this was the "ten toes" of the Beast. Then the illusion was shattered when other countries joined. Those who expected Jesus to return exactly six thou-

And You Thought You Had a Year 2000 Problem

A few years ago if one spoke about "the Year 2000 Problem" in prophetic circles it probably would have been interpreted as the problem one would encounter if he or she predicted Christ would return during that year and he didn't. Now we are all readily aware of the computer glitch that has been variously dubbed the Year 2000 Problem, Y2K, or the Millennium Bug—what *Newsweek* has called "the greatest technological problem in the history of mankind." The problem began with the software designers' answer to saving memory. They chose a two-digit format for dates, for example 99 instead of 1999. This worked well but didn't allow for the issues raised by the year 2000. Thus, at the onset of that year uncorrected computers could read 00 as 1900 rather than 2000, malfunction, and cause the loss of billions of dollars of time-sensitive information. Much discussion has taken place regarding who is taking this forecast seriously and who will be adequately prepared (i.e., year 2000 compliant). As they say, only time will tell.

The problem dovetails with long-held prophetic beliefs that associate powerful computers with the Beast of the Apocalypse. Thus, date setters and millennial entrepreneurs did not miss their opportunity to weigh in on the apocalyptic implications of the computer crisis.

Fig. 6.6 Dining in the Apocalypse. Here is one group's proactive response to the potential dangers that they believe could be brought on by the Y2K problem.

An advertisement for Grant Jeffrey's *The Millennium Meltdown* claimed that "at midnight on December 31, 1999, millions of computers throughout the world will begin to crash." This technological failure and resulting crisis "*may* [emphasis ours] set the stage for the coming world government that was prophesied to arise in the last days." For those who did not care for this approach, Jeffrey also offered a fictionalized forecast of the Y2K phenomenon. His *Flee the Darkness,* coauthored by Angela Hunt, was also released in the fall of 1998.

Another Y2K "consumer advocate," as he is described, Michael Hyatt, also offered two takes on the crisis. One was a novel, *Y2K: The Day the World Shuts Down,* offering a fictional account of the crisis, and the other, *The Millennium Bug Personal Survival Kit: Everything You and Your Family Must Know to Get from One Side of the*

Fig. 6.7 Panic Predictions. Human attempts at theologizing the Y2K problem should not be confused with the inscrutable judgments of God.

Crisis to the Other, included audio tapes and a resource manual and offered (we assume) a nonfictional account of the crisis. The survival guide was offered for a limited time price of $89 (a 50% savings) with a "100% Satisfaction Guarantee." If things turn out to be as bad as Hyatt forecasts and the kit helps one to survive, then it will be money well spent. However, if the crisis does not reach apocalyptic proportions, one wonders how long the publisher will offer the "complete, no-questions-asked refund."

Not to be outdone in missing the latest prophetic bandwagon, Hal Lindsey and Cliff Ford released a video in late 1998, *Facing Millennial Midnight: The Y2K Crisis Confronting America and the World,* which promised the answers to "what will ultimately happen, and why" in regards to the Year 2000 crisis.

Now a technological apocalypse is before us. And we were just wondering if our VCRs would still be working.

Sources: *The Millennium Meltdown* advertisement, *CBA Marketplace,* July 1998, 110–11; *The Millennium Bug Personal Survival Kit* advertisement, *World,* 3 October 1998, 33; *Facing Millennial Midnight* advertisement, *Christian Retailing,* 24 October 1998, 36–37.

sand years after the creation of Adam and two thousand years after his birth in Bethlehem and to usher in the thousand-year Sabbath rest of the millennial kingdom also have had their hopes dashed. The tribulation did not begin in 1988 or 1989, nor did Jesus come down from the skies in 1995 or 1996 as he should have. (Bible scholars knew that the date of Jesus' birth in A.D. 1 was incorrect; it actually was 4 or 5 B.C.)

These Christians failed to grasp that the prophetic accounts mentioned in the Gospels are not like a road sign that warns:

"Freeway ends in 2 miles." Rather, the prophecies are like signals that caution of danger along the way. Jesus did not post these signs so we could calculate when the end would come but rather to warn believers and strengthen their faith as they endeavored to live and walk in his ways. They call attention to the struggle between good and evil that will continue through time until Christ finally defeats evil and brings in his kingdom. The main intent of these prophetic passages is not prediction but to provide warnings and promises for those who follow the Lord. Thus, Jesus cautions believers: "Everyone will hate you because of me, but those who stand firm to the end will be saved," and "No one knows about that day or hour, not even the angels in heaven, nor the Son, but only the Father. Be on guard! Be alert! You do not know when that time will come" (Mark 13:13, 32–33 NIVILE).

The quest for signs and the interpretation of contemporary events in a sensationalist fashion sadly reveals that many Christians have bought into the mentality of our age. Sensationalism is the driving force behind the secular mass media, and things are little different in the Christian media. One need only sample the offerings of talk shows on Christian television, glance at the prophecy section in any Christian bookstore, or listen to the sermons of popular preachers to see how true this observation is. For the secular media, and especially the movie makers, the end of the millennium opened a Pandora's box of sensationalism, complete with spectacular depictions of traumatic occurrences—earthquakes, volcanic eruptions, global warming scenarios, asteroids crashing into the earth, terrorist seizures of innocent people, threat of nuclear attacks, and even alien invasions. Christian writers and artists tried to match the sensationalism of the secular media with their portrayals of events at the rapture, the horrors of the great tribulation, the battle of Armageddon, and the glorious return of Christ. Instead of comprehending the signs of the times, the Christian media have unwittingly conformed to the values of the times.

Some Christians are so caught up in this millennial madness and positive that Jesus will come as the year 2000 dawns that the tourist hotels in Jerusalem are completely booked far in advance of January 2000. A few of these travelers have even bought one-way tickets to Israel. They are confident that Jesus will appear then and they will begin reigning with him. They see no need to plan a return trip home. In fact, Israel's National Parks Authority is even fueling such speculation. Aware of the Christian pilgrim market, they are rushing by the year 2000 to turn the mundane archaeological site at Mount Megiddo (Armageddon) "into a park with apocalyptic appeal, using advanced computer graphics to bring to life the final showdown as it is prophesied in the Bible."[14]

Such an emphasis upon the dramatic and sensational aspects of Christ's return, linked with millenarian date setting, completely misses the importance of the second advent. It puts humans at the center of the event instead of the reigning Lord. The stress is on the external circumstances and how they benefit us rather than on Christ and his glorification.

Apocalyptic Social Action

A significant problem with millennial preaching is the way it has often cut the nerve to social action on the part of its hearers. Historically, premillennialism has been the main culprit in discouraging social involvement by Christians, although some contemporary forms of postmillennialism advocate little more than an individualistic approach to societal problems and an acceptance of the economic values of the present age. The soft-pedaling of social involvement has not always been as flagrant as it has been subtle. For example, look at the attitude toward the modern world that one classic prophecy writer expressed. Although put on paper over thirty years ago, the advice would still play well among heavenly minded millenarians today.

Understanding prophecy produces poise in a person. Poise is defined as balance and stability. But how can anyone be stable in a world like ours? A dog-eat-dog attitude pervades business affairs. The materialism of this day of plenty puts pressure on all of us. . . . Parents are afraid for their children, races fight each other, and nations compete to see who can first destroy the others. . . . We cannot help but wonder where the trend will lead. . . . The answer to these questions is in the Bible, and particularly in an understanding of God's program for the future. This sort of knowledge will impart to you a certainty and confidence not available elsewhere.[15]

So the message is clear. Things are going from bad to worse, and there is little any of us can do about it. Another example of this view is the statement from a prominent evangelist who, on the basis of his millennial understanding, raises doubts about social improvement programs:

I am afraid the church is trying to speak out on too many issues that really do not concern the church. There are certain issues we know to be wrong—racial injustice, crime, gambling, dishonesty, pornography. On these matters we must thunder forth as the prophets of God. However, I am not so sure that the corporate body of the church has a right to make political decisions. . . . Although Christ said that a man's life does not consist of the things he has, we in the church are very dangerously near to teaching the people that "things" are life's most important possessions. I live in Appalachia . . . I know families who . . . are considered poor. . . . However, they have a joy, a radiance, and a peace rooted deep in their spiritual faith that gives them contentment and peace. I know millionaires in New York, Texas, and California who are almost ready to blow their brains out. . . . Which is the wealthiest? Who is the richer?[16]

Statements such as these discourage Christians from actively engaging in social action and foster a supernatural social ethic that effectively supports the status quo in society. With considerable justification a major sociological study concluded that "Conservative Protestantism tends to take a miraculous view of social justice. . . . Thus they concentrate their energies on conversion and evangelism and largely ignore social issues except for occasional efforts to make unlawful what they judge to be personal vices. They also largely ignore the empirical fact that 'born-again' and regenerated Christians remain noticeably sinful and thus offer their followers little guidance in ethical behavior."[17] In short, evangelicals in particular do not support purposive social change to improve the lot of humanity despite the clear teaching of Scripture about loving our neighbors and helping those who are in need (the bodily needs are certainly not excluded here—cf. Matt. 25:31–46).

But this approach misunderstands the meaning of the millennium. Although the fulfilled kingdom is in the future, the church ought to be a pilot project for the coming millennial society. As one theologian explained, the second coming is the great floodlight that illumines history, the clearest picture of what God wants now as well as then:

> The landscapes of the Bible's future are not polluted with the sights of injustice, the sounds of war, or the pangs of deprivation. Peace, righteousness, and plenty dwell there as celebrated achievements of the King of kings. It is the ethical perfection of that kingdom which both prods and guides us to get on with the task of loving our neighbors, living as peacemakers, and offering the cups of cold water in the Savior's name. Christian ethics flow from our view of the future: we not only pray for God's will to be done on earth as it is in heaven, but we work to be part of the answer to that prayer.[18]

The Meaning of the Millennium

How shall we then live? D. S. Russell, commenting on the messages of Daniel and Revelation, points the way to understanding and living out the Bible's apocalyptic message.

> [The Bible is] a word that has something relevant to say to politicians as well as preachers, a word that is more concerned with fact than fantasy, a word that carries with it an authority that is undiminished with the passing of the years. To read these biblical books simply as "tracts for the times" is to deny their prophetic power; to read them simply as speculative forecasts is to reduce them to the level of cosmic horoscopes;

Pastoral Counsel
for an Apocalyptic Age

1. Hold high the blessed hope of Jesus' return. It is too precious a doctrine to be co-opted by self-proclaimed prophets who lack training in historical theology and biblical interpretation.

2. Reject the fallacy of date setting and place setting. Friends, there simply is no countdown to Armageddon. The future is contingent upon the give and take of God's initiative and our response. Faith, not some artificial calendar scheme, is the catalyst for divine providence.

3. Get some solid education in eschatological language. We have been in the last days for nearly two thousand years now, and none of us knows whether it will continue on for two years or two thousand years or two million years. Some basic education in apocalyptic literature will go a long way in helping you distinguish good interpretation of the text of Scripture from holy baloney.

4. Avoid mixing nationalistic myths with the everlasting gospel of the kingdom. Have you noticed how many endtime scenarios give favored-nation status to the United States? Or demonize enemy nations? . . . I plead with you, do not be a part of this misguided nationalistic fervor.

5. Please, for God's sake, refuse to exploit the hopes and fears of your people with speculative prophecy preaching. Don't weaken the gospel by tickling the ears of your people with the latest apocalyptic scheme. . . . Preach the kingdom of God here, now, and coming. Make eschatological hope a foundation for faithful living and growing conformity to Christ, not an escape from discipleship. Stoutly refuse to demean the gospel by mixing hope of the second coming with reckless speculation.

Source: Adapted from Richard J. Foster, "Heart-to-Heart: A Pastoral Letter," *Renovaré*, November 1995, 8. Inverness Drive East, Suite 102, Englewood, CO 80112-5609.

to read them as forms of spiritual escapism into a fantastic world of mysteries and monsters is to demean and degrade them. They proclaim a message that is every bit as powerful now as it was those many years ago, a message that is at one and the same time personal and political, temporal and eternal.[19]

When the apocalyptic writers of the Bible proclaimed the kingdom's coming, they spoke of its nearness in time; Jesus had the same message of immediacy, but he also emphasized its urgency. The kingdom was not merely a future phenomenon but a powerful, cataclysmic force in the here and now.[20]

The Call for Justice

Consequently, the Christian must struggle now for kingdom issues. But what should this involve? In addition to sharing the faith with others through preaching and personal testimony, one must support the Christian witness with acts of decency, kindness, and justice. It is here that those who proclaim the theology of liberation have much to teach the church. One need not agree with all of their theological views to second the comment of South African Bishop Desmond Tutu: "If you are neutral in a situation of injustice, you have chosen the side of the oppressor. If an elephant has his foot on the tail of the mouse, and you say you are neutral, the mouse will not appreciate your neutrality."[21]

There is an enormous divergence between the rich and poor of today's world, a contrast often described geographically in terms of the North-South divide. Demographic experts calculate that by the year 2000 the world's population will be 6.3 billion, and by 2025 it may reach as high as 8.5 billion. Moreover, 95 percent of the global population growth over the next quarter century will be in the developing countries of Latin America, Africa, and Asia. It is estimated that by 2025 Mexico will have replaced Japan as one of the ten most populous countries on the earth, and Nigeria's population will exceed that of the United States. The implications of such projections are startling.

Despite progress made in economic growth, public health, and literacy in the developing world, hundreds of millions of people still live in "absolute poverty," defined as a condition of life in which malnutrition, illiteracy, disease, squalid housing, high infant mortality, and low life expectancy are beyond any reasonable definition of human decency. The stark reality is that the North (including Eastern Europe) has a quarter of the world's population and 80 percent of its income, while in the South (including China) three-quarters of the world's people live on one-fifth of its income. Also, approximately 90 percent of the global manufacturing industry is in the North. While the quality of life in the North rises steadily, in the South every two seconds a child dies of hunger or disease.

Still, the contrast between wealth and poverty does not correspond exactly with the North-South division. Some of the oil-producing OPEC countries are rich, while poverty is found in North America and Europe. Even in the industrialized United States 14 percent of the population, including 20 percent of the children, live beneath the poverty line. In Britain over 10 percent live below the legal definition of poverty, and another 10 to 15 percent are close to this point. A great disparity between wealth and poverty is found both between nations and within them.

Many Christians today are tempted to use the complexities of economics as an excuse to do nothing. However, God's peo-

Fig. 6.8 How Much Is Enough? Wealthy Western Christians should struggle with questions of economic disparity.

ple need to dedicate themselves not only to verbal evangelism but also to relieving human needs as part of sharing the Good News (Luke 4:18–19), both at home and to the ends of the earth. This explains why Christians in what some term the "two-thirds world" place issues of poverty and economic development at the top of their theological agendas. Some Christians in the North have difficulty understanding why liberation is so central to the thinking of their counterparts in Latin America, Africa, and Asia, but they have never faced the stark, dehumanizing reality of grinding poverty. God has provided enough resources to meet the needs of all. Christians in the more-developed lands must share their material means with others by supporting public and private efforts to aid the poor, by scaling down our high standard of living, and by working to empower those who do not have the ability

to help themselves to become equal participants in the global economy.

One recent observer cogently frames the eschatological implications on economics by asking "whether the church will view the millennium primarily 'from above'—implicitly blessing the American economic vision for the event—or whether we will use the opportunity to stand with those 'from below,' on the margins or *eschata* of society."[22]

The Call for Peace

The vision of the millennial kingdom also projects into our time a desire for peace. The closing chapters of the Book of Revelation portray an image of the future in which there is a peaceful existence. City gates are never shut, the kings of the earth are bringing their glory to God, and the nations are being healed. Are we working for peace? Surely today it is needed more than ever.

The relaxation of the Cold War tensions following the demise of the Soviet Union led many into complacency about the continuing threat of war. The menace of international communism faded and with it the fear of a nuclear holocaust, but a fragmenting nationalism took its place. A variety of mini-nationalisms pointed to the great paradox of our times: bitter divisions in what otherwise is an increasingly unifying world. Since the end of World War II, over one hundred new entities have declared their independence and started on the road to nationhood. Usually politically unstable and economically weak, these states face severe problems. The existence of so many new nation states is a serious matter because they are precarious in nature. Given their small land areas and limited resources, the hopes to which independence gave rise cannot be fulfilled by peaceful development. Consequently, they may resort to force to gain what they want. These wars may be fought with conventional weapons, but there is always the temptation to turn to atomic, biological, and chemical (ABC) warfare. The use of chemical weapons by the Iraqis in the 1980s illustrates this point.

What makes this even more frightening is the proliferation of atomic weapons. In the 1980s only five countries had them—the United States, the Soviet Union, Britain, France, and China. By the early 1990s it was known that seventeen more countries had the capability to produce such arms. In the first decade of the twenty-first century, the "nuclear club" will have many more members. As the number of countries who possess nuclear arms increases, the possibility that these weapons may be used in a war exponentially increases. Christians should sense the urgency to make efforts on behalf of peace. As Jesus said, "Blessed are the peacemakers, for they will be called children of God" (Matt. 5:9 NIVILE).

An objective observer from another planet would undoubtedly conclude that earth is indeed a strange place. There is such a surplus of weapons and yet a scarcity of food for the hungry and shelter for the homeless. Thus, the task confronting believers is an urgent one. They must teach people to build a peace in the world that is based on a true knowledge of God and just relationships among nations. The quest for peace consequently involves more than the struggle against violence. As many have observed, "If you want peace, work for justice." This brings one to the universal scope of the eschatological hope. The Revelator claimed that all nations would flow into the final kingdom (Rev. 15:4). The prophecies of the Old and New Testaments indicate an acceptance of people from all tribes and tongues who turn to God (Isa. 66:18; Joel 3:2; Rev. 5:9; 21:24). When we compare this outlook with the present age, we should be challenged to join the struggle against racism and ethnic hatred.

The Call for Equality

Racism and ethnicity are global matters, not something limited to the West. Before European expansion (c. 1500), the

Fig. 6.9 John the Revelator. Exiled to the island of Patmos, John received strange visions from God that have led to centuries of apocalyptic speculation.

various races of the human family lived in relative isolation. Mass migrations, both free and forced, gradually modified this situation, and presently varying degrees of racial mixture exist throughout the world. The change in the racial map of the world did not necessarily make conflict inevitable. What actually promoted it was the nature of European expansion. Possessing technological and military superiority, the Western Europeans conquered vast colonial possessions in Africa, Asia, and the Americas. In the process, Westerners developed a myth of racial superiority to justify their conduct.

The racial and ethnic tensions created in history have been steadily increasing in the contemporary world. Christians are especially equipped to deal with this situation, as the apostle Paul made clear in his remarkable address to the Athenians (Acts 17:22–31). Athens was perhaps the most racially, ethnically, and culturally diverse city in the Roman Empire. Paul addressed the questions of their differences in the sight of God. His sermon emphasized four points.

First, he affirmed the unity of humanity because God is the Creator, Sustainer, and Father of all humankind. Consequently, racism is not only foolish but evil since it violates the creative purposes of God.

Second, Paul acknowledged the diversity of ethnic cultures. Despite the fact that God made all nations from one human being, "he determined the times set for them and the exact places where they should live" (v. 26). Scripture acknowledges that cultures enrich the total picture of human life, so Christians may affirm both the unity of humankind and the diversity of ethnic existence.

Third, although the missionary preacher accepted the richness of the various cultures as a reflection of the created order, he did not carry this over into the realm of religion. He did not accept the idolatry on which they were based or the idea that each people should have its own distinctive gods and religious faith. God does not tolerate rivals to his Son, Jesus Christ, the one and only Savior and judge of humankind.

Finally, the apostle declared the importance of the church, which would be

CALVIN & HOBBES
Bill Watterson

Fig. 6.10 The Trouble with the Future. Everyone's favorite comic strip philosopher weighs in on the human condition's impact on the future.

a new and reconciled community to which all may belong (Acts 17:34).

John R. W. Stott eloquently sums up the thrust of Paul's address to the Athenians:

> Because of the unity of humankind, we demand equal rights and equal respect for racial minorities. Because of the diversity of ethnic groups, we renounce cultural imperialism and seek to preserve all those riches of inter-racial culture which are compatible with Christ's lordship. Because of the finality of Christ, we affirm that religious freedom includes the right to propagate the gospel. Because of the glory of the church, we must seek to rid ourselves of any lingering racism and strive to make it a model of harmony between races, in which the multiracial dream comes true.[23]

The Call to Stewardship

According to the final chapter of the Bible, in the future kingdom the water will be clear as crystal, and the trees will bear abundant fruit in every month. In short, the Adamic curse will be removed from creation, and Edenic conditions will return (Rev. 22:1–5; cf. Rom. 8:22). This model vision should encourage Christians to begin tackling perhaps the most serious challenge facing humankind, that of preserving the earth. While the creation may be cursed, that is no excuse to abandon earth care.

The extent of environmental devastation is alarming, represented by such recent disasters as the 1984 leak of poisonous gas from a chemical plant at Bhopal in India, the 1986 Chernobyl nuclear power plant accident in the Ukraine, the 1989 Exxon *Valdez* oil spill in Alaska,

Fig. 6.11 A Peaceable Kingdom. John Sartain's mezzotint engraving, *The Harmony of Christian Love*, paints a mid-nineteenth-century vision of the millennial kingdom.

and the 1998 forest fires in Indonesia and Mexico. Such alarming events as the destruction of the tropical rain forests, the southward advance of the Sahara desert, the prevalence of acid rain, the extinction of innumerable species of animals and plants, the devastation caused by nuclear and chemical weapon sites in the United States and Russia, and other crises cry out to Christians to assume responsibility for environmental protection.

Those who forego facing the pollution of the planet problem often argue that our efforts will be futile until Christ returns. But such thinking falls short spiritually. Environmental neglect that excuses its posture because of prophetic schedules falls prey to an odd modern phenomenon—eschatological idolatry. Those who "conceive of history as a blueprint instead of a story"[24] perpetuate a stewardship of neglect. But this is God's world, and he expects his children to exercise responsible stewardship here and now.

Conclusion

The following words are inscribed on a wall by the headquarters of the United Nations in New York: "They shall beat their swords into plowshares, and their spears into pruninghooks: nation shall not lift up sword against nation, neither shall they learn war any more" (Isa. 2:4 KJV). This passage affirms the transformation of the world states that will occur when Christ returns to redeem the world. While the United Nations can reduce conflict, there will be no final peace until his coming. Likewise, until then there will be no final solutions to the problems plaguing society. Yet respect for the natural world; love for all people regardless of race, gender, or class; justice for the poor; and the establishment of peace are important goals that the Christian vision of the kingdom puts before society even now.

As Stephen Travis affirms:

Even though we know that we are "strangers and pilgrims on the earth," we should do all we can to improve the conditions of [human] lives. Why? Because love and justice and all the values which will be basic in heaven are God's will for men now. The church is to be a sign of God's kingdom, pioneering things which are God's will for [humanity]. That is what the church at its best has always been. Who pioneered mass education? Who pioneered hospitals? Who pioneered the abolition of slavery? In each case Christians played a leading

Fig. 6.12 Going Home. Contemporary sculptor George Lorio has crafted a piece that captures our longing for eternity.

role in causing progressive change. . . . If there has been progress in the past, there can be progress in the future.[25]

We can pursue these goals with a certainty born of the conviction that the Christian hope leads somewhere—to the triumph of God. As people who have heard God's loving invitation to share in his victory, we long for the day when the shout will resound throughout the heavens and earth: "Praise God! For the Lord, almighty, is king!" It is this assurance that gives the millennial hope such power. We look forward to a time when peace and justice will embrace, prevailing on earth as in heaven. Millennialism constantly reminds believers that no matter how discouraging the situation is today, millennial glory awaits us in the future. Perhaps your social class is declining or your theological viewpoint is on the wane or some great personal tragedy has arisen. Take heart. One day assuredly believers will rule the world with Christ. All that is broken will be repaired, and the entire earth and its population will be renewed.

However, in the meantime we are to continue working faithfully at the tasks to which God has called us. We are not to pause but to proceed, not to repose but to reform. We are to labor in the vineyard until we are called for the banquet. As C. S. Lewis put it so well, the joyous anticipation of the return of Christ and his establishment of the millennial kingdom must never preclude

sober work for the future within the limits of ordinary morality and prudence. . . . For what comes is judgment: happy are those whom it finds laboring in their vocations, whether they were merely going out to feed the pigs or laying good plans to deliver humanity a hundred years hence from some great evil. The curtain has indeed now fallen. Those pigs will never in fact be fed, the great campaign against white slavery or governmental tyranny will never in fact proceed to victory. No matter; you were at your post when the inspection came.[26]

This is sage advice for millennial travelers, appropriate for the ages and into eternity. Pilgrims, by definition, are peripatetic, on the move. And so should we be as we enter the new millennium, proclaiming good news and performing good works as we confidently await the Lord's promised sure and certain return.

Notes

Introduction

1. Richard Landes, "On Owls, Roosters, and Apocalyptic Time: A Historical Method for Reading a Refractory Documentation," *Union Seminary Quarterly Review* 49, nos. 1–2 (1996). Available from http://www.uts.columbia.edu/~usqr/LANDES.HTM.

2. J. R. R. Tolkien, *The Return of the King* (New York: Ballantine, 1968), 280, quoted in Everett L. Wilson, *Jesus and the End-Time: An Interpretation* (Chicago: Covenant Press, 1977), 166.

Chapter 1: Apocalypse Wow

1. Henry Grunwald, "Can the Millennium Deliver?" *Time,* 11 May 1998, 88.

2. *Atlantic Monthly,* June 1891, 860.

3. George Gallup Jr. and Sarah Jones, *100 Questions and Answers: Religion in America* (Princeton, N.J.: Religion Research Center, 1989), 18–21.

4. Princeton Religion Research Center, *Emerging Trends* 16 (June 1996): 4.

5. Princeton Religion Research Center, *Emerging Trends* 13 (February 1991): 1.

6. William Ecenbarger, "Comes the Millennium," *Chicago Tribune Magazine,* 18 February 1996, sec. 10, p. 21.

7. Asa Briggs and Daniel Snowman, *Fins de Siècle: How Centuries End 1400–2000* (New Haven: Yale University Press, 1996), 1.

8. Ibid., 3.

9. Ibid.

10. Henri Focillon, *The Year 1000* (New York: Frederick Ungar, 1969), 60.

11. Robert J. L. Burrows, "The Coming of the New Age," in *The New Age Rage,* ed. Karen Hoyt (Old Tappan, N.J.: Fleming H. Revell, 1987), 19–20.

12. Fritjof Capra, *The Turning Point* (New York: Simon & Schuster, 1982).

13. The most lucid discussion of this aspect of New Age thought is found in Hoyt, *New Age Rage,* 34–45.

14. Alvin Toffler, *The Third Wave* (New York: William Morrow, 1980).

15. James Finn Garner, *Apocalypse Wow! A Memoir for the End of Time* (New York: Simon & Schuster, 1997).

Chapter 2: The Eschatological Smorgasbord

1. Stanley J. Grenz, *Created for Community: Connecting Christian Belief with Christian Living,* 2d ed. (Grand Rapids: Baker, 1998), 253.

2. David B. Barrett, "Annual Statistical Table on Global Mission: 1997," *International Bulletin of Missionary Research* 21 (January 1997): 25.

3. Note to Genesis 1:28, *The Scofield Reference Bible* (New York: Oxford University Press, 1917), 5.

4. Elwood McQuaid, *The Zion Connection* (Eugene, Oreg.: Harvest House, 1996), 79.

5. Ibid.

6. Note to Ezekiel 38, *The Scofield Reference Bible,* 883.

Chapter 3: It's the End of the World as We Know It

1. David Briggs, "Millennium's Approach Raises Hopes, Fears," *The Grand Rapids Press,* 15 November 1997, p. B6.

2. Stanley N. Gundry, "Hermeneutics or Zeitgeist as the Determining Factor in the History of Eschatologies," *Journal of the Evangelical Theological Society* 20, no. 1 (1977): 50.

3. "Justin Martyr Dialogue with Trypho, a Jew," 80, in *The Ante-Nicene Fathers: Translation of the Fathers Down to A.D. 325,* ed. A. Roberts and J. Donaldson (Grand Rapids: Eerdmans, 1975), 2:201.

4. Lactantius, *Divine Institutes,* 3.1, in *Ante-Nicene Fathers,* 21:478.

5. D. H. Kromminga, *The Millennium in the Church* (Grand Rapids: Eerdmans), 76.

6. Augustine, *The City of God,* trans. Marcus Dodds (New York: Modern Library, 1993), 20.7.

7. Ibid., 20.8.

8. Ibid., 20.17, 19.

9. Matthew Spinka, *John Hus: A Biography* (Princeton: Princeton University Press, 1968), 266.

10. John Calvin, *Joannis Calvini Opera* (Braunschweig: Schwetschke, 1889), 41:302.

11. Henry Drummond, *Dialogues on Prophecy* (London: 1827), 1:ii–iii.

12. Paul Boyer, *When Time Shall Be No More: Prophecy Belief in Modern American Culture* (Cambridge: Harvard/Belknap, 1992), 88.

13. Billy Graham, *World Aflame* (New York: Doubleday, 1965), 217.

14. Ibid., 216–29.

15. Ibid., 206.

16. Ibid., 207.

17. Billy Graham, *Approaching Hoofbeats: The Four Horsemen of the Apocalypse* (Waco: Word, 1983), 10.

18. Ibid., 9–10.

19. Ibid., 27.

20. Helen Lee Turner, "Myths: Stories of This World and the World to Come," in *Southern Baptists Observed,* ed. Nancy Tatom Ammerman (Knoxville: University of Tennessee Press, 1993), 102.

21. Ibid., 120.

22. The flowering of their thought is best represented in the following works: Craig A. Blaising and Darrell L. Bock, eds., *Dispensationalism, Israel and the Church* (Grand Rapids: Zondervan, 1992); Robert L. Saucy, *The Case for Progressive Dispensationalism* (Grand Rapids: Zondervan, 1993); and Craig A. Blaising and Darrell L. Bock, *Progressive Dispensationalism* (Wheaton: Victor/BridgePoint, 1993).

Chapter 4: Does Anyone Really Know What Time It Is?

1. David Briggs, "Millennium's Approach Raises Hopes, Fears," *The Grand Rapids Press,* 15 November 1997, p. B6.

2. LeRoy Edwin Froom, *The Prophetic Faith of Our Fathers* (Washington, D.C.: Review and Herald, 1948), charts on II, 786–87; III, 252–53.

3. Charles Finney, *Lectures on Revival* (Cambridge: Harvard University Press, 1960), 306.

4. Quoted in George R. Knight, *Millennial Fever and the End of the World* (Boise, Idaho: Pacific Press, 1993), 305.

5. M. J. Penton, "The Eschatology of Jehovah's Witnesses," in *The Coming Kingdom,* ed. M. Darrol Bryant and Donald W. Dayton (Barrytown, N.Y.: International Religious Foundation, 1983), 181.

6. Ibid., 184.

7. Melvin D. Curry, *Jehovah's Witnesses* (New York: Garland Books, 1992), 126.

8. Quoted in Dwight Wilson, *Armageddon Now!* (Grand Rapids: Baker, 1977), 63.

9. Leonard Sale-Harrison, *The Resurrection of the Old Roman Empire* (London: Pickering Inglis, 1939), 96.

10. Ibid., 60.

11. Ibid., 118.

12. *Publishers Weekly,* 14 March 1977, 30–32.

13. Jeffrey L. Sheler, "Dark Prophecies," *U.S. News & World Report,* 15 December 1997, 69.

14. Hal Lindsey, *Satan Is Alive and Well on Planet Earth* (New York: Inspirational Press, 1994), 221.

15. Hal Lindsey, *The Late Great Planet Earth* (Grand Rapids: Zondervan, 1970), 54.

16. Ibid., 181.

17. Ibid., 89.

18. Ibid., 114.

19. Hal Lindsey, *Apocalypse Code* (Palos Verdes, Calif.: Western Front, Ltd., 1997), 36–37.

20. For more on this see the discussion by Mark G. Toulouse, "Pat Robertson: Apocalyptic Theology and American Foreign Policy," *Journal of Church and State* 31 (winter 1989): 73–99.

21. Pat Robertson, *The New World Order* (Dallas: Word, 1991), 37.

22. Ibid., 68.

23. Ibid., 68–71.

24. Ibid., 122.

25. Ibid., 96.

26. Ibid., 75–76, 31.

27. Ibid., 176–77.

28. Ibid., 215–16.

29. Ibid., 220.

30. Ibid., 253–55.

31. Ibid., 263–64.

32. Ibid., 264.

33. Ibid., 268.

34. Henry Grunwald, "Can the Millennium Deliver?" *Time,* 11 May 1998, 84–88.

Chapter 5: Apocalyptic Bebop

1. Gareth G. Cook, "New Age: The Next Plane of Consciousness," *U.S. News & World Report,* 19 December 1994, 66.

2. CMS homepage. Cited in the mission of the Center for Millennial Studies. Available from http://www.mille.org/indexA.html#introduction.

3. See H. Richard Niebuhr, *The Kingdom of God in America* (Chicago: Willett, Clark, 1937).

4. Ernest Lee Tuveson, *Redeemer Nation: The Idea of America's Millennial Role* (Chicago: University of Chicago Press, 1968).

5. Quotations are from Reagan's official speeches contained in Richard V. Pierard and Linder, *Civil Religion and the Presidency* (Grand Rapids: Zondervan, 1988), 275–76.

6. Tim LaHaye, *The Bible's Influence on American History* (San Diego: Master Books, 1976), 59.

7. Timothy E. Fulop, "'The Future Golden Day of the Race': Millennialism and Black Americans in the Nadir, 1877–1901," *Harvard Theological Review* 84 (January 1991): 75–99.

8. James M. Rhodes, *The Hitler Movement: A Modern Millenarian Revolution* (Stanford: Hoover Institution Press, 1980).

9. Norman Cohn, *The Pursuit of the Millennium: Revolutionary Millenarians and Mystical Anarchists of the Middle Ages* (New York: Oxford University Press, 1957, 1970).

10. Rhodes, *Hitler Movement,* 39–41.

11. Ibid., 60.

12. Ibid., 65–66.

13. Ibid., 66.

14. Ibid., 76–79.

15. Karl Marx and Friedrich Engels, *The Communist Manifesto,* in *Birth of the Communist Manifesto,* ed. Dirk J. Struik (New York: International Publishers, 1971), 89.

16. Ibid., 91.

17. Ibid., 103.

18. Ibid., 111.

19. Karl Marx, *Critique of the Gotha Program* (New York: International Publishers, 1938), 10.

20. Marx and Engels, *Communist Manifesto,* 113.

21. Rastafarians have made the deepest inroads into popular culture through reggae music. Bob Marley (d. 1981) brought reggae international attention in the late 1970s; his "Legend" is the best-selling reggae album ever, with more than five million copies sold. See David Yonke, "Ziggy Marley Puts His Message of Peace in a Musical Bottle of Reggae," *The Grand Rapids Press,* 3 July 1998, p. B7.

22. Anthony Wallace, *Religion: An Anthropological View* (New York: Random House, 1966), 30.

23. Sandra L. Zimdars-Swartz, *Encountering Mary: From La Salette to Medjugorje* (Princeton: Princeton University Press, 1991), 4–9.

24. Fulton J. Sheen, quoted in ibid., 207.

25. Michael W. Cuneo, *The Smoke of Satan* (New York: Oxford University Press, 1997), 4–5, 150.

26. "Millennium Watchers Predicting 'Juicy Time' for Apocalyptic Views," *Chicago Tribune,* 2 January 1997, sec. 1.

27. William Alnor, *Soothsayers of the Second Advent* (Old Tappan, N.J.: Revell, 1989), 179.

28. Wilbur Smith, *Egypt in Biblical Prophecy* (Boston: W. A. Wilde, 1957), 223–25.

29. See John Warwick Montgomery, *Principalities and Powers* (Minneapolis: Bethany House, 1973), 53.

30. Quoted in Grant Jeffrey, *The Handwriting of God: Sacred Mysteries of the Bible* (Toronto: Frontier Research Publications, 1997), 117.

31. Ibid.

Chapter 6: The Final Chapter

1. Paul Boyer, *When Time Shall Be No More: Prophecy Belief in Modern American Culture* (Cambridge: Harvard University Press/Belknap Press, 1992).

2. Stanley J. Grenz, *The Millennial Maze: Sorting Out Evangelical Options* (Downers Grove, Ill.: InterVarsity Press, 1992).

3. Timothy P. Weber, "How Evangelicals Became Israel's Best Friend," *Christianity Today,* 5 October 1998, 49.

4. Richard Kyle, *The Last Days Are Here Again* (Grand Rapids: Baker, 1998), 187.

5. James West Davidson, *The Logic of Millennial Thought* (New Haven: Yale University Press, 1977), 256.

6. Ibid., 258–60.

7. This saying has been attributed to Isaac Newton, who used it on various occasions. However, it can be traced back to the ancient Roman poet Lucan, and numerous writers over the last three centuries have used various forms of it. Robert K. Merton, *On the Shoulders of Giants* (New York: Free Press, 1965).

8. G. K. Chesterton, "The Ethics of England," in *The Collected Works* (San Francisco: Ignatius Press, 1986), 1:251.

9. Lindsey, *Late Great Planet Earth,* 161.

10. Pat Robertson, quoted in Grace Halsell, *Prophecy and Politic: Militant Evangelists on the Road to Nuclear War* (Westport, Conn.: Lawrence Hill, 1986), 16.

11. James Robison, quoted in ibid.

12. A. J. Mojtabi, *Blessed Assurance: At Home with the Bomb in Amarillo, Texas* (Boston: Houghton Mifflin, 1986).

13. Weber, "How Evangelicals Became Israel's Best Friend," 49.

14. Michael Miller, "Israel Plans Tourist Park with Apocalyptic Feel," *The Grand Rapids Press,* 16 February 1997, p. B7.

15. Charles C. Ryrie, *The Bible and Tomorrow's News* (Wheaton: Scripture Press, 1969), 12.

16. Billy Graham, *World Aflame* (New York: Doubleday, 1965), 181, 186.

17. Rodney Stark and Charles Glock, *American Piety: The Nature of Religious Commitment* (Berkeley: University of California Press, 1968), 75.

18. David Hubbard, *The Second Coming: What Will Happen When Jesus Returns?* (Downers Grove, Ill.: InterVarsity Press, 1984), 10.

19. D. S. Russell, *Prophecy and the Apocalyptic Dream: Protest and Promise* (Peabody, Mass.: Hendrickson, 1994), 108.

20. Ibid., 120.

21. Quoted in Robert McAfee Brown, *Unexpected News: Reading the Bible with Third World Eyes* (Philadelphia: Westminster Press, 1984), 19.

22. Barbara Rossing, "Standing at the Door of a New Millennium: Economy, Eschatology, and Hope," *Dialog: A Journal of Theology* 37, no. 4 (fall 1998): 268.

23. John R. W. Stott, *Decisive Issues Facing Christians Today* (Old Tappan, N.J.: Revell, 1990), 225–26.

24. Lewis H. Lapham, ed., *History: The End of the World* (New York: History Book Club, 1997), 287.

25. Stephen Travis, *The Jesus Hope* (London: Word, 1974), 125–26.

26. C. S. Lewis, "The World's Last Night," in *The World's Last Night and Other Essays* (New York: Harcourt Brace, 1959), 111–12.

Select Bibliography

Abanes, Richard. *American Militias: Rebellion, Racism and Religion*. Downers Grove, Ill.: InterVarsity Press, 1996.

———. *End-Time Visions: The Road to Armageddon*. New York: Four Walls Eight Windows, 1998.

Alnor, William A. *Soothsayers of the Second Advent*. Old Tappan, N.J.: Revell, 1989.

———. *UFOs in the New Age: Extraterrestrial Messages and the Truth of Scripture*. Grand Rapids: Baker, 1992.

Anderson, Robert. *The Coming Prince*. Grand Rapids: Kregel, 1975.

Ankerberg, John, and John Weldon. *One World: Biblical Prophecy and the New World Order*. Chicago: Moody Press, 1991.

Ariel, Yaakov S. *On Behalf of Israel: American Fundamentalist Attitudes toward Jews, Judaism, and Zionism, 1865–1945*. Brooklyn, N.Y.: Carlson, 1991.

Armerding, Carl E., and W. Ward Gasque, eds. *Handbook of Biblical Prophecy*. Grand Rapids: Baker, 1977.

Aune, David E. *Prophecy in Early Christianity and the Ancient Mediterranean World*. Grand Rapids: Eerdmans, 1991.

Aveni, Anthony F. *Empires of Time: Calendars, Clocks, and Cultures*. New York: Basic Books, 1989.

Ball, Bryan. *A Great Expectation: Eschatological Thought in English Protestantism to 1660*. Leiden: E. J. Brill, 1975.

Barkun, Michael. *Crucible of the Millennium*. Syracuse: Syracuse University Press, 1986.

———. *Disaster and the Millennium*. New Haven: Yale University Press, 1974.

———. *Religion and the Racist Right: The Origins of the Christian Identity Movement*. Chapel Hill: University of North Carolina Press, 1994.

Bass, Clarence B. *Backgrounds to Dispensationalism*. Grand Rapids: Baker, 1960.

Bettis, Joseph, and S. K. Johannesen, eds. *The Return of the Millennium*. Barrytown, N.Y.: New Era Books, 1984.

Biederwolf, William E. *The Second Coming Bible*. Grand Rapids: Baker, 1980.

Blackstone, William E. *Jesus Is Coming*. New York: Revell, 1908.

Blaising, Craig A., and Darrell L. Bock. *Progressive Dispensationalism*. Wheaton: Victor/BridgePoint, 1993.

Blevins, Gary D. *666: The Final Warning*. Kingsport, Tenn.: Vision of the End Ministries, 1990.

Bloch, Ruth H. *Visionary Republic*. New York: Cambridge University Press, 1985.

Boff, Leonardo. *Introducing Liberation Theology*. Maryknoll, N.Y.: Orbis Books, 1987.

————. *Way of the Cross—Way of Justice*. Maryknoll, N.Y.: Orbis Books, 1980.

————. *When Theology Listens to the Poor*. San Francisco: Harper & Row, 1988.

Borst, Arno. *The Ordering of Time: From the Ancient Computus to the Modern Computer*. New York: Polity Press, 1993.

Botting, Heather and Gary. *The Orwellian World of Jehovah's Witnesses*. Toronto: University of Toronto Press, 1984.

Boyer, Paul. *When Time Shall Be No More: Prophecy Belief in Modern American Culture*. Cambridge: Harvard University Press, 1992.

Briggs, Asa, and Daniel Snowman. *Fins de Siècle: How Centuries End 1400–2000*. New Haven: Yale University Press, 1996.

Brown, Robert McAfee. *Gustavo Guttierez: An Introduction to Liberation Theology*. Maryknoll, N.Y.: Orbis Books, 1990.

Bryant, M. Darrol, and Donald W. Dayton. *The Coming Kingdom: Essays in American Millennialism and Eschatology*. Barrytown, N.Y.: New Era Books, 1983.

Brummett, Barry. *Contemporary Apocalyptic Rhetoric*. New York: Praeger, 1991.

Bull, Malcolm, ed. *Apocalypse Theory and the Ends of the World*. Oxford: Blackwell, 1995.

Camping, Harold. *1994?* New York: Vantage Press, 1992.

Capp, B. S. *The Fifth Monarchy Men: A Study in Seventeenth-Century English Millenarianism*. Totowa, N.J.: Rowman and Littlefield, 1972.

Carpenter, Joel A. *Revive Us Again: The Reawakening of American Fundamentalism*. New York: Oxford University Press, 1997.

Chandler, Russell. *Doomsday: The End of the World—A View through Time*. Ann Arbor, Mich.: Servant Publications, 1993.

Clark, David S. *The Message from Patmos: A Postmillennial Commentary*. Grand Rapids: Baker, 1989.

Clifford, Paula. *A Brief History of End-Time*. Oxford: Lion, 1997.

Clouse, Robert G., ed. *The Meaning of the Millennium*. Downers Grove, Ill: InterVarsity Press, 1977.

————, Richard V. Pierard, and Edwin M. Yamauchi. *Two Kingdoms: The Church and Culture through the Ages*. Chicago: Moody Press, 1993.

Coder, S. Maxwell. *The Final Chapter*. Wheaton: Tyndale House, 1984.

Cohen, Daniel. *Prophets of Doom*. Brookfield, Conn.: Millbrook Press, 1992.

————. *Waiting for the Apocalypse*. Buffalo: Prometheus Books, 1983.

Cohn, Norman. *Cosmos, Chaos and the World to Come*. New Haven: Yale University Press, 1993.

————. *The Pursuit of the Millennium: Revolutionary Millenarians and Mystical Anarchists of the Middle Ages*. New York: Oxford University Press, 1974.

Conyers, A. J. *The End: What Jesus Really Said about the Last Things*. Downers Grove, Ill.: InterVarsity Press, 1995.

Couch, Mal, ed. *Dictionary of Premillennial Theology*. Grand Rapids: Kregel, 1996.

Cuneo, Michael W. *The Smoke of Satan: Conservative and Traditionalist Dissent in Contemporary American Catholicism*. New York: Oxford University Press, 1997.

Curry, Melvin D. *Jehovah's Witnesses: The Millenarian World of the Watch Tower*. New York: Garland, 1992.

Davidson, James West. *The Logic of Millennial Thought*. New Haven: Yale University Press, 1977.

De Jong, James A. *As the Waters Cover the Sea: Millennial Expectations in the Rise of Anglo-American Missions 1640–1810*. Kampen, The Netherlands: J. H. Kok, 1970.

DeMar, Gary. *Last Days Madness: Obsession of the Modern Church*. Atlanta: American Vision, 1997.

————, and Peter J. Leithart. *The Legacy of Hatred Continues: A Response to Hal Lindsey's* The Road to Holocaust. Atlanta: American Vision, 1989.

————. *The Reduction of Christianity: A Biblical Response to Dave Hunt*. Atlanta: American Vision, 1988.

Doan, Ruth Alden. *The Miller Heresy: Millenarianism and American Culture*. Philadelphia: Temple University Press, 1987.

Dobson, Ed. *The End: Why Jesus Could Return by A.D. 2000.* Grand Rapids: Zondervan, 1997.

Dublin, Max. *Futurehype: The Tyranny of Prophecy.* New York: Dutton, 1991.

Duncan, David Ewing. *Calendar: Humanity's Epic Struggle to Determine a True and Accurate Year.* New York: Avon Books, 1998.

Dyer, Charles H. *The Rise of Babylon: Sign of the End Times.* Wheaton: Tyndale House, 1991.

———. *World News and Bible Prophecy.* Wheaton: Tyndale House, 1993.

Ehrlich, Paul R. *The Population Bomb.* New York: Ballantine, 1968.

Ellul, Jacques. *Jesus and Marx: From Gospel to Ideology.* Grand Rapids: Eerdmans, 1988.

Emmerson, Richard K. *Antichrist in the Middle Ages.* Seattle: University of Washington Press, 1981.

———, and Bernard McGinn, eds. *The Apocalypse in the Middle Ages.* Ithaca: Cornell University Press, 1992.

Erdoes, Richard. *A.D. 1000: Living on the Brink of Apocalypse.* San Francisco: Harper & Row, 1988.

Erickson, Millard J. *Contemporary Options in Eschatology: A Study of the Millennium.* Grand Rapids: Baker, 1977.

Feinberg, Charles L. *Millennialism: The Two Major Views.* Winona Lake, Ind.: BMH Books, 1985.

Festinger, Leon, Henry W. Riecken, and Stanley Schacher. *When Prophecy Fails.* Minneapolis: University of Minnesota Press, 1956.

Firth, Katherine R. *The Apocalyptic Tradition in Reformation Britain, 1530–1645.* Oxford: Oxford University Press, 1979.

Friedländer, Saul, et al., eds. *Visions of Apocalypse: End or Rebirth?* New York: Holmes and Meier, 1985.

Friedrich, Otto. *The End of the World: A History.* New York: Fromm International, 1982.

Froom, LeRoy Edwin. *The Prophetic Faith of Our Fathers.* 4 vols. Washington: Review and Herald, 1954.

Fukuyama, Francis. *The End of History and the Last Man.* New York: Free Press, 1992.

Fuller, Robert. *Naming the Antichrist: The History of an American Obsession.* New York: Oxford University Press, 1995.

Garrett, Clarke. *Respectable Folly: Millenarians and the French Revolution in France and England.* Baltimore: Johns Hopkins University Press, 1975.

Glason, T. Francis. *His Appearing and His Kingdom.* London: Epworth, 1953.

Goetz, William R. *Apocalypse Next.* Camp Hill, Pa.: Horizon House, 1991.

Graham, Billy. *Approaching Hoofbeats: The Four Horsemen of the Apocalypse.* Waco: Word, 1983.

———. *Storm Warning.* Dallas: Word, 1992

———. *Till Armageddon.* Waco: Word, 1981.

———. *World Aflame.* Garden City, N.Y.: Doubleday, 1965.

Grenz, Stanley J. *The Millennial Maze: Sorting Out Evangelical Options.* Downers Grove, Ill: InterVarsity Press, 1992.

Griffin, William, ed. *Endtime: The Doomsday Catalog.* New York: Macmillan, 1979.

Grosso, Michael. *The Millennium Myth: Love and Death at the End of Time.* Wheaton: Quest Books, 1995.

Gundry, Robert H. *First the Antichrist: Why Christ Won't Come before the Antichrist Does.* Grand Rapids: Baker, 1997.

———. *The Church and the Tribulation.* Grand Rapids: Zondervan, 1973.

Hagee, John. *Beginning of the End: The Assassination of Yitzhak Rabin and the Coming of Antichrist.* Nashville: Nelson, 1996.

Halsell, Grace. *Prophecy and Politics: Militant Evangelists on the Road to Nuclear War.* Westport, Conn.: Lawrence Hill, 1986.

Harrison, J. F. C. *The Second Coming: Popular Millenarianism, 1780–1850.* New Brunswick, N.J.: Rutgers University Press, 1979.

Heilbroner, Robert. *Visions of the Future: The Distant Past, Yesterday, Today, Tomorrow.* New York: Oxford University Press, 1995.

Hendricksen, William. *Israel and the Bible.* Grand Rapids: Baker, 1968.

———. *More Than Conquerors.* Grand Rapids: Baker, 1939.

Hewitt, V. J., and Peter Lorie. *Nostradamus: The End of the Millennium, Prophecies 1992 to 2001.* New York: Simon & Schuster, 1991.

Hill, Christopher. *Antichrist in Seventeenth-Century England*. London: Verso, 1990.

Hill, Clifford. *Prophecy Past and Present: An Exploration of the Prophetic Ministry in the Bible and Church Today*. Ann Arbor, Mich.: Servant Publications, 1991.

Hindson, Ed. *Approaching Armageddon: The World Prepares for War with God*. Eugene, Ore.: Harvest House, 1997.

————. *End Times, the Middle East, and the New World Order*. Wheaton: Victor Books, 1991.

Hoekema, Anthony A. *The Bible and the Future*. Grand Rapids: Eerdmans, 1979.

Hogue, John. *The Millennium Book of Prophecy*. San Francisco: Harper, 1994.

————. *Nostradamus and the Millennium: Last Predictions*. Garden City, N.Y.: Doubleday, 1987.

Hoyt, Karen, ed. *The New Age Rage*. Old Tappan, N.J.: Revell, 1987.

Hubbard, David Allan. *The Second Coming: What Will Happen When Jesus Returns?* Downers Grove: InterVarsity Press, 1984.

Hunt, Dave. *A Cup of Trembling*. Eugene, Ore.: Harvest House, 1995.

————. *Global Peace and the Rise of Antichrist*. Eugene, Ore.: Harvest House, 1990.

————. *How Close Are We?* Eugene, Ore.: Harvest House, 1993.

————. *Peace, Prosperity, and the Coming Holocaust*. Eugene, Ore.: Harvest House, 1983.

————. *A Woman Rides the Beast: The Roman Catholic Church and the Last Days*. Eugene, Ore.: Harvest House, 1994.

Ice, Thomas, and Timothy Demy, eds. *When the Trumpet Sounds*. Eugene, Ore.: Harvest House, 1995.

James, William T. *Storming toward Armageddon: Essays in Apocalypse*. Green Forest, Ark.: New Leaf Press, 1992.

Jay, Peter, and Michael Stewart. *Apocalypse 2000*. New York: Prentice-Hall, 1987.

Jeffrey, Grant R. *Armageddon: Appointment with Destiny*. New York: Bantam, 1990.

————. *The Handwriting of God*. Toronto: Frontier Research Publications, 1997.

————. *The Signature of God*. Toronto: Frontier Research Publications, 1996.

Jewett, Robert. *Jesus against the Rapture: Seven Unexpected Prophecies*. Philadelphia: Westminster, 1979.

Jonsson, Carl Olof, and Wolfgang Herbst. *The "Sign" of the Last Days—When?* Atlanta: Commentary Press, 1987.

Kaplan, Jeffrey. *Radical Religion in America*. Syracuse: Syracuse University Press, 1997.

Keller, Catherine. *Apocalypse Now and Then*. Boston: Beacon Press, 1996.

Kermode, Frank. *The Sense of an Ending*. New York: Oxford University Press, 1967.

Kik, J. Marcellus. *An Eschatology of Victory*. Phillipsburg, N.J.: Presbyterian and Reformed, 1975.

Kirban, Salem. *Countdown to Rapture*. Irvine, Calif.: Harvest House, 1977.

————. *Guide to Survival*. Chattanooga: AMG Publishers, 1990.

————. *666*. Wheaton: Tyndale House, 1970.

Klaassen, Walter. *Armageddon and the Peaceable Kingdom*. Scottdale, Penn.: Herald Press, 1999.

————. *Living at the End of the Ages*. Lanham, Md.: University Press of America, 1992.

Knight, George R. *Millennial Fever and the End of the World*. Boise, Idaho: Pacific Press, 1993.

Körtner, Ulrich H. J. *The End of the World*. Louisville: Westminster John Knox Press, 1995.

Kromminga, D. H. *The Millennium in the Church*. Grand Rapids: Eerdmans, 1945.

Kyle, Richard. *The Last Days Are Here Again: A History of the End Times*. Grand Rapids: Baker, 1998.

————. *The Religious Fringe: A History of Alternative Religions in America*. Downers Grove, Ill.: InterVarsity Press, 1993.

Ladd, George E. *The Blessed Hope*. Grand Rapids: Eerdmans, 1956.

LaHaye, Tim. *The Coming Peace in the Middle East*. Grand Rapids: Zondervan, 1984.

————. *No Fear of the Storm: Why Christians Will Escape All of the Tribulation*. Sisters, Ore.: Multnomah, 1992.

————. *The Race for the Twenty-First Century: What Christians Must Do to Survive*. Nashville: Nelson, 1986.

Landes, Richard. *Whilst God Tarried: Disappointed Millennialism and the Genealogy of the Modern West.* New York: Basic Books, 1999.

Lapham, Lewis H., ed. *History: The End of the World.* New York: History Book Club, 1998.

Larkin, Clarence. *Dispensational Truth or God's Plan and Purpose in the Ages.* Santa Fe, N.M.: Sun Publishing, 1998.

LaSor, William Sanford. *The Truth about Armageddon: What the Bible Says about the End Times.* Grand Rapids: Baker, 1982.

Leslie, John. *The End of the World: The Science and Ethics of Human Extinction.* London: Routledge, 1996.

Lewis, C. S. *The World's Last Night and Other Essays.* New York: Harcourt Brace, 1987.

Lewis, David Allen. *Prophecy 2000.* Green Forest, Ark.: New Leaf Press, 1990.

———. *Smashing the Gates of Hell in the Last Days.* Green Forest, Ark.: New Leaf Press, 1987.

Lewis, James, ed. *From the Ashes.* New York: Rowman & Littlefield, 1994.

Lightner, Robert P. *The Last Days Handbook.* Nashville: Nelson, 1990.

Lindsell, Harold. *The Armageddon Spectre.* Westchester, Ill.: Crossway Books, 1984.

Lindsey, Hal. *Apocalypse Code.* Palos Verdes, Calif.: Western Front, 1997.

———. *The Late Great Planet Earth.* Grand Rapids: Zondervan, 1970.

———. *The Liberation of Planet Earth.* Grand Rapids: Zondervan, 1974.

———. *Planet Earth—2000 A.D.* Palos Verdes: Western Front, 1994.

———. *The Rapture.* New York: Bantam, 1983.

———. *The Road to Holocaust.* New York: Bantam, 1989.

———. *Satan Is Alive and Well on Planet Earth.* Grand Rapids: Zondervan, 1972.

———. *There's a New World Coming.* New York: Bantam, 1973.

———. *The 1980s: Countdown to Armageddon.* New York: Bantam, 1980.

Lorie, Peter. *Nostradamus: The Millennium and Beyond.* New York: Simon & Schuster, 1993.

MacPherson, Dave. *The Great Rapture Hoax.* Fletcher, N.C.: New Puritan Library, 1983.

———. *Three R's: Rapture, Revisionism, Robbery. Pretribulation Raputurism from 1830 to Hal Lindsey.* Simpsonsville, S.C.: P.O.S.T., Inc., 1998.

Mann, A. T. *Millennium Prophecies: Predictions for the Year 2000.* Rockport, Mass.: Element, 1992.

Manuel, Frank E. *Shapes of Philosophical History.* Stanford, Calif.: Stanford University Press, 1965.

Marrs, Texe. *Millennium.* Austin: Living Truth Publishers, 1990.

Marsden, George. *Fundamentalism and American Culture.* New York: Oxford University Press, 1980.

Martin, Ralph. *The Catholic Church at the End of an Age.* San Francisco: Ignatius Press, 1994.

———. *Is Jesus Coming Soon? A Catholic Perspective on the Second Coming.* San Francisco: Ignatius Press, 1997.

Mauro, Philip. *The Wonders of Bible Chronology.* Swengel, Pa.: Reiner, 1970.

McBirnie, W. S. *2000 AD!: Nine Years to Doomsday?* Glendale, Calif.: Voice of Americanism, 1991.

McCall, Thomas S., and Zola Levitt. *Coming: The End! Russia and Israel in Prophecy.* Chicago: Moody Press, 1992.

McClain, Alva J. *Daniel's Prophecy of the Seventy Weeks.* Grand Rapids: Zondervan 1940.

McConnell, Janice T. *The Visions of the Children.* New York: St. Martin's Press, 1992.

McGinn, Bernard. *Antichrist.* San Francisco: Harper, 1994.

———. *Visions of the End.* New York: Columbia University Press, 1979.

McQuaid, Elwood. *The Zion Connection.* Eugene, Ore.: Harvest House, 1996.

Miller, Elliot, and Kenneth R. Samples. *The Cult of the Virgin.* Grand Rapids: Baker, 1992.

Mitchell, David J. *Queen Christabel: A Biography of Christabel Pankhurst.* London: Macdonald and Jane's, 1977.

North, Gary. *Millennialism and Social Theory.* Tyler, Tex.: Institute for Christian Economics, 1990.

Numbers, Ronald L., and Jonathan M. Butler. *The Disappointed.* Knoxville: University of Tennessee Press, 1993.

O'Leary, Stephen D. *Arguing the Apocalypse: A Theory of Millennial Rhetoric.* New York: Oxford University Press, 1994.

Oropeza, B. J. *99 Reasons Why No One Knows When Christ Will Return.* Downers Grove, Ill.: InterVarsity Press, 1994.

Parise, Frank, ed. *The Book of Calendars.* New York: Facts on File, 1982.

Pate, C. Marvin, and Calvin B. Haines Jr. *Doomsday Delusions: What's Wrong with Predictions about the End of the World.* Downers Grove, Ill.: InterVarsity Press, 1995.

Penton, M. James. *Apocalypse Delayed: The Story of the Jehovah's Witnesses.* Toronto: University of Toronto Press, 1985.

Peters, George N. H. *The Theocratic Kingdom of Our Lord Jesus, the Christ.* 3 vols. Grand Rapids: Kregel, 1978.

Peters, Ted. *Fear, Faith, and the Future: Affirming Christian Hope in the Face of Doomsday Prophecies.* Minneapolis: Augsburg, 1980.

———. *Futures—Human and Divine.* Atlanta: John Knox, 1978.

Polak, Frederick. *The Image of the Future.* San Francisco: Jossey-Bass, 1973.

Petersen, Rodney L. *Preaching in the Last Days.* New York: Oxford University Press, 1993.

Price, Walter K. *The Coming Antichrist.* Chicago: Moody Press, 1974.

Reagan, David. *The Master Plan: Making Sense of the Controversies Surrounding Bible Prophecy Today.* Eugene, Ore.: Harvest House, 1993.

Reavis, Dick J. *The Ashes of Waco: An Investigation.* New York: Simon & Schuster, 1995.

Reeves, Marjorie. *The Influence of Prophecy in the Later Middle Ages.* New York: Oxford University Press, 1969.

———. *Joachim of Fiore and the Prophetic Future.* New York: Harper & Row, 1976.

Reiter, Richard, et al. *The Rapture: Pre-, Mid-, or Post-Tribulational?* Grand Rapids: Zondervan, 1984.

Relfe, Mary S. *When Your Money Fails . . . The "666 System" Is Here.* Montgomery, Ala.: Ministries, 1981.

Robertson, Marion G. "Pat." *The New Millennium.* Dallas: Word, 1990.

———. *The New World Order.* Dallas: Word, 1991.

———. *The Secret Kingdom: Your Path to Peace, Love, and Financial Security.* Dallas: Word, 1992.

Rosenthal, Marvin. *The Pre-Wrath Rapture of the Church: A New Understanding of the Rapture, the Tribulation, and the Second Coming.* Nashville: Nelson, 1990.

Rowley, H. H. *The Relevance of Apocalyptic.* Greenwood, S.C.: Attic Press, 1980.

Rubinsky, Yuri, and Ian Wiseman. *A History of the End of the World.* New York: William Morrow, 1982.

Russell, D. S. *Prophecy and the Apocalyptic Dream: Protest and Promise.* Peabody, Mass.: Hendrickson, 1994.

Ryrie, Charles C. *The Bible and Tomorrow's News.* Wheaton: Scripture Press, 1969.

———. *Dispensationalism.* Chicago: Moody Press, 1995.

———. *The Living End: Enlightening and Astonishing Disclosures about the Coming Last Days of Earth.* Old Tappan, N.J.: Revell, 1976.

St. Claire, Michael J. *Millenarian Movements in Historical Context.* New York: Garland, 1992.

Samples, Ken, Erwin de Castro, Richard Abanes, and Robert Lyle. *Prophets of the Apocalypse: David Koresh and Other American Messiahs.* Grand Rapids: Baker, 1994.

Sandeen, Ernest R. *The Roots of Fundamentalism.* Chicago: University of Chicago Press, 1970.

Saucy, Robert L. *The Case for Progressive Dispensationalism.* Grand Rapids: Zondervan, 1993.

Schmithals, Walter. *The Apocalyptic Movement.* Nashville: Abingdon Press, 1975.

Schwartz, Hillel. *Century's End: A Cultural History of the Fin de Siècle from the 990s through the 1990s.* New York: Doubleday, 1990.

Scotland, Nigel. *Charismatics and the Next Millennium.* London: Hodder & Stoughton, 1995.

Smith, Wilbur M. *Egypt in Biblical Prophecy.* Boston: W. A. Wilde, 1957.

———. *Israeli/Arab Conflict and the Bible.* Glendale, Calif.: Regal, 1967.

———. *This Atomic Age and the Word of God.* Boston: W. A. Wilde, 1948.

Stearns, Peter N. *Millennium III, Century XXI.* Boulder, Colo.: Westview Press, 1996.

Still, William T. *New World Order: The Ancient Plan of Secret Societies*. Lafayette, La.: Huntington House, 1990.

Stokes, John, ed. *Fin de Siècle/Fin du Globe: Fears and Fantasies of the Late Nineteenth Century*. New York: St. Martin's Press, 1992.

Stone, Jon R. *A Guide to the End of the World: Popular Eschatology in America*. New York: Garland, 1993.

Strozier, Charles B. *Apocalypse: On the Psychology of Fundamentalism in America*. Boston: Beacon, 1994.

Swihart, Stephen D. *Armageddon 1998?: God's Plan for the End Times*. Plainfield, N.J.: Logos, 1980.

Terrell, Steve. *The 90's: Decade of Apocalypse*. South Plainfield, N.J.: Bridge Publishing, 1994.

Thompson, Damian. *The End of Time: Faith and Fear in the Shadow of the Millennium*. Hanover, N.H.: University Press of New England, 1996.

Toon, Peter, ed. *Puritans, the Millennium, and the Future of Israel*. Greenwood, S.C.: Attic Press, 1970.

Travis, Stephen. *I Believe in the Second Coming of Jesus*. Grand Rapids: Eerdmans, 1982.

———. *The Jesus Hope*. London: Word, 1974

Tuveson, Ernest Lee. *Millennium and Utopia*. New York: Harper, 1964.

———. *Redeemer Nation: The Idea of America's Millennial Role*. Chicago: University of Chicago Press, 1968.

Van Impe, Jack. *Israel's Final Holocaust*. Nashville: Nelson, 1979.

———. *2001: On the Edge of Eternity*. Dallas: Word, 1996.

Van Kampen, Robert. *The Sign*. Wheaton: Crossway Books, 1992.

Wagar, W. Warren. *Next Three Futures: Paradigms of Things to Come*. New York: Praeger, 1991.

———. *Terminal Visions*. Bloomington, Ind.: Indiana University Press, 1982.

Wainwright, Arthur W. *Mysterious Apocalypse: Interpreting the Book of Revelation*. Nashville: Abingdon Press, 1993.

Walvoord, John F. *Armageddon, Oil and the Middle East Crisis*. Grand Rapids: Zondervan, 1990.

———. *Israel in Prophecy*. Grand Rapids: Zondervan, 1988.

———. *The Nations in Prophecy*. Grand Rapids: Zondervan, 1988.

Watt, David H. *A Transforming Faith: Explorations of Twentieth-Century American Evangelicalism*. New Brunswick, N.J.: Rutgers University Press, 1991.

Weber, Timothy P. *Living in the Shadow of the Second Coming*. Chicago: University of Chicago Press, 1987.

West, Nathaniel. *The Thousand Year Reign of Christ*. Grand Rapids: Kregel, 1993.

Whisenant, Edgar C. *88 Reasons Why the Rapture Is in 1988*. Nashville: World Bible Society, 1988.

———, and Greg Brewer. *The Final Shout: Rapture Report 1989*. Nashville: World Bible Society, 1989.

Whitrow, G. J. *Time in History: Views of Time from Prehistory to the Present Day*. New York: Oxford University Press, 1989.

Wilcock, Michael. *I Saw Heaven Opened: The Message of Revelation*. Downers Grove, Ill.: InterVarsity Press, 1975.

Wilson, Dwight. *Armageddon Now! The Premillenarian Response to Russia and Israel since 1917*. Grand Rapids: Baker, 1977.

Wilson, Everett L. *Jesus and the End-Time: An Interpretation*. Chicago: Covenant Press, 1977.

Wright, Stuart A., ed. *Armageddon in Waco*. Chicago: University of Chicago Press, 1995.

Yamauchi, Edwin M. *Foes from the Northern Frontier: Invading Hordes form the Russian Steppes*. Grand Rapids: Baker, 1982.

———. *The World of the First Christians*. San Francisco: Harper & Row, 1981.

Zamora, Lois Parkinson, ed. *The Apocalyptic Vision in America*. Bowling Green, Ohio: Bowling Green State University Popular Press, 1982.

Zimdars-Swartz, Sandra L. *Encountering Mary: From La Salette to Medjugorje*. Princeton, N.J.: Princeton University Press, 1991.

Credits and Permissions

Credits are listed in the order in which the illustrations appear.

Chapter 1

Internet home page: Courtesy of Armageddon Books.

Jezreel Valley photograph: Courtesy of Melinda Van Engen.

Clockmaker: From *Trade and Occupations: A Pictorial Archive from Early Sources,* Dover Publications.

Pontius Puddle comic: Courtesy of Joel Kauffman, 111 Carter Road, Goshen, Indiana 46526.

Augustine image from mid-fifteenth-century book, *The Lives of the Saints,* MS Tanner 17, folio 111: Courtesy of Bodleine Library, Oxford University.

David Koresh 1981 file photograph from Mount Carmel compound: AP/WIDE WORLD PHOTOS.

Richard Butler photograph: Courtesy of Craig Buck.

Cover from *The Rise of Babylon: Sign of the End Times* by Charles H. Dyer with Angela Elwell Hunt: Copyright © 1991 by Charles H. Dyer. Used by permission.

Chapter 2

Tract in bottle: Mr. and Mrs. H. H. Mayes, courtesy of the Billy Graham Center Museum, Wheaton, Illinois.

"The Angel with the Key . . ." woodcut by Albrecht Dürer: Courtesy of the Billy Graham Center Museum, Wheaton, Illinois.

Jonathan Edwards painting: Courtesy of the Billy Graham Center Museum, Wheaton, Illinois.

"Social Progress" hymn: From *Hymns for the Living Age* by H. Augustine Smith. Copyright © 1923. Used by permission of Fleming H. Revell, a division of Baker Book House, Grand Rapids, Michigan.

Cover from *More Than Conquerors* by William Hendricksen: Copyright © 1939. Used by permission of Baker Books, a division of Baker Book House, Grand Rapids, Michigan.

Comic by John Lawing as it appeared in *Christianity Today:* Copyright © 1978 John V. Lawing Jr. Used by permission.

C. I. Scofield photograph: Courtesy of the Billy Graham Center Museum, Wheaton, Illinois.

Dispensational chart: Courtesy of Rev. Clarence Larkin Est., P.O. Box 334, Glenside, PA 19038. Used by permission.

Dispensational chart comparison: From *Progressive Dispensationalism* by Craig A. Blaising and Darrell L. Bock. Copyright © 1996. Used by permission of Baker Books, a division of Baker Book House, Grand Rapids, Michigan.

Rapture painting by Charles Anderson, distributed by Bible Believer's Evangelistic Association, Inc., Sherman, Texas: Courtesy of the Billy Graham Center Museum, Wheaton, Illinois.

Rapture index: Courtesy of Todd Strandberg. Used by permission.

Bumper sticker: Courtesy of the Billy Graham Center Museum, Wheaton, Illinois.

Cover from *Armageddon, Oil and the Middle East Crisis* by John R. Walvoord: Copyright © 1990 by John R. Walvoord and John E. Walvoord. Used by permission of Zondervan Publishing House, Grand Rapids, Michigan.

Millennial chart: From *Created for Community,* 2d ed., by Stanley J. Grenz. Copyright © 1998. Used by permission of Baker Books, a division of Baker Book House, Grand Rapids, Michigan.

Chapter 3

Tertullian painting: Copyright © 1966 by The Canton Baptist Temple Company, Canton, Ohio. Used by permission.

Constantine bust: Courtesy of the Italian Government Travel Office.

"The New Jerusalem" painting by Gustave Doré: Courtesy of the Billy Graham Center Museum, Wheaton, Illinois.

Monk: From *Men: A Pictorial Archive of Nineteenth-Century Sources,* Dover Publications.

Anti-papist image: From *Picture Book of Devils, Demons and Witchcraft,* Dover Publications.

Christopher Columbus, seal and preface, from *Libro de las Profecías,* trans. Delno C. West and August Kling (Gainesville, Fl.: University Press of Florida, 1991): Courtesy of University Press of Florida.

Cover from *The Millennium Bible* by William Edward Biederwolf: Copyright © 1964. Used by permission of Baker Books, a division of Baker Book House, Grand Rapids, Michigan.

John Nelson Darby photograph: Courtesy of the Billy Graham Center Museum, Wheaton, Illinois.

Dispensational chart: From *Jesus Is Coming* by W. E. Blackstone. Copyright © 1898. Used by permission of Fleming H. Revell, a division of Baker Book House, Grand Rapids, Michigan.

Page spread: From *The Scofield Reference Bible,* edited by C. I. Scofield. Copyright © 1909, 1917, 1937, 1945. Used by permission of Oxford University Press, New York.

Billy Graham photograph: Courtesy of the Billy Graham Center Archives, Wheaton, Illinois.

"Four Horsemen of the Apocalypse" woodcut by Albrecht Dürer: Courtesy of the Billy Graham Center Museum, Wheaton, Illinois.

Cover of pamphlet by Mission for the Coming Days: Courtesy of the Billy Graham Center Museum, Wheaton, Illinois.

Millennial cereal comic: Courtesy of Mary Chambers. Used by permission.

Chapter 4

End-Time Handmaidens, July 5, 1997, photograph by Ruth Fremson: AP/WIDE WORLD PHOTOS.

Miller's end of the world illustrations: Courtesy of the Billy Graham Center Museum, Wheaton, Illinois.

Miller's prophecy chart: Courtesy of the Billy Graham Center Museum, Wheaton, Illinois.

Christabel Pankhurst photograph: Reproduced from the Collections of the Library of Congress.

Woman in bookstore comic: Courtesy of Wayne Stayskal, Tampa, Florida.

Cover and photo from *The Late Great Planet Earth* by Hal Lindsey: Copyright © 1970 by Zondervan Publishing House, Grand Rapids, Michigan. Used by permission.

Pat Robertson photograph: Credit: CBN.

Tim LaHaye photograph: Used by permission of Tim LaHaye.

Revival meeting poster: Courtesy of the Billy Graham Center Museum, Wheaton, Illinois.

Chapter 5

Ronald Reagan photograph by Michael Evans: Used by permission of the Ronald Reagan Library.

Cover from *The Light and the Glory* by Peter Marshall and David Manuel: Copyright © 1977. Used by permission of Fleming H. Revell, a division of Baker Book House, Grand Rapids, Michigan.

Adolf Hitler photograph: Reproduced from the Collections of the Library of Congress.

The Great Assize, or Day of Judgment poster: Reproduced from the Collections of the Library of Congress.

Haile Selassie photograph from Haile Selassie home page, http://www.angelfire.com/ak/selassie: Courtesy of Esther Selassie Antohin.

Lourdes, France: Used by permission of Betty Crowell, Faraway Places Stock Photos.

Pyramid drawing: From *Soothsayers of the Second Advent* by William Alnor. Copyright © 1989. Used by permission of Fleming H. Revell, a division of Baker Book House, Grand Rapids, Michigan.

"The Resurrection" woodcut by Albrecht Dürer: Courtesy of the Billy Graham Center Museum, Wheaton, Illinois.

Chapter 6

COUNTDOWN TO THE MILLENNIUM 1998–1999: Copyright © 1997. Reprinted with permission of Andrews and McMeel Publishing. All rights reserved.

"Adoration of the Lamb" woodcut by Albrecht Dürer: Courtesy of the Billy Graham Center Museum, Wheaton, Illinois.

"Gift of Vision from God" painting by Howard Finster: Used with artist's permission. Courtesy of the Billy Graham Center Museum, Wheaton, Illinois.

Woman being tatooed with 666 photograph: Courtesy of Salem Kirban from his book *666*.

Millennium Market advertisement: Used by permission.

Pontius Puddle comics: Courtesy of Joel Kauffman, 111 Carter Road, Goshen, Indiana 46526.

St. John the Revelator: From the *Sunday School Almanac and Calendar for 1854,* Methodist Tract Society. Courtesy of the Billy Graham Center Museum, Wheaton, Illinois.

CALVIN AND HOBBES: © Watterson. Reprinted with permission of UNIVERSAL PRESS SYNDICATE. All rights reserved.

"The Harmony of Christian Love" mid-nineteenth-century engraving by John Sartain: Reproduced from the Collections of the Library of Congress.

"Mem's Going Home" sculpture by George Lorio: Used with artist's permission. Courtesy of the Billy Graham Center Museum, Wheaton, Illinois.

Subject Index

Scripture Index

Robert G. Clouse (Ph.D., University of Iowa) is professor of history at Indiana State University in Terre Haute, Indiana. He is the (co)author or editor of twelve books, including *The Meaning of the Millennium* and *Two Kingdoms: The Church and Culture through the Ages*. He writes and lectures regularly on millennial topics.

Robert N. Hosack (M.A., Trinity Evangelical Divinity School) is acquisitions editor at Baker Books and a freelance writer and editor.

Richard V. Pierard (Ph.D., University of Iowa) is professor of history at Indiana State University in Terre Haute, Indiana. He is the (co)author or editor of eight books and over one hundred articles, including *Twilight of the Saints: Biblical Christianity and Civil Religion in America* and *Two Kingdoms: The Church and Culture through the Ages*. He specializes in global Christianity.